Back to America

....

Anthropology of Contemporary North America

Back to America

Identity, Political Culture,
and the Tea Party Movement

William H. Westermeyer

University of Nebraska Press | Lincoln

Portions of this book first appeared as "Local Tea Party
Groups: The Vibrancy of the Movement" in *Political and
Legal Anthropology Review* 39, no S1 (2016): 12–38; and
"Progressives' Plantation: The Tea Party's Complex
Relationship with Race," in *Political Sentiments and Social
Movements: The Person in Politics and Culture*, ed. Claudia
Strauss and Jack Friedman (New York: Palgrave Macmil-
lan, 2018), 61–89.

Library of Congress Control Number: 2019013754

Contents

Acknowledgments

I owe more than acknowledgment but deeply felt appreciation and gratitude to many people who made the completion of this work possible. The first acknowledgment must go to my father, Dr. Vaughn W. Westermeyer. Though his parenting skills left much to be desired, he instilled in me a desire for knowledge, a dynamic curiosity, and a desire to understand how things work and why things are as they are. Up until his death he still was attempting to steer me away from political work and toward graduate school. He would be amused to see how the two ended up complementing each other.

When I eventually entered academia, Dr. Nora Haenn opened my eyes regarding ways to study politics and social movements made possible by anthropology. Nora has continued to be a steady, encouraging mentor and a very good friend.

More than anybody else Dottie Holland, who passed away just prior to publication, made this work possible. My first meeting with Dottie was similar to countless meetings we had in the following years. Sitting in her office discussing my interests, Dottie asked the right questions, prompting me to expand my ideas and think in different directions, all the while showing patience and encouragement. In many ways Dottie was as interested in my research as I was, and we *both* lived a profound learning experience in the production of this research. Yet beyond the academics, Dottie and I shared many wonderful learning experiences, whether it was dinner and conversation or the many political protests and rallies that Dottie and I attended together.

I must acknowledge the guidance offered by Don Nonini. Don is a brilliant anthropologist who shared many of my interests and was also a strong motivation throughout the production of this book. I will never forget the afternoons of one-on-one time with him discussing core works of political anthropology. I realize now the large amount of time Don spent with me on these core works. Other faculty members in the Anthropology Department at University of North Carolina at Chapel Hill in their own ways were each instrumental in my education. Charles Price, a wonderful teacher and human being, offered numerous invaluable suggestions for improving the manuscript and its theoretical foundations. Jean Dennison was so enthusiastic about my research topic from the start and provided important suggestions regarding the fundamental direction of my argument. And Christopher Nelson challenged me to unwrap some of the more difficult theoretic and philosophical principles of anthropology.

Many others provided important feedback and encouragement throughout the research and writing: Jeff Boyer, Claudia Strauss, Jeff Juris, Jack Freidman, Peter Hervik, Sarah Dempsey, and the late Sandra Morgen.

Two other people deserve my deepest and heartfelt gratitude and love. My brother, Geoff, was a constant presence from two thousand miles away and was never lacking of support and love. I don't know where to start with Monica Montgomery Westermeyer. Monica always had the no-nonsense attitude that kept a lot of problems in perspective. Her kindness and regular conversations had a huge influence on making this project possible.

Several students in the University of North Carolina anthropology graduate program made this journey easier, more educational, and fun. Most important are Caela O'Connell and Julianna Parks, whose love and friendship are beyond description. Yet I also want to thank Lindsay Bloch, Martha King, Claire Novotny, Emily Cubbon Ditto, Tomas Gallaretta Cervera, Andrew Ofstehage, Laura Wagner, Erin Stevens Nelson, and David Cranford.

The success of my research was largely a function of the years I spent as a political organizer and manager. I never worked harder than during those years. They were stressful, exhilarating, mundane, comical, and the best years of my life. Though I worked with hundreds of people, several have had and continue to have profound effects on my thinking, analysis, and perspective. Eric Hacopian, Charles Chamberlain, Klinton

Kinder, Sihya Smith, Robert Grocholski, Debra Macisco, Heather Bennett, Dane Morgan, Amy Donaldson, Angelo Paparella, and our departed friend Michelle Jose—all were brilliant and energetic friends with whom I shared the best and sometimes the worst of times. I learned so much from them. Among this group, special thanks go to Joan Mitchell, who read and proofed the manuscript, helping polish the final product.

So much appreciation is due to the people at University of Nebraska Press, especially Alicia Christensen and Abby Stryker, who patiently guided me through the initial peer review stages. Elizabeth Zaleski, Ann Baker, Tish Fobben, and copyeditor Julie Kimmel kept me on task and made the publishing process relatively painless. Much gratitude is reserved for the Anthropology of Contemporary North America series editors, James Bielo and Carrie Lane, and the faculty advisory board who saw the potential contribution of this book to the series and anthropology in general. Three anonymous peer reviewers provided useful, encouraging feedback that greatly improved the manuscript, making it attractive to an even wider audience.

Finally, I thank my Tea Party consultants, who placed their trust in me to translate their movement to a broader audience.

I feel indebted to all these people for the time and effort that they've given me, and I feel a heavy but vitalizing responsibility to produce a work that all these people can be proud of.

Introduction

The high school gym was hot, humid, and quickly reaching its seating capacity. It was, after all, August on the coastal plain of North Carolina, a time when air conditioners are running day and night. Several hundred voters from North Carolina's First Congressional District had gathered on that sultry night in 2009 for a town hall meeting organized by Democratic representative C. K. Butterfield, hoping for details about President Barack Obama's health care reform proposal that was being drafted by the Democrats. However, many in attendance were not interested in details; they had heard enough from media accounts and talk radio. Over the course of two hours, there were many questions and many accusations against the congressman. The tension was high, with jeers and boos for the congressman's answers and loud cheers for citizens expressing opposition to the measure. I assumed that many of the detractors were supporters of the emerging Tea Party, a loud and extensive protest movement that had been growing since the inauguration of President Obama six months before.

The Tea Party movement (TPM), characterized by large and small protests and rallies across the nation, had been growing over the prior months. Media were avidly portraying Tea Party protests of the policies and person of Barack Obama and the economic recovery legislation passed in response to what subsequently became known as the Great Recession. Tea Party events were populated by older, middle-class, and typically conservative protesters emulating the founding fathers and demanding strict adherence to a literal interpretation of the U.S. Constitution.

My first actual exposure to the Tea Party movement occurred on that night at Congressman Butterfield's town hall. This town hall was not unique. Dozens of confrontational constituent meetings with similar atmospheres were held across the nation that month. Typically mundane and sparsely attended constituent town hall meetings were transformed that August into well-attended, dramatic, and contentious political theater (Isenstadt 2009). The excitement of some that the United Sates would finally pass comprehensive health care reform was tempered by this groundswell of opposition to creeping "statism." Although the TPM had been growing for the prior six months, the congressional town hall meetings of August 2009 indicated that American political culture was undergoing a dramatic shift characterized by the emergence of an aggressive conservative populist backlash.

Viewing from the sidelines, I initially found these town halls puzzling. The people speaking (or rather, yelling) in opposition to health care reform seemed to be neither experienced citizen activists nor professional advocates expressing policy positions. The statements were often accompanied by highly emotional displays and more often evoked symbolic concerns and moral panics (S. Cohen 1972; Hall et al. 1978) punctuated with charges that the Congress member was "un-American" or "socialist" or "fascist." At the same time the sheer number of attendees was remarkable. During my earlier thirteen-year stint in full-time political work, I had organized protests and street theater and knew that getting large numbers of people to an event was no easy task. Yet this event and dozens of others across the nation were standing-room only. Furthermore, despite the wide dispersion of the town halls across the country, the messages conveyed by the protesters were unusually consistent.

Was this emerging movement spontaneous or contrived? Was it driven by elite and corporate interests or the grassroots? I was leaning toward elite and contrived given the large numbers of people in attendance, the consistent discourses, and my knowledge that the Republican Party, conservative think tanks such as the Heritage Foundation, and the U.S. Chamber of Commerce were all opposed to the Patient Protection and Affordable Care Act. Was this simply a better-organized repeat of fifteen years earlier, when those same groups successfully defeated the Clinton-era health care reform? The early media coverage of the movement was of little help in dispelling my opinion. Although there was some excellent work by journalists attempting to understand the Tea Party phenomenon (Gardner 2010; McGrath 2010; Zernike 2010; Zernike and Thee-Brenan 2010), some argued that the TPM was "Astroturf" organized by the GOP or the billionaire industrialists Charles and David Koch. The protesters, they argued, were an example of how conservatives were being duped into acting against their self-interest (e.g., DiMaggio 2010; Krugman 2009).

Nonetheless, as I continued ethnographic research in the Piedmont of North Carolina that following year, I found that "Tea Partyists" were organizing locally, meeting in small, typically county-level, face-to-face groups that assembled regularly in restaurants or American Legion halls. Welcomed as a researcher into what I term "local Tea Party groups" (LTPGS), I was struck by how the groups created spaces for political discussion, political action, and the fashioning of political identities as Tea Partyists. These groups became the focus of my research. I wanted to understand the actions and perceptions of the everyday Tea Party participants. This book builds an argument about how these small, yet multiple, widely dispersed groups were playing a large role in the success of the movement.

Those who maintained that elites such as the Koch brothers were orchestrating the TPM were not entirely wrong; their picture was simply incomplete and grossly oversimplified. The movement was constituted from elite *and* grassroots actors (Skocpol and Williamson 2012). I describe the TPM as being composed of three broad sets of political actors: national-level Tea Party organizations (NTPOs), conservative broadcast media, and as mentioned, local groups of activists or LTPGS.[1] Established national-level conservative organizations, such as the Koch-supported Americans for Prosperity (AFP), were organizing protests and adapting their outreach to the emergent grassroots movement (Mayer 2016; Zernike 2010). At the same time new NTPOs specifically focused on the TPM, such as Tea Party Patriots, were compiling massive memberships and building networks linking LTPGS. Conservative broadcast media—mainly Fox News and syndicated conservative talk radio—were not simply reporting on the new movement but actively helping to organize it (Zernike 2010; Williamson, Skocpol, and Coggin 2011;

Banerjee 2013). Fox News and Tea Party Patriots were present in the small local groups in the form of discourses circulating through and between them. Yet LTPGs in the area of my study were spontaneous and autonomous without formal links to the national-level groups. Each group re-created a Tea Party cultural world, yet also fashioned particular political organizations with their own priorities, actions, and characteristics. The following description of a meeting of the Hamilton County Tea Party (HCTP) gives a feel for the complexity of the local groups and sets the stage for describing the central questions of this book.[2] On this occasion the Hamilton group meeting took place in a crowded private dining room of a local restaurant.

The meeting included approximately fifty people who were primarily middle-aged with some retirees, upper and upper-middle class, and white. When I arrived, Sandy, the cofounder of the group and facilitator of the meeting, was identifying leaders of different projects and asking them to provide updates. She began by announcing that the planning for the April 15 Tax Day Tea Party Rally at the county courthouse plaza was well underway. The updates began with John, an aspiring writer and lifelong reader of conservative philosophy. He reported that he had been in contact with schools, asking them to publicize an essay contest that HCTP was sponsoring for schoolchildren on the importance of the U.S. Constitution in their lives. Next, Gloria, a mother of four and a former volunteer coordinator for Tea Party Patriots, mentioned that the John Locke Foundation, a North Carolina think tank and advocacy organization similar to the Heritage Foundation, was offering workshops on understanding the U.S. Constitution. For a fee the organization would send a representative to any locale in North Carolina to conduct a full-day class on the details and historical bases of the document's contents. Another woman rose next to give a report on "disaster planning." Echoing recent forebodings by Fox News personality Glenn Beck, she warned of societal disruptions from unforeseen natural calamities, electromagnetic pulse, and the current financial crises in Greece and Iceland. She had compiled information on how to set up a survival plan and to stockpile food and seed banks, and she recommended that members read the book *Patriots: Surviving the Coming Collapse* (Rawles 2009).

Several members reported on the "budget team," a project to evaluate and research the Hamilton County government budget with the goal of identifying wasteful spending they wanted the Democrat-controlled board of commissioners to cut. Subsets of members organized themselves into working groups, each to address a different budget category— transportation, human resources, and so forth. They were planning on presenting an alternative budget to the county board of commissioners in three months.

Closing the evening, Dan related the story of his attending a talk by Van Jones, a liberal former "green jobs czar" in Barack Obama's administration whom Glenn Beck had fashioned into a tangible symbol of "progressives'" plan to destroy America. Dan filmed the event, during which an audience member asked Jones to define "social justice." Jones replied, "Would you be willing to take your life, write it on a card, throw it in a big pot with everybody else's, reach in and pull out another life with total confidence that it would be a good life? No? Then you have some work to do [to make everyone's life a good life]." Dan inserted text reading, "ISN'T THIS COMMUNISM?" at the end of this video clip and posted it to HCTP's Facebook page and YouTube channel. Members of the Hamilton County group also sent a link to the video to Glenn Beck's and Bill O'Reilly's email accounts. (It was broadcast during their shows later that month.) As Dan concluded, he said, displaying a combination of purpose and exuberance, that he felt like the Old Testament figure Nehemiah with his sword and trowel rebuilding Jerusalem and purifying the faith—only that his sword was a video camera.

In that one fast-paced hour of the Hamilton County meeting, a snapshot of the priorities and practices of a local Tea Party group emerged, providing a clue to the role these groups filled in the wider movement. The participants stressed familiar Tea Party themes of fiscal austerity and reverence for the Constitution. Additionally, though the group was autonomous, it was nonetheless drawing on packaged printed information from regional and national organizations, such as the John Locke Foundation, and circulating discourses from conservative popular, nationally distributed media—most notably here, Glenn Beck.

Yet despite the overlap of its content with familiar images of the Tea Party movement, the Hamilton County Tea Party demonstrates how

LTPGS constitute an important component of the movement. Noteworthy was the *local focus* of the group's activism, which in this case, was the county board of commissioners. In addition, the group was *developing its own tactics*—rewriting the county budget and using video and YouTube in innovative ways. Through the internet this group, like others that I studied, was able to *feed the "cultural resources" they had produced back into the trans-local Tea Party* and conservative universe. As I argue in more detail in later chapters, they formed a semi-independent component vital to the circulation and production of the symbolic and discursive components of the movement. Some of the tactics of HCTP were different from those of the other seven groups I observed, reflecting the backgrounds of the participants and the particular organizational culture developed within the group.

As exemplified by the Hamilton County group, LTPGS were key to the vitality of this emerging movement. They created social spaces where the nationally circulating symbolic themes of the Tea Party gained expression in local political activities. In these spaces participants were reproducing and repurposing discourses, symbols, and practices circulating via broadcast media, new media, and social media. As time went by, I also began to realize that these groups were not only sites of local performance of these nationally circulating discourses; they were also sites of innovative local application of the cultural resources and sites of cultural production for the broader community. They were, in some cases, producing new symbolic and discursive components that fed the wider Tea Party universe of media, political personalities, and elite advocacy groups. Finally, and perhaps most important, these local groups were also facilitating the development of many everyday citizens as informed and effective political actors eager to influence the local, as well as the national, political landscape.

The Tea Party and Social Movement Theory

The perspectives offered in this book build on two lines of inquiry within social movement theory. First, the elite–grassroots–mass media network of the TPM is uncommon, especially among movements on the left. Second, ethnographic research of Tea Party groups provides an intimate view of the transformation of everyday people into activists as they fashion collective and *personal* political identities within submerged spaces of practice.

GRASSROOTS-ELITE-MEDIA NETWORK

This study of the Tea Party draws attention to a different kind of social movement form—the association of autonomous elite and grassroots units of a movement networked through broadcast media, social media, and face-to-face interaction. Many social movement scholars study groups of relatively powerless people often on the sociopolitical left. In contrast, the Tea Party movement presents a special challenge in the application of social movement theory. Theoretically, one of the biggest differences between some right-wing movements and left-wing movements in the current historical period is the incorporation of elite and mass media components in a populist movement. The TPM is essentially an *elite-grassroots-media network*. Beginning fifty years ago, Gerlach and Hine (1970) described what would later be called "New Social Movements" as "segmented, acephalous and reticulate," or simply networks containing no true center. The idea of network organization—"social movement networks"—grew as an important paradigm in the study of social movements (Castells 2000; Melucci, Keane, and Mier 1989; Melucci 1996). The paradigm was used by McAdam (1982) and Morris (1984) in studies of the civil rights movement, Diani (1995) in the environmental movement, and Juris (2008a) in the alter-globalization movement. The TPM is a type of social movement network composed of commercial broadcast media, everyday citizens, and elite advocacy groups (Skocpol and Williamson [2012] make a similar observation). Nonetheless, the network model is rarely applied to the TPM because, to many, the presence of elite organizations implies ipso facto orchestration by elite organizations. This is a position my ethnographic material disputes.

Political power today is often contested through movements constituted by communication networks (Castells 2007), and thus the newer organizational forms are characterized by some as "connective action" (Bennett and Segerberg 2012) in which the "resources" consist of information shared through networks. Yet social movement networks still display different degrees of member autonomy and central control (Flanagin, Stohl, and Bimber 2006). Organizations will vary between strong hierarchical control, such as the National Rifle Association, at one extreme and wide individual autonomy and responsibility, as exhibited in the Occupy movement, at the other. However, some political organizations are "hybrid," characterized by multiple forms. The Christian Coalition of the 1990s is an example of a centralized political organization complemented by relatively autonomous individuals and small local chapters scattered across the nation (W. Martin 1996; R. Reed 1994). Was the Christian Coalition "spontaneous or contrived"? It was both. The TPM is similarly a hybrid characterized by local groups with unrestricted individual and local-group latitude and a collection of national, formal organizations—often corporate-backed—that are connected to only a few local groups, and then only loosely.

New technologies are another feature of changes in social movements, and most likely one that is driving transformations. The social movement network model took new form through, among other information technologies, social networking websites like Twitter in the Arab Spring (Khondker 2011) and the Occupy movement (Juris 2012). LTPGs and NTPOs use digital social networks, such as Facebook, to share information, coordinate actions, and construct meaning. However, the Tea Party is somewhat unique in that conservative broadcast media, such as corporate powerhouses Fox News and talk radio syndicator Premier Networks, play an important role sending the cultural resources of the movement over the nation's airwaves and cable networks (see also Boykoff and Laschever 2011; Skocpol and Williamson 2012; Williamson, Skocpol, and Coggin 2011). Moreover, since the proliferation of twenty-four-hour cable news, corporate media consolidation, and the dismantling of the fairness doctrine, which mandated equal time for opposing viewpoints on federally licensed media outlets, the Tea Party information network is robust and insular.[3] Conservatives and others pursuing a particular ideological bent are able to easily and effectively circumscribe their media exposure to one consistent perspective across multiple media sources (Jamieson and Cappella 2008). The extensiveness of this possibility in the U.S. has only come about recently, so the oversized role that the commercial media play was much less feasible when much of the classical social movement literature was created. At this point in time, the Tea Party is a truly a different sort of movement network.

My analysis of local Tea Party groups reflects an approach to social movements that emphasizes meaning making as opposed to resources and organization. Several existing studies of the TPM (e.g., Van Dyke and Meyer 2014; Skocpol and Williamson 2012) develop effective resource mobilization approaches (Jenkins 1983; McCarthy and Zald 1977) with their focus on the material conditions, organizational capacities (including skills and networks), and tactics that enable organizations to mobilize support to address grievances. Yet that approach offers less understanding of the role of identity and personal transformation in the wider success of the movement. As Shapira (2013) has written, "In the process of focusing on the organizational dimensions of movements, resource mobilization scholars have mostly abandoned the project of understanding movements through understanding their participants." Directing attention to the role of LTPGs and everyday citizens in the wider movement requires a different approach. Anthropologists of social movements, along with other social movement scholars involved in the "cultural turn" (Kurzman 2008), are more helpful in understanding the centrality of LTPGs as these scholars tend to focus on the construction of meanings and identities (e.g., Allen, Daro, and Holland 2007; Escobar 2008; Alvarez and Escobar 1992; Holland, Fox, and Daro 2018; Price 2009; Satterfield 2002).[4] Entering the meetings and activities of local Tea Party groups, one is struck by the presence of submerged spaces (Melucci, Keane, and Mier 1989), where the distinctive cultural resources of the movement are used in the fashioning and performance of cultural or "figured worlds" (Holland et al. 1998), collectively constructed systems of meaning against which events, developments, self, and others are interpreted.[5] The LTPGs, in short, created the possibility for everyday citizens to produce, materialize, and perform practices and activities understood in terms of the Tea Party's political vision.

While these approaches will be discussed in more detail later, the participants in the Hamilton County Tea Party meeting provide a good entry point for thinking about actors forming in the spaces created by the TPM. For example, participants were forming a relationship between their own intimate (personal) sense of themselves as political actors and the meanings circulated by the Tea Party–supportive media. They were using these political discourses to identify themselves and, just as important, to try to change others as political actors. John, for example, used his love of writing to help the next generation appreciate and understand the Constitution. The shift in participants' politics was not simply about understanding the meanings of issues and symbols, but about the way people actually practiced their political personhood. The Hamilton County participants were taking on new political activities and positions, such as researching budgets, speaking at county meetings, and planning rallies. Local groups were circulating the resources, yet also appropriating, recombining, and contextualizing them within local-historical particularities. Their work created conditions for a powerful transformation of members' political identities and for the emergence on the local political scene of spirited new political actors.

I utilize different conceptions of identity in my analysis. By "personal" or "intimate" political identity, I refer to senses of self as political actors that individuals construct using cultural resources. By "collective" political identity, I refer to the sense of one's group as a political actor. "Social" identity refers to the broad categories of socially constructed groups that are often the basis of "identity politics," such as race, gender, and ethnicity. Identities, political and otherwise, are fashioned around shared cultural resources, practices, and emotional investments. They are negotiated, performed, and sometimes opposed in social practice, often becoming self-defining (e.g., Holland, Fox, and Daro 2008; Melucci 1995). The social practice theories of identity that I draw on provide an effective means for conceptualizing an important aspect of people's relationship to politics.[6] Politics requires individuals to confront and make sense of multiple, often abstract, and sometimes unfamiliar concepts and discourses. How they do so is mediated to a significant degree by their identities; social actors form emotionally invested senses of self, which inform how they plan and evaluate their own action and performance and that of others (Holland et al. 1998).

Additionally, senses of self are always in process and may be destabilized by sociocultural change resulting for some in ill-defined senses of anger, fear, and confusion. Social movements may anchor "unfixed" identities by supplying a logic of articulation or nodal points around which meaning and identities can be fixed (Escobar 2008).

Portions of the book are addressed to my analysis of the collective political identities that are forming in the Tea Party, to the intimate (personal) identities as Tea Partyists that some participants form, and to the social identities constructed in the Tea Party that are assigned to others.[7] My ethnographic material allows me insight into identity processes and goes beyond common and sometimes overly broad uses of "identity" in political analyses. Indeed, one key drawback of a popular form of political analysis that I aim to address is the attribution of uniformity to large, demographically defined categories of individuals, such as white, male Southerners, that are often neither collectively symbolized, unified agentive groups nor necessarily aggregates with empirically shared interests sufficiently significant to motivate them to common political action.

From my research and data analysis, a perspective on the TPM emerged that I describe in this book. I build the argument that the roles of everyday citizens and of the LTPGs they form are crucial to understanding the effectiveness of the Tea Party movement. The movement's emerging discourses produced and circulated by elite conservative organizations, media, and everyday citizens were employed to forge a figured world that not only gave meaning to many people's concerns over the direction of the country early in the Obama presidency, but established connections between those concerns and more long-term, ongoing anxieties about social and cultural change in America. The local Tea Party groups were and continued to be central to the movement's success by providing the space for collective political identities to be developed, lived, and performed. The results were vibrant local spaces of cultural production and effective political activism.

Yet this is not meant to imply that the microcultures produced in the LTPGs were carbon copies of each other. I observed variation across the first few LTPGs I observed; therefore, I conducted a multi-sited ethnography to better investigate different characteristics of the groups and to see whether my observation of local group autonomy was widespread. My choice of the American South as the site of my research proved to be a good decision. As more scholarly work on the movement emerged in 2011, I found very little reference to Tea Party groups in the American South and no focus whatsoever on how LTPGs may reflect the regions of the country in which they are situated. Ethnography of Southern Tea

Partyists provides a particularly vivid illustration of the fashioning of political identities given many of my consultant's attachment to the South's rich history and their connection to evangelical Christianity.[8]

Is an ethnography of Tea Party groups in one corner of the American South representative of the Tea Party in general? Absolutely not. Are many of my findings applicable to Tea Party groups nationwide? Yes. Some of my arguments on race, gender, and activism styles are discussed elsewhere with similar conclusions (Braunstein 2017; Burke 2016; Deckman 2016). Moreover, the network structure that I conceptualize was affirmed by Skocpol and Williamsons (2012). My discussions on faith (which Skocpol and Williamson discuss very little) are similar to those presented by Braunstein (2017). Furthermore, the cultural resources that constitute the figured world of the Tea Party that I ground this analysis in emerge in many of the later qualitative works published on the Tea Party.

However, as an anthropologist, I am less concerned with generalizability than a sociologist or a political scientist would be. Anthropology is a discipline that explores diversity, a quality that should not be confused with difference. Although difference is an aspect of diversity, so too is similarity. As a comparative discipline, anthropology seeks to explain the presence of sameness and difference across cultures. My anthropological analysis of the Tea Party will demonstrate a constant shift between similarity and difference both among the different LTPGs and across the movement.

I conducted participant observation and interviews with *active* participants in local Tea Party groups. Early research on the Tea Party was characterized by different conceptions of who actually represented the movement. In some quantitative studies, the Tea Party is represented through the opinions of those who "support" the movement. I argue that these methodological classifications are problematic. One can personally support many movements and in different ways (financial support, moral support, spiritual support, and physical support such as volunteering). Some movements represent core aspects of one's identity while others are viewed as simply better than the alternative. However, loose definitions of "the Tea Party" have been used to draw rather significant conclusions such as racism (I return to this in chapter 3) and other core grievances.

Strangers in Their Own Land is a recent volume by sociologist Arlie Hochschild (2016). The book contains rich ethnographic data drawn from several years of research among Louisiana conservatives, or what she calls "Tea Party advocates." She is largely successful drawing out and describing the lived experiences as well as the emotional aspects or "feeling rules" of her consultants. However, the conclusions she reaches and assigns to the Tea Party come from individuals, many of whom simply voiced agreement with the movement. The book seems to conflate Far Right fiscal/social conservatives and Tea Partyists. Consequently, I found her conclusions to be more consistent with non–Tea Party, right-wing conservatives.[9] Let me be clear, however, that this and other works provide very important insights into the opinions and outlooks of conservative Americans at the time of the Tea Party's emergence. Yet to capture the essence of what motivates and mobilizes Americans to *become Tea Party activists*, one must engage over an extended time with those *physically and emotionally* invested in the movement.

For eighteen months beginning in July 2010 and ending in January 2012, I conducted participant observation with eight LTPGs in the Piedmont region of North Carolina. The Piedmont is an economically and culturally diverse region of medium-size cities and small towns in picturesque rural settings. The region includes a range of rural and urban landscapes from the glittering southern banking capital of Charlotte to small towns, some still reeling from the departure of textile and furniture manufacturing and the decline of tobacco cultivation. I chose LTPGs with which to conduct participant observation on the basis of the different landscapes they occupy. Hamilton and Revere County Tea Parties were in counties anchored by relatively large cities of 100,000 or more. Hawthorne, Franklin, and Pierce County Tea Parties were in primarily rural counties anchored by small cities of fewer than 30,000 people. Adams and Greene County Tea Parties were in rural counties abutting the Appalachian Mountains with no nearby municipalities larger than a small town. Finally, the Burgoyne County Tea Party was in a region that had become a haven for middle- and upper-middle-class retirees. As will be seen, this combination of LTPGs produced a good variation of group characteristics, activities, and memberships. Table 1 provides basic characteristics of each LTPG and some of the key consultants I quote.

TABLE I. Local Tea Party groups in study

COUNTY	GEOGRAPHY	MEMBERS	AUDIENCE/ ACTIVIST	KEY CONSULTANTS
Adams	rural/small town	working class / middle aged	activist	Paul, Randy
Burgoyne	suburban	middle-/upper- class retirees	activist	Sue
Franklin	small city	middle/working class	audience	Sharon, Peter
Greene	rural/small town	working class/ middle aged	audience	David
Hamilton	urban	upper-middle class/middle aged	activist	Sandy, Robert
Hawthorne	small city	working class/ middle aged	audience	Mike, Trey, Sandra, Darrell
Pierce	small city, semirural	working class/ diverse ages	audience	Dale, Diane
Revere	urban	middle/upper- middle class	audience	Richard, Cheryl

My primary participant observation was conducted in regularly held meetings of the local Tea Party groups and in group events such as candidate forums and talks by invited speakers. During these meetings I observed the dialogue and interaction between members, the dynamic between leaders and nonleaders as well as the airing of members' concerns, and even open-ended discussions. When I completed my fieldwork, I had attended seventy-five different meetings and events, including large rallies outside the regular meetings. From these events I recruited consultants for semistructured interviews. I conducted fifty-nine semistructured interviews, which included the one or two primary organizers and several members of each group. I approached most of the interviews as political autobiographies (Holland and Nonini 2007), asking people to relate their history of political involvement and political awakening. Although I did want to understand some of the ideological positions of Tea Partyists, understanding the path my consultants took to the Tea

Party movement was of greater interest to me. Understanding ideology only gets one so far in understanding movement participation (Shapira 2013). Tea Partyists were committing themselves to a cultural world of practices and emotions, which is best captured by probing into activities, experiences, and relationships.

I also immersed myself in the Tea Party information network. I created a Facebook profile so that I could observe and participate in the social network of the groups and the wider Tea Party universe. Finally, I joined most of the listservs of NTPOs, such as Americans for Prosperity, FreedomWorks, and Heritage Action, in order to receive the same organizational messages as my consultants.

I situated myself in the research cognizant of my outlook toward political and social issues, the sense of stigma many Tea Partyists felt, and the sense of mistrust many of my consultants felt toward people whose politics were to the left of theirs. I presented myself as a researcher working to translate the Tea Party and the outlooks of its grassroots participants to the general public. Whereas militant and activist research (Hale 2006; Juris 2008) position the researcher within the struggle, I worked at pains to remove myself from it as much as possible. I told consultants up front that I would prefer not to discuss my own views on issues because I did not want people to feel that they needed to defend theirs'. I spent at least six months simply observing meetings and rallies and getting to know participants before ever sitting down for an interview. My purpose in these early months was to demonstrate my true desire to understand a fascinating political phenomenon, which regardless of the political implications, was driven by people who, like most other Americans, were trying to grasp and respond to dramatic social and economic change. I told them I disagreed with some of their beliefs and agreed with some; for example, I said I believed that government has a role in public life, yet I was fearful of many actions of the state, such as National Security Agency (NSA) wiretapping. My interests also came out in my interviewing given that I spent less time on the details of specific issues (which I was less interested in) and more time discussing biography, the meaning of experiences, and political activity. My consultants were satisfied with my explanation, I believe, because the desire for their movement to be understood outweighed their concern that I might, as one consultant said, "make us look like a bunch of idiots." When I left the field, it was apparent that many of my consultants, some of whom I had built friendships with, placed strong trust in me to describe their movement to a wider audience, not as a partisan, but as a social scientist. This is the goal I believe is apparent in this work.

With respect to my own political sentiments, the research was decidedly a challenge for me. At times it was difficult to quietly study conservative Americans at a point in history when many conservative ideas I vehemently disagreed with were becoming policy. Nonetheless, I am sure that conducting research with consultants whose views I often (though not always) disagreed with was made easier by the nonpartisan political organizing I had done for over a decade in the 1980s and 1990s. Saul Alinsky (1971), in *Rules for Radicals*, a book read by many young political organizers like myself (and thanks to Glenn Beck, many Tea Partyists as well), writes that organizers must overcome "psychological barriers to communication" (xix) by subverting personal preferences that may run counter to the community with which one is organizing. When campaigning for ballot initiatives, which address singular topics, I learned and taught other campaign workers to focus on gaining support for the topic at hand regardless of whether a potential supporter held views on unrelated issues that one found distasteful. This disposition translated well to anthropological research conducted with conservatives, and I am certain that my previous experience with political campaigns aided my effort to set aside my own political sensibilities in order to understand those animating local Tea Party participants.

Structure of the Book

In the following pages, I describe the Tea Party's prominence in the American political landscape and the way the movement provides a space for everyday citizens to realize a sense of political agency and activism. I direct attention to the local Tea Party groups, showing their importance to the success of the movement and their role as influential actors in the local political landscape. To capture the importance of the movement in these different regards, the chapters shift from a wide perspective of the Tea Party in the context of American political culture; a narrower focus on individuals' personal histories and their paths to the TPM; and finally a longer analysis of the local groups, their members, and actions.

The book consists of five chapters. Chapter 1 lays out an analysis of the different components of the movement and the movement's construction of a figured world or meaning system that resonated with a large number of conservative citizens.

Chapter 2 discusses how my Tea Party consultants found or constructed a meaningful relationship between their personal lives and the movement. The chapter, employing data from political autobiography interviews, underscores the personally significant connections between their lives and the figured world of the Tea Party movement. Providing a more people-centered perspective on the dynamics mentioned in chapter 1, chapter 2 illustrates how everyday citizens easily built "equivalences" between their own grievances and concerns and the perceived goals of the movement, an indicator of a successful movement as argued by Laclau (2005).

Chapter 3 discusses how the interpretive frame of the Tea Party figured world and the Tea Partyists' attendant collective political identities were used to make sense of a particular ongoing political struggle. Racism was and continues to be a consistent charge made against Tea Partyists and was the source of great frustration for those in my study. This chapter describes how Tea Partyists come to understand racial difference and inequality and how that understanding reflects how race is conceptualized in contemporary conservative and mainstream American politics.

Chapters 4 and 5 are devoted to a description of the local Tea Party groups and their significance in the wider Tea Party movement. Chapter 4 describes some typical Tea Party meetings and some of the activities within the LTPGs. I build on theories of submerged social movement spaces (e.g., Hetherington 1998; Melucci, Keane, and Mier 1989; Taylor and Whittier 1999) and communities of practice (Lave and Wenger 1991) to show how LTPGs provide the basis for figured worlds performed in these spaces and fashion collective political identities.

Chapter 5 discusses the considerable variation across groups, including the different types of political activism practiced by local Tea Party groups. I explore in this chapter the different characteristics of LTPGs and the way these characteristics relate to the types and fields of political activity. The chapter shows that Tea Party organizing and protest focused on local political bodies and policies are a crucial and often overlooked aspect of the Tea Party's success.

I conclude with what I see as the importance of linking social movement studies, political anthropology, and mainstream electoral politics. I will also draw attention to what the study of contemporary conservative political movements and projects can contribute to anthropology and social movement studies.

As the book goes to press, the legacy of the Tea Party is still unfolding, and the reader is likely seeing connections between the TPM and the most recent form of right-wing populism, Trumpism. The Tea Party is not Trumpism, but as Mark Twain might have said, they sure rhyme. One could argue that Trump continued to exploit fissures in the American political culture that, though not necessarily opened by the TPM, were definitely exacerbated by it. Occasionally in the analysis and in the epilogue, I will make attempts to draw connections between the two movements, though the profound shifts in American political culture are ongoing.

1   Patriots

FASHIONING A FIGURED

WORLD OF TEA PARTY POLITICS

This analysis builds an understanding of the Tea Party's emergence, attraction, and spread as a combination of messages and practices that provided participants with meaningful interpretations of sociopolitical struggles at a specific and unique point in time. These interpretations and practices combined with other circulating cultural resources contributed to the fashioning of durable political identities within local Tea Party groups. This chapter describes the emergence of those cultural resources and their formation into a cultural world that provided the foundation for these Tea Party identities.

Conservative, nativist, and populist movements have emerged throughout American history (Berlet and Lyons 2000). Yet each emerged in the context of unique historical conjunctures and were driven by people with specific values and fears. Since several authors have thoroughly discussed the history of the Tea Party's emergence (Formisano 2012; Rosenthal and Trost 2012; Skocpol and Williamson 2012; Zernike 2010), a detailed description is unnecessary. However, a discussion of the meanings that my consultants attached to the emerging movement is crucial to understanding the theoretical concepts I will employ. Moreover, since I have described the TPM as a network of citizens, elites, and media, it is important to understand how those entities together contributed to the fear and concerns of conservative Americans in early 2009 and participated in the circulation of symbols, narratives, and frames that mobilized my consultants. This section will focus less on the history of the movement and the arrangement of resources and more on the words of Tea Partyists fashioning meaning from those processes.

In the first months of 2009, the United States was at a unique point in its history. During the final months of 2008, the economy had continued to deteriorate to a point where the financial crisis was being compared to the Great Depression. In January Barack Obama was inaugurated as the first Democratic president in eight years and the nation's first African American to assume the office. To many Americans, the time was electric. There was a sense that America was in a place it had never been before, yet one that was slightly familiar. There were comparisons to Franklin Roosevelt, such as the *Time* magazine cover for November 24, 2008, showing a Rooseveltesque Obama with cigarette holder, pince-nez, and crumpled fedora under the headline "The New New Deal."

Many conservative Americans, however, found the prospects of this new era unsettling. Media played a leading role in developing these fears long before Election Day. Understanding the emergence of new outlooks requires the researcher to consider not only the sociopolitical landscape but also the media messages available to consumers for making sense of the new developments (Hall et al. 1978; Hervik 2011). Media, in other words, reshape, amplify, and circulate cultural resources that their consumers may take up to understand political events and issues. The media-driven discourses employed throughout the 2008 campaign acted to "other" the future president, portraying him as being foreign and possessing beliefs that were out of sync with mainstream America. Videos began circulating of the pastor at Barack Obama's home church in Chicago. The Rev. Jeremiah Wright was reported to practice a religious perspective termed "black liberation theology," portrayed as Marxist, violent, antiwhite, and reminiscent of the social unrest of the 1960s. There were also reports of Obama sitting on an educational oversight board that included William Ayers, a professor of education at the University of Chicago and a former member of the violent, antiwar organization the Weather Underground. Stories such as these and countless references on talk radio created alarm among conservatives and many others regarding Barack Obama.

By Election Day many conservatives saw Barack Obama as someone foreign to American sensibilities. Not only was he considered a Marxist, but like Wright, he seemed to hark back to the conflict and turmoil of the 1960s, an era many of these Americans would just as soon not revisit. My consultants portrayed Barack Obama as dangerous and out of step with "mainstream" sensibilities. To those who would make up the primarily older and white demographic of the TPM, these themes were frightening.

In a later chapter I will draw some conclusions regarding how my Tea Party consultants conceptualized racial difference and conflict in America. In this description one can see how what I believe are overly simplistic conclusions regarding race and the Tea Party may have emerged in those early months. I maintain that it is easy to take a shortcut here and attribute Tea Partyists' concerns as simple racism. But my data in chapter 3 complicate that charge with ideas of national membership and cultural citizenship.

Conservative Americans were also concerned about government spending and the national debt. In 2008 the United States was experiencing the worst financial crisis since the Great Depression. This crisis itself was alarming, yet the massive government expenditure to address the crisis was also alarming. Before the election the Bush administration had initiated large government expenditures to prevent the collapse of the banking sector. As Barack Obama took office, this program was extended (the total expenditure would be reduced later) and a flurry of new programs were begun.

Moderate and liberal Americans tended to see the 2009 increase in spending and debt as a troubling yet necessary or even inadequate government reaction to the economic crisis. To many conservatives, in contrast, it seemed to shift the world as they knew it. Spending, debt, new responsibilities of government, and the seemingly foreign values of the new president all contributed to what Perrin et al. (2011), drawing on Anthony Giddens (1991), term "ontological insecurity," the destabilization of one's sense of self and one's place in the social world. Most Americans had not witnessed such massive and sudden deficit spending on domestic and social programs and job creation in their lifetime. The most recent instance of spending increases of that magnitude, not spent on tax cuts or defense, was during the Great Society programs of Lyndon Baines Johnson and the creation of Medicare, half a century before. Simply, in the months leading up to late winter 2009, there were numerous sources contributing to a general unease and fear on the part of conservative Americans.

Scholars of the Tea Party have attributed varying degrees of causation to the media circulation of an emotional outburst by CNBC reporter Rick Santelli broadcast live from the floor of the Chicago Mercantile Exchange on February 19, 2009. Most, however, will agree that it was a moment that crystalized many conservative grievances emerging at the time. Most would also agree that the rapid and widespread circulation of the outburst foreshadowed the importance of media in the mobilization of the movement. However, from the perspective of my Tea Party consultants, "Santelli's rant" was meaningful. My interest is to show how the episode combined a set of powerful symbols into a compelling and concise description of the concerns some Americans had regarding their perception of the country's direction in the early weeks of the Obama administration. It was an important moment in the emergence of the movement yet was one of many cultural resources employed by all three components of the Tea Party network to fashion a cultural world of the Tea Party.

With palpable emotions of indignation and anger, Santelli directed his ire at federal legislation that would provide subsidies to homeowners needing to renegotiate mortgage terms. This program was designed to slow the high foreclosure rates—1 in 45 households experienced a foreclosure filing in 2009 (Christie 2010)—that were intensifying the economic downturn. Santelli's statement, laying the onus of the mortgage crisis at the feet of irresponsible "losers," was wrapped in themes of personal responsibility, fairness, misplaced entitlement, ill-conceived government priorities, patriotism, and a less-than-serious call for a "tea party" on the shores of Lake Michigan. These themes, which I will analyze later in this chapter, raise some of the important discourses and other cultural resources that will enable the imagination and performance of the Tea Party's complex of meaning and cultural world.

The CNBC anchors in the studio were discussing the new legislation when they referred to Santelli for his comment. His response took the anchors by surprise.

The government is promoting bad behavior! . . . How is this, president and new administration? Why don't you put up a website to have people vote on the internet as a referendum to see if we really want to subsidize the losers' mortgages; or would we like to at least buy cars and buy houses in foreclosure and give 'em to people that might have a chance to actually prosper down the road and reward people that could carry the water instead of drink the water. This is America!

From the first sentence, Santelli enunciates moral claims wrapped in everyday economic resentment that became a hallmark of the Tea Party: those who (are likely to) do the work should be the ones to receive support and the rewards. Then turning to a group of floor traders behind him, he asks, "How many of you want to pay someone else's mortgage?" He then focused that statement by saying, "How would you like to pay the mortgage for someone who bought a bigger house than they could afford?" To Santelli, the economic crisis was not caused by loose regulation of the financial industry and lax underwriting standards for mortgages but by the personal choices of individuals not living within their means. Moreover, government through its bailouts was enabling this bad behavior at the expense of those who make responsible choices and fulfill their responsibilities.

Santelli then shifts to a second theme: America's Revolutionary history and patriotism. "We're thinking of having a Chicago Tea Party in July. All you capitalists that want to show up to Lake Michigan, I'm going to start organizing." Then, just before the viewers were returned to the anchors in the studio, Santelli drew in one more historical referent. "I'll tell you what, if you read our founding fathers, people like Benjamin Franklin and Jefferson, what we're doing in this country now is making them roll over in their graves." Although Santelli's use of the Boston Tea Party as an organizing symbol was not new in American politics (Lepore 2010; Mayer 2016), his use in this instance linked conservative moral claims of self-reliance and choice to the nation's founders. Simply, in Santelli's portrayal the founders practiced and instilled in the nation— both its people and its government—a set of values that have been betrayed by contemporary Americans and their government.

Noteworthy is how Santelli effectively frames fiscal issues as an instance of ongoing cultural politics (Alvarez, Dagnino, and Escobar 1998) that was meaningful to many different groups of conservative

Americans.[1] Sandra Morgen (2011) describes a years-long effort that she terms "taxpayer identity politics," a historical process of identification begun during the New Deal and driven by conservative and corporate interests. The taxpayer is cast as an overburdened producer of funding for irresponsible and insatiable government spending that invariably goes to an undeserving "other," such as welfare recipients and, more recently, public employees. Moreover, Santelli's frame also resonates with conservative evangelicals who constituted an oversized share of early Tea Party supporters (Jones 2016; Jones and Cox 2010). Christian evangelicals' more individual relationship with Christ and salvation relates to more conservative socioeconomic outlooks, or what Emerson and Smith (2000) term "accountable freewill individualism." Many conservative Protestant evangelicals are less willing to blame people's misfortune on structural factors, such as lax banking regulations and structural inequality, than they are to blame Santelli's "losers." Individualism, personal responsibility, and distrust that government programs will alleviate social ills become moral claims regarding who truly demonstrates American cultural membership.

I maintain that Santelli and the emerging Tea Party discourse tapped into several resentments—taxpayer identity politics, cultural identity politics, and Christian identity politics—all enunciating deep-seated cultural anxieties. Santelli reflected what Cohen and Arato (1984) term "the cultural politics of neo-conservatism," that is, the root of the national crisis is figured as a worsening culture of dependency at the expense of historic and defining American values such as achievement, self-reliance, and "principles of order," including private property. Robert Jones (2016) writes that this narrative of cultural loss and an idealized past was also meaningful to large numbers of conservative white Protestants experiencing with dismay the dramatically changing social and moral landscape of America. Some of my consultants would use the term "American exceptionalism" in this context, while others would phrase the problem as a rejection of "founding principles."

Santelli and the emerging Tea Party combined decades-old cultural politics with constitutional literalism and compelling patriotic images. In short, the diffuse confusion, fear, and anger over seemingly out-of-control government, negligent politicians, and faulty citizenship were clearly framed for many conservative Americans as an outcome of a government that was not being held in check by the firm boundaries specified in the Constitution. These boundaries are supposed to be upheld by citizens motivated by patriotism, responsibility, and morality as extolled in the Revolutionary era and personified in the moral examples set by George Washington, Benjamin Franklin, and other of the nation's founders.

The widely and repetitively circulated clip of Santelli's rant set in motion an "articulation" or linkage between different symbolic elements in a new single discourse (S. Hall 1996; Laclau and Mouffe 1985) encompassing patriotism, history, capitalism, and emotions of indignation, fear, and betrayal of history and the country's greatness. None of these separate elements were necessarily new as conservative themes (Berlet and Lyons 2000; Diamond 1995; McGirr 2001; Phillips-Fein 2009), but they were merged at a unique historical moment when new meanings emerged in particular arrangements of social forces and events. The importance of this articulation was that it brought together a "package" (Gamson and Modigliani 1989) of symbolic devices, moral appeals, and metaphors that formed interpretive frames of an issue that resonated (Benford and Snow 2000; Gamson 1992) with many and motivated them to seek out the emerging movement.

Santelli's rant effectively forged an interpretation of events that was meaningful and emotionally appropriate for a large number of Americans. The episode could easily have disappeared as the news cycle moved on to something else. However, the discourses were quickly picked up by different political actors who supplemented the frames with new concerns, visions, emotions, and imagined worlds and lay a foundation for the forging of a distinctive collective political identity.

Santelli's rant was a dominant story on that news day, and it also set in motion concerted organizing strategies by what would become the three components of the movement network mentioned earlier. National-level conservative advocacy organizations—some existing, some emerging—became closely associated with the Tea Party movement as national Tea Party organizations. Conservative media, primarily Fox News and conservative talk radio, supplied the movement with a constant stream of relevant images and material. Last, local groups of everyday citizens formed local Tea Party groups.

Shortly after Santelli's outburst, approximately fifty small protests occurred on February 27, 2009. These were organized by a group of activist conservatives who came together shortly after Barack Obama's inauguration under the Twitter hashtag #TopConservativesOnTwitter (Lo 2012). Jenny Beth Martin, a former conservative political consultant, began a social network on Ning.com to organize like-minded conservatives that within months became Tea Party Patriots, an organization that developed into one of the primary NTPOs (Zernike 2010).

Two corporate-backed conservative advocacy organizations found in the emerging Tea Party discourse an opportunity to further their policy goals and recruit and train grassroots-level activists, lending their organizations a semblance of grassroots support (Mayer 2016). Americans for Prosperity and FreedomWorks emerged from the split of Citizens for Sound Economy, which had been organized by industrialists Charles and David Koch. FreedomWorks, which also provided assistance to Tea Party Patriots (Fetner and King 2014), began organizing within hours of Santelli's rant. The organization established a website through which people were encouraged to plan protests for April 15 and receive tips and guidelines for organizing a protest, making signs, writing press releases, and giving soundbites. Later in 2009, Americans for Prosperity began playing a large role in the movement, providing issue information, grassroots trainings, and subsidized charter buses to large events.

In addition to what became national Tea Party organizations, conservative media also began to organize around Tea Party themes soon after the Santelli episode. Fox News and conservative talk radio were the primary media-based organizers of the nascent Tea Party movement. Beyond simply repetitive news coverage of the emerging Tea Party, Fox News was actively cultivating the movement (Williamson, Skocpol, and Coggin 2011). Fox News host Sean Hannity aired the Santelli clip on the same day, and like FreedomWorks, the Fox News Channel also created a website and actively promoted April 15 "Tax Day Tea Parties." Fox produced its own map showing events around the country and directed viewers to its own website. The network also sent anchors to several of the events and advocated the views of the nascent movement (Hananoki 2009).

Working through these networks and others were thousands of everyday citizens inspired by Santelli, media sources, and the spectacle of people protesting. These citizens themselves organized rallies or sought them out in their areas. Most of my consultants made spontaneous statements indicating they quickly identified with the people they saw on television at that time and were inspired by the images. In an interview Paul and his wife described their first impression of the Tea Party: "When we first saw the Tea Party on television, we understood exactly what they were trying to do. They wanted to make a change in this country at the grassroots. They were just pissed off at both sides just like we were. And I thought, 'Wow, there's people out there like me.'" In a sense these images provided a kind of relief for many who saw other people displaying their deep patriotism and willingness to stand up to an out-of-control government. As Trey put it, "I felt that the people were speaking for me. The people were echoing my sentiments that . . . I think it was a sense of comfort. I felt comfortable knowing that other people saw what I saw." Wendell had spent years as a local Republican Party official in rural Greene County, watching the grassroots party structure slowly decline: "When I saw that many people who were moved politically and they had decided to stop griping and be active, I thought 'at last there is hope for this country.'"

Several of my consultants stated that soon after they had heard Santelli's outburst and seen reports of the emergence of protests, they searched online for demonstrations in their areas. Some drove miles to stand tentatively on the sidewalk in front of a post office or federal courthouse with handmade signs, along with others, mostly strangers, similarly unsure of what precisely to do, but confident because of media images that there were others like them marching and chanting and holding signs.

"Stop the Bailouts—that was my first Tea Party sign," said Darrell, a retired civilian military employee who, before the Tea Party, had never considered protesting anything—"except maybe if they had run out of beer or something." Seeing the protests on television, he said, "I felt like I wanted to do something. I didn't want to just be a bystander. I wanted to at least carry a sign. I would feel like I was doing something. The first protest I went to was in Fayetteville. I drove all the way down there. There were only about twenty-five of us, and we marched around for a while with our signs at the federal courthouse." Marshall, in the adjacent county to Darrell but unacquainted with him, searched online for "anything Tea Party" after seeing Santelli. He also headed to the Fayetteville protest. Marshall later met local Tea Party organizers in his own county at one of the Tax Day protests and became a leader in the group, the Burgoyne County Tea Party. Farther west another of my consultants, Peter, was also motivated by Santelli and the burgeoning movement.

I was listening to one of the [conservative talk radio] shows and I heard Rick Santelli's rant. Then I saw the video. He's right, the government is overspending. Our government is doing this to the people and then all of a sudden, these little Tea Party groups start popping up. I started googling 'tea party groups' and came upon Tea Party Patriots. Right around March, the Charlotte Tea Party had a rally regarding spending. I went to Charlotte and made a sign. I was hearing people speaking that were pretty good. The people around me were pretty like-minded.

Peter later founded the Franklin County Tea Party.

These three components operating in those early months of 2009 provided an important beginning of the movement and illustrate the construction of meaning through its networked architecture. The components were separate and were made up of multiple and separate actors within them. Yet like many other contemporary social movements, the TPM did not have a hierarchical structure; it was "reticulated" (Gerlach and Hine 1970), having connections through different networks (e.g., Castells 2012). Radio and TV, social media, and the personal networks of everyday citizens were all able to circulate strikingly similar cultural resources, including symbols, narratives, and emotional displays focused on similar grievances.

The initial attraction of the TPM cannot be attributed to any one factor. Initial concerns varied yet were crystalized by a specific historic arrangement of forces and conditions. Some were concerned about the economy. Others about a seemingly unresponsive political system and ever-expanding government. Still others were frightened by the Barack Obama represented by conservative media.

The key was not those concerns per se but rather how through symbols, circulated through media networks, those concerns were condensed into a common interpretive framework. Santelli's rant took peoples inchoate concerns and condensed them by linking them to metaphors, images, and narratives that were particularly meaningful to conservative, primarily white Americans. Fears and concerns took material form when placed alongside the founders, America's Revolutionary heritage, and the moral and cultural aspects of class politics. This frame was then expanded and circulated by conservative media, elite organizations like FreedomWorks, and everyday citizens.

It is also important to stress that the three different components—media, large organizations, and everyday people—all played a role in the emergence of the movement. FreedomWorks and Koch-affiliated Americans for Prosperity are accorded different degrees, and sometimes oversized degrees, of responsibility for the rise of the Tea Party by different scholars (e.g., DiMaggio 2011; Mayer 2016; Skocpol and Williamson 2012). My data show that national Tea Party organizations were necessary for the emergence of the movement yet insufficient to be solely responsible for its rise and longevity. The three components working separately yet networked together constructed the movement. The TPM did assume a specific form owing to the influence of those organizations. However, local groups I observed made clear to me that they received no direct funding from NTPOs. However, more significant, FreedomWorks and AFP had been organizing efforts and actions for two decades (sometimes even using the Boston Tea Party theme) without ever achieving the notoriety they did with the TPM (Mayer 2016). Finally, the local Tea Party groups I participated with declined after 2012. Attendance at meetings declined, and several groups no longer met on a regular basis. However, FreedomWorks and AFP were no less active at events and meetings of other LTPGs. In short, those groups had their best years because of the other aspects of the movement.

A Figured World of the Tea Party

Santelli's rant functioned as an effective collective action frame that resonated with the concerns of many nascent Tea Partyists and motivated them to seek out the emerging movement. Framing theory is employed in social movement studies to account for aspects of meaning-making by social movements through appeals that situate the movement's discourse and symbols within a target group's cultural understandings (Snow and Benford 1988). And while framing effectively provides a language for capturing these first moments of the TPM, the theory proves limited for appreciating what developed after those initial moments. The movement grew into a dynamic, polycephalous, multivocal formation of shifting components, each involved in the cultural production of new meanings, practices, and identities. People were not just hearing descriptions and interpretations of Tea Party grievances on television and radio; they were also hearing and seeing rallies and protests portraying everyday citizens developing, performing, and displaying dispositions characterized by emotional displays and colorful practices and sentiments.

Popular media can provide resources for interpreting events and even fashioning subjectivities (e.g., Abu-Lughod 2002; Anderson 1984), but the Tea Partyists, drawing on these media images, were together creating productive social spaces and relations in connection with these resources. They were forging, performing, and expressing collective identities. They themselves became generative. They added new cultural resources, such as dressing in Revolutionary era garb, and drew in additional historical props, such as the Gadsden flag's Don't Tread on Me. This dynamic and productive quality also resulted in meanings unwelcome by many in the Tea Party, such as the display of Confederate flags and overtly racist images and references to President Obama.

Therefore, much more than simply providing interpretations, all three components were involved in the production of a widespread collective political identity that forefronted action and reinforced basic themes applicable across a wide variety of political concerns. In its most basic sense, a collective identity is based on the sharing of cognitive, moral, and emotional connections (Polletta and Jasper 2001). More specifically, people fashion collective identities under specific historical circumstances using cultural resources at hand in response to changing circumstances (Holland, Fox, and Daro 2008). These cultural resources may become especially potent when articulated in relation to a "figured world" and the identities relevant to that world (Holland et al. 1998). The concept of figured worlds is part of the theoretical perspective of social practice theory. A social practice theory of identity (see, for example,

Escobar 2008; Holland et al. 1998; Holland and Lave 2001; Satterfield 2002; Urrieta 2007) builds on the school of identity theory developed by social psychologist G. H. Mead (1912, 1934), as modified by the theories of social theorists Pierre Bourdieu and Mikhail Bakhtin. A primary line is drawn from cultural-historical psychologist Lev Vygotsky's recognition of human's penchant for conjuring imaginary or play worlds (Vygotsky 1978). While we are familiar with children figuring themselves in an imaginary world of firefighters or parents, throughout their lives, groups of people fashion cultural worlds for different domains of institutional life, for example, academia, restaurant work, or commodity trading. Each of these worlds is a "tradition of apprehension" (Urrieta 2010) in which people are recognized and words and events acquire meanings unique to that world. People "figure" senses of self-based on the persons, ideas, and symbols established in the world, where specific characters, symbols, practices and discourses are recognized and differentially valued. In the spaces where these figured worlds are performed, selves, others, and their actions are interpreted against these horizons of meaning and often form sensibilities and dispositions recognized in these worlds.

In her ethnography of the northwest logging disputes of the 1990s, Terre Satterfield (2002) found that the collective identities of pro-logging and anti-logging activists were characterized by distinct figured worlds associated with each side's practices, narratives, and symbolic meanings. As the two sides of the dispute interacted indirectly through the media and sometimes directly in spaces such as demonstrations, hearings, and debates, intimate and collective identities developed and shifted. Both sides of the dispute were constituted by cohesive solidarities that valued the forest and nature, though in different ways. Distinct ways of dress characterized these solidarities, which were also marked by contrasting emotional practices and content, such as loggers' sense of stigma as the public rejected their occupations, and by opposing narratives of the conflict. Furthermore, between the two figured worlds, the past differed, as did visions and commitments to the future. These conflicting cultural worlds indicated an alternate way of interpreting the conflict and certain aspects of the world in general. Satterfield referred to the two sides as "talking past each other yet sounding similar" because each side often claimed ownership over some of the same objects or "cultural resources," though investing those resources with their own meanings. For example, the northern spotted owl, an endangered species whose presence sparked the entire conflict, evoked dissimilar yet equally strong meanings depending on whether one was an environmentalist or a pro-logger activist.[2]

This example shows that different sides in a conflict don't simply possess opposing ideas but actually occupy opposing cultural worlds. Furthermore, using this concept provides a richer explanation of the bitter conflict that occurred in the Northwest in the 1980s and 1990s. As I will show in further chapters, the figured world of the Tea Party movement provides an equally nuanced explanation for the movement's success both in its breadth and, more significant, in the deep level of commitment by participants.

Figured worlds are more analytically useful than and should not be confused with the concepts "worldview" or "ideology," which connote an all-encompassing belief system that transcends most domains of life. While Tea Partyists may hold a conservative worldview or a Christian evangelical worldview, these are only factors in the construction of political identities fashioned *within* the context of the figured world.

As compared to worldview, a figured world is best considered as a conceptual space that is constructed in practice by people, media, and organizations. It differs from worldview in several qualities that make it a more useful theoretical concept. First, figured worlds are situated in different places by people with different histories. Thus, unlike a worldview, the figured world will vary across space and time. However, figured worlds may be remarkably consistent across space as actors, developing similar outlooks, are connected through networks (Niesz and Krishnamurthy 2014). Consistency is most commonly achieved through mass communication, and media discourses have been shown to be appropriated and used as artifacts to constitute shared cultural worlds (Anderson 1984; Hervik 2011; Spitulnik 2002).

Second, worldviews imply transcendence and a foundational mental orientation. People are instead "recruited" into figured worlds and move into and out of multiple ones. One may occupy and perform the figured world of a member of academia during the week and then perform a different figured world when she practices her religion on the weekend.

Finally, ideologies and worldviews are primarily ideational or cognitive, whereas figured worlds are performed by the body and actively rely on cultural resources—symbols, words, and objects in the practice of constructing the world. In other words, figured worlds have materiality.

One of the most vivid illustrations of cultural resources and face-to-face recruitment of neophytes into a figured world is a description of Alcoholics Anonymous (AA) by Carol Cain (1991; see also Holland et al. 1998). Those who come to Alcoholics Anonymous by choice are seeking to change the unmanageable life of a "practicing alcoholic."[3] Cain writes that as one proceeds through AA, one is drawn into a new figured world of the sober alcoholic. This figured world is created and reproduced in the individual AA meetings, an alternative world of socially produced and culturally constructed activities that the "newcomer" learns to participate in as part of his or her new sober identity. The figured world is also populated by cultural resources or artifacts, symbolically marked objects that become a link to and a materialization of the figured world. These include the tokens (poker chips in Cain's study) that mark milestones of sobriety (twenty-four hours, one month, five years, etc.); texts such as the book *Alcoholics Anonymous*, called the "big book"; and emotional accounts and the ritualized practices of telling stories about one's path to sobriety. "These objects originate outside the performers and are imposed upon people through the current institutional treatments and within interaction to the point that they are self-administered" (Holland et al. 1998, 62).

Anyone observing the Tea Party can easily discern a distinctive cultural world. The Tea Party has created a set of identities, practices, emotions, and symbols that constitute what it means to be a Tea Party member. In the case of the TPM, cultural resources are objects such as the Constitution, historical figures such as the founding fathers, social identities such as "liberals" and "patriots," discourses such as those that construe government spending as out of control, historical narratives such as America's Judeo-Christian moral foundation, and emotional expressions such as defiant anger. These elements make up the collective identity of the Tea Party. Tea Party members perform their version of the collective identity in a range of activities and practices, including organizing political rallies, counterprotesting, making and displaying signs, dressing in colonial era outfits, and telling stories of outrage at meetings of LTPGs. Their grievances and claims are framed in expressions of indignation, assertions of patriotism, and a sense of felt danger. They share visions and symbols with other Americans, such as freedom and the Constitution, but they have invested specific meanings in and have made claims of their own over those symbols.

As noted, I characterize the TPM as a cultural movement. Its grievances are the demise or abandonment of specific collective (and sometimes imagined) understandings, values, practices, and meanings that are the essence of American exceptionalism. They speak to the meaning of citizenship and community. Excessive taxes, bailouts, and wasteful government spending are the symptoms and results of the decay. The source of the problem is forsaking those moral qualities or "trading the burdens of greatness for the relief of mediocrity" (Steele 2011). The Tea Party figured world assumes a core narrative that committed patriots can end the tyranny of bailouts, excessive taxes, dependency, and dishonest politicians by reconnecting Americans to the historical legacy of the nation's founding, by restoring the founding principles of personal freedom and responsibility, and by reinstating firm constraints on government.

This narrative undergirds the valorization and championing of three broad and overlapping sets of practices and dispositions evident in gatherings of Tea Party groups. The three, which I will expand on in the next section, are as follows: *patriotism*, the demonstration of patriotism in public and in everyday practice, including the forthright honoring of heroic and virtuous episodes from American history and the willingness to stand for fiscal restraint and other principles no matter what; *fundamentalism*, an insistence on cultural, political, and economic fundamentalism most vividly displayed in adherence to the literal meaning of the Constitution and the rejection of "RINOs" (Republicans in name only) in favor of all but the most inflexible conservatives; and *emotional expression*, the emotional display of indignation and resolve. Before discussing the three sets of dispositions in more depth, an event I attended with some of my Tea Party consultants will illustrate the figured world in the context of those dispositions.

The Washington DC sky was clear, and a bright sun was shining that first week of April 2011. I was emerging from a chartered bus at the west front of the U.S. Capitol with a couple dozen members of the Burgoyne County Tea Party. We had left the county before dawn on one of several busses chartered by the NTPO Americans for Prosperity to ferry people on the Eastern Seaboard to the Stop Spending Now rally. The rally was organized by AFP to show support for conservative Republican congress members who were blocking an increase in the government's debt ceiling, the periodic resolution passed by Congress to maintain the federal government's borrowing authority. Empowered by many newly elected "Tea Party conservatives," these Republicans had been holding up the resolution, threatening to allow the federal government to continue to function only in exchange for broad and deep cuts in spending.

During the six-hour bus ride, I met several members of the Burgoyne County Tea Party. According to Sue, the co-founder of this chapter, those present were seasoned activists who had been involved in seventeen protests and grassroots lobbying events since the chapter was formed two years before. As we walked along the path from the west front to the east front, where the rally was to be held, I surveyed the group. Most of the members were of retirement age (it was also a weekday). Most wore red T-shirts emblazoned with the Burgoyne Tea Party logo over their button-down shirts and blouses. Two of our group were dressed in colonial attire. John had on a navy-blue coat with gold trim that resembled an officer in the Continental Army. Travis wore a coat of a much brighter blue, cream-colored breeches and high socks, and white wig—more the looks of a noncombatant. John, the more outgoing of the two, carried a hand-drawn sign that said, "Shut 'Er Down," signifying the demand that Republicans should risk a government shutdown and the accompanying fiscal chaos in order to get the spending cuts they desired. Also in our group were a couple of younger women and a sixteen-year-old high school student who would later dash between the House and the Senate office buildings (beyond the opposite ends of the capitol—no short distance) in order to meet both of his heroes, Congressman Ron Paul and his son, Senator Rand Paul, before the buses departed again for North Carolina.

As we came around to the east side of capital, there was a crowd of six hundred or seven hundred people, which, though large, was dwarfed by the vast expanse of lawn and trees between the House of Representatives side of the Capitol and the Library of Congress. In the center of the group was a podium where speakers would address the rally. People milled about, some carrying 16 × 24–inch cardboard signs distributed by AFP that read, "Cut Spending Now."[4] Others carried their own handmade signs with such slogans as "We Want Liberty, Not Tyranny—No Obamacare!" There were several more signs which simply stated, "Shut It Down," and one with a cartoon drawing of a sinister-looking Barack Obama with the caption which read, "Liar, Liar, America on Fire."

The rally included remarks from several conservative officeholders popular with Tea Partyists. Then-congressman Mike Pence of Indiana announced, "The debt stops here! If liberals in the Senate would rather play political games than accept a modest down-payment on fiscal discipline and reform, then I say, 'Shut It Down!'" The crowd responded with a chant of "Shut It Down! Shut It Down!"

Rep. Jim Jordan of Ohio warned, "This spending fight is the central fight of our time. This is why we need patriots like you to step forward and say that this matters for our country and for our kids and for our grandkids." He then evoked the biblical story of David and Goliath encouraging them as underdogs.

Tim Phillips, AFP leader, in just a few sentences was able to associate President Barack Obama with criminality, racial discord, and elitism in his remarks: "President Obama told Republican leaders to act like adults. You know where he is today? He's in New York having lunch with [civil rights activist] Al Sharpton, who owes the government $1.8 million in back taxes. . . . Tell President Obama to put the golf clubs away and stop hanging out with tax cheats and start acting like an adult himself!"

The highlight of the rally was a speech by Tea Party favorite Rep. Michele Bachmann of Minnesota: "You came here because you care more about your government and your country than your own comfort and enjoyment. You are reasonable, fair-minded people who are fed up with government spending and who are saying to Congress: 'be principled, be practical, be reform-minded, and do these three things: One, don't tax us anymore. We are taxed enough already. Two, stop spending.

Stop spending more money than you have. And three, start operating within the limits of the Constitution."

The rally was finished by 2 p.m., and by 4 p.m. we were back on the bus. We arrived at our starting point at 10 p.m., seventeen hours after we had departed.

This is a scene that most Americans observing a televised Tea Party protest in 2011 would have been familiar with: a large rally of primarily white, conservative citizens carrying handwritten signs, the Stars and Stripes, and a few yellow Gadsden flags. Some are dressed in colonial garb, but all advocate uncompromising positions justified by their patriotism and the words of the Constitution. Those who considered the Tea Party "Astroturf," or fake grassroots, would have focused on the placards supplied by the AFP. Those who knew that the local groups were independently organized and operated would have known the groups were a hybrid of grassroots and NTPO organizing.

This description provides a glimpse of how the themes of the core narrative of the figured world were performed. The speakers addressed the existential danger of national debt and runaway spending using carefully chosen words that match the symbols and convictions of the attendees. Michele Bachmann stressed the Constitution as the ultimate test of legislation. She mentioned reasonable people who have a duty to save the republic. Tim Phillips evoked the "otherness" of President Obama. Finally, Mike Pence evoked an uncompromising stance of fundamentalism: sending the nation into a fiscal crisis overweighs any compromise. Patriotism, fundamentalism, and emotional displays of indignation were each present in the protest there in Washington, creating a bricolage understandable to any Tea Partyist. Less obvious in this scene was the way in which these discrete qualities were interwoven and imbricated into a complex political style.

PATRIOTISM AND HISTORY

In my analysis of the figured world constructed by the Tea Party movement, patriotism and history stand out as a quality and disposition central to many of the cultural resources used in the movement. The meanings of "patriot" are complex. It is a term used by many of my Tea

Party consultants and is in the names of many of the LTPGs. The anthropological literature suggests that patriotism is likely tied to nationalism.[5]

Nationalism, as an ideology, assigns a near-religious quality and mission to the nation-state, figuratively placing it above politics (Kapferer 1988). This mission is grounded in an imagined past or "retrospective illusion" of national founding and a future invested with purpose and destiny. Carried to the present, nationalism acts to resuscitate a love of nation often asserted in a language of ethnic unity and purity and a shared cultural identity.

These aspects of nationalism characterize the patriotism of the Tea Party figured world. As mentioned, the Tea Party labors to reawaken a shared, single-minded, and primordial American culture, including its honored narratives, heroes, and texts. The identity grounded in that culture is the key to American renewal. In many ways the shared cultural identity and history is primarily white or, as will become apparent, colorblind and based in the hegemonic understanding of American history familiar to those educated in mid-twentieth-century America.

Part of the Tea Party's version of American cultural identity is the open demonstration of pride and patriotism, which is seen by many as no longer socially acceptable in America. As Roberta, an upper-middle-class retiree, put it:

> People are not as patriotic as they used to be. I think there is a reawakening of patriotism because we are getting ready to lose our country and our freedom. But when I grew up, we put your hand over your heart for the Pledge of Allegiance. We sang "God Bless America," and we sang religious songs. I learned all the armed services songs. Today it is considered poor taste. Are you going to step on somebody's toes? Well, you are going to step on people's toes anyway. Step on them for the right reasons.

The nationalist voice of homogeneity is also apparent in this utterance as the consultant is essentially saying there is one interpretation of America and that interpretation must be enunciated regardless of others who may hold different interpretations.

But the most evident of patriotic practices in the Tea Party figured world involves emulating, learning, and evoking particular interpretations of Revolutionary era American history. In many cases when I asked consultants about their patriotism, the response centered on the sacrifices of the founding fathers. Kapferer, discussing nationalism, describes a form of worship of things defined as "the founding myths and legends of the nation and the customs and traditions and language of the nation" (Kapferer 1988, 1).

While many movements have used American history and the American Revolution as a frame, historical accounts are considered foundational by the Tea Party. For my Tea Party consultants, understanding American history provides the necessary lens for grasping the grave condition of American exceptionalism and cultural identity. When I met Darrell, a retiree and original member of the Hawthorne County Tea Party, he was in the process of building a parade float for the Tea Party group that would be used in the many holiday parades planned in the small towns and cities of the county. When the float was completed, three members of the group dressed in Revolutionary era costumes would stand it, waving to spectators. Other members would walk alongside handing out small American flags. Darrell saw this symbolic activity as more important than the more instrumental political activity of speaking at the meetings of the Board of Commissioners, the county legislative body. As he put it, "You want to go to [county] commissioners meetings, that's nice. But I don't really care that much about it. Because I care if our country is going back to the Constitution and our leaders are going to bring pride back our country. And that we get back to our founding fathers' great experiment. All this other stuff doesn't matter anyway." Implicit in Darrell's description is the sense that reconnecting with the historical roots of American greatness is the primary task.

As members of the Burgoyne County group mentioned earlier, dressing in colonial attire was intended to reconnect people with the meaning of the founders and the American Revolution. As Brad explained to me, "It draws attention back to the basics of what the Tea Party stands for." Brad and others were attempting to use symbols to revive forgotten ideas and themes they thought were crucial to the nation's greatness. The decline of American exceptionalism, they contended, flows from the rejection of founding principles. The Tea Partyists attempted to draw attention to historical principles and combat their neglect in contemporary America by re-signifying objects representing those principles and attributing to them the power to evoke those principles. To Darrell and many of my consultants, reconnecting Americans to their Revolutionary past is as important, if not more so, than political advocacy.

Glenn Beck, especially during his previous television show on the Fox News Channel, best illustrates the urgent connection between current national problems and historical themes. During the summer of 2010, Beck continually returned to a theme based on the final words of the Declaration of Independence. The closing sentence of the document reads, "With a firm reliance on the protection of Divine Providence, we mutually pledge to each other our Lives, our Fortunes, and our sacred Honor." In addition to stressing the spiritual content of this phrase, Beck stressed the founders' willingness to commit their lives, fortunes, and sacred honor as foundational characteristics and a model for a person's own personal and spiritual renewal. These episodes were extremely significant for Tea Party members, I maintain, because Beck effectively sutured the founding fathers to the moral themes of the figured world through a practice of patriotism that people could follow. Moreover, given the "pedagogical" style of Beck's program, many saw Beck as providing keys that would lead to a personal transformation in which one would possess the same qualities that made the founders so exemplary.

The use in everyday life of "our Lives, our Fortunes, and our sacred Honor" proved to hold strong meaning among Tea Party members as indicated in several discussions I had with them. As will be discussed later in this chapter, words from the founding fathers are often given literal and near divine meaning; however, here, in these simple words and in the context that most Tea Partyists knew from childhood, the founders are shown to have extraordinary qualities. The founders were aware that their signature on the Declaration of Independence could, if they were captured, lead to their execution. They also expected to lose their material comfort and well-being in what was expected to be a difficult war for independence against the world's preeminent power. But above the more tangible qualities of life and possessions was a pledge of honor to the other signers. In this manner, the signers were committed to a cause that, in Kapferer's words, is above politics—the good of the new nation and the protection of its patriots were above any political differences and conflicts that might have been apparent as members of the Continental Congress.

The words "honor" and "sacrifice" were used by those I interviewed several times with some using the exact phrase "sacred honor." This sense of sacrifice and commitment was brought out as people engaged in the activities of the Tea Party. Robert alludes to this meaning while describing how his Tea Party organizing was interfering with his home and work life: "My wife asked me before the event [a rally he was organizing]—it was the busiest time of year and here I was applying energy and time away from my family and business to do this. Someone had called me at like 9:30 at night and she asked me when this was going to stop. I told her that I didn't think it was ever going to stop. I loved it [before] when I just lived my life without any intrusion and not worry about stuff."

Richard, an officer in the U.S. Navy Reserve, was torn by his duty to uphold the Constitution and his sense that his loyalty to the Constitution may someday conflict with orders from leaders who were not, in his view, adhering to the document: "I'm still in the Navy Reserve. I took the same oath as congressmen and senators take. My oath is not to elected officials. It is to the Constitution. I sit around on reserve weekends and ask [myself] what our responsibilities are under that oath when elected officials are not following the Constitution. That led me to thoughts that I didn't want to think about. I have had these conversations with other officers. Joining the Tea Party was another way for me to support and defend the Constitution."

As seen in these examples, historical narratives of patriotism are cultural resources used in the fashioning of figured worlds and in the forging of intimate political identities. However, history is also a terrain of struggle, a source of "inspiration and tools of battle" (Skocpol and Williamson 2012). Indeed, in his classic work on a headhunting tribe in the Philippines, Renato Rosaldo uses similar words, arguing that Ilongot act as "partisans using their version [of stories] . . . as weapons against their opponents" (1980, 20).

In several cases Tea Partyists and media personalities would merge the temporality of history by reordering the relationship of past to present. Tea Partyists bring the past into the present as a touchstone for current policies, what Jill Lepore (2010, 8) terms "antihistory." The founders and their ideas are contemporaneous with the debate over health care, for example. And by claiming the founders would hold a conservative interpretation of the reform, the founding fathers are described as "rolling over in their graves." I experienced this weaponized antihistory firsthand in the presentation by a founding father impersonator that I saw several times during my research.

Ernest spends a busy retirement running a Tea Party group and giving presentations as his alter ego, Benjamin Franklin. I watched Ernest appear as Ben Franklin three times and learned that a large majority of my consultants, across central and western North Carolina, had seen his portrayal at least once. He dressed in colonial attire, wore wire-rimmed glasses, and used a cane. Portraying Franklin, he claimed he had come to our time on a type of sacred mission to "bring the *truth* of the founders and the original documents they signed," adding "not what you have been taught," employing the familiar theme of uncovering truths that secular and liberal society have hidden. In another presentation he said, "I was in a school recently and was asked by a young man, 'Dr. Franklin, how did you get here? And why did you come?' To tell you what it was like over two hundred years ago. To tell you what we did and why we did it and to help educate you in the arena of truth."

Ernest's portrayal employed understandings about Franklin that many Tea Party members have come to know from watching Glenn Beck. Discussing the Declaration of Independence, Ernest as Ben stated with authority that "happiness," as in the pursuit of happiness, "means property. It means that the government shouldn't take it. It means that you have the right to the just rewards of your hard work. And the thing that breaks my heart, you are not getting all of your just rewards from your hard work."

In another instance Franklin confessed, "though in my younger years I was an atheist and a deist, I have concluded that God governs in the affairs of the state and intervenes in the lives of those who believe." Whether Franklin took these positions has been argued over and sometimes dismissed by historians, but to Tea Party members what Ernest as Ben said is more than plausible, especially when considered in light of what they consider the secularization of society and government and the leftist bias of the educational institutions and academics that are the keepers of that history. The Tea Party cultural world revolves around a core narrative of a decaying America. To them, there is no doubt that if Ben Franklin (or Washington or Adams) could come to our time, they would scold us for straying far from the ideals that the founders outlined.

Ernest's portrayal also shows that history is something to possess, that by a specific (sometimes false) interpretation, history becomes a form of capital to enrich a particular ideological position. To push that metaphor further, Tea Party supporters and media will sometimes uncover hidden treasures—historical "facts"—that buttress their vision of America. Of course, to them, this treasure was not lost but hidden by liberalism and political correctness. One such example was the claim made by one of my consultants that half the signers of the Declaration of Independence were pastors. I found several references to the claim being made by author David Barton and more recently by former Arkansas governor Mike Huckabee. Detractors attempt to clarify the claim that those signers attended colonial era universities, such as Harvard and William and Mary, which were founded as religious institutions. Degrees from those universities were essentially degrees of theology and divinity. However, having such a degree did not necessarily mean that those graduates were clergymen. The interpretation and deployment of stories becomes a point of contact in this battle over the meaning of America. In a manner similar to today's charges of "fake news," history becomes something that is either real or not real and becomes associated with the goals and ideologies of one's opponent, in this case, liberal society. The "real history" is hidden, is stolen, or has been forsaken.

The past is often used as a medium for articulating and assigning meaning to these broader discourses. But it also demands a particular and narrow reading of America's Revolutionary era history in what Lepore terms "historical fundamentalism." History and texts are seen as sacred and ageless and need to be understood with the same original intent as Christian fundamentalists understand much of the Bible. This historical fundamentalism reflects a more general fundamentalist approach by Tea Partyists that entails political, cultural, and religious fundamentalism.

"Fundamentalism" is a broad term used in several contexts typically to describe a commitment to the essence of some traditional way and often a desire to return to a period in the past considered to represent the pure form. An early instance of a movement for fundamentalism in the U.S. arose in the late nineteenth and early twentieth centuries within American Protestantism. It was a reaction against "modernist" theology such as the "social gospel," biblical criticism, and changes in the nation's cultural and social terrain (Wilcox 1992; Wilcox and Robinson 2011). This movement took its name from *The Fundamentals* (1910–15), a twelve-volume set of essays designed to combat liberal theology. Anthropologist Judith Nagata (2001) defines fundamentalism as "entailing special forms of identity politics, meaning and labeling characterized by a quest for certainty, exclusiveness and unambiguous boundaries where the 'Other' is the enemy demonized." This broad definition effectively describes a central disposition of the Tea Party's approach to the world and politics. The concept of "cultural fundamentalism" is especially useful for thinking about the TPM's notions of American cultural identity and, as I will discuss later, the stance of the TPM in the cultural politics over immigration. Anthropologist Verena Stolcke (1995) writes that cultural fundamentalism "reifies culture conceived as a compact, bounded, localized, and historically rooted set of traditions and values transmitted through the generations." This definition is applicable to many aspects of the Tea Party already discussed, such as harking back to an idealized time, primarily Revolutionary era America. In an interview Janine and her husband saw this theme as so important that they considered it as their LTPG's motto: "We need to go back to basics. As a matter of fact, we were toying with that as a slogan or motto for the website. 'Back to the basics.' We feel like we should get back to a time when the Tea Parties were going on. A smaller government. A government for the people, by the people. It's not that anymore. It seems like a government for the government by the government." Many also believe fundamental truths lie in the simplicity of mid-twentieth-century America, seen as a time one of my consultants describes as when "people did not need to lock doors and children could play outdoors unsupervised."

This fundamentalist type of rhetoric Stolcke describes was apparent in many utterances of Tea Partyists when discussing undocumented immigrants. While the issue of undocumented workers came up frequently in my research, the nature of the concerns was quite varied and sometimes contradictory. Teasing out the degree to which race and ethnicity are mixed with what Tea Partyists assumed to be cultural traits is difficult. Yet when considered in the context of the Tea Party figured world and the ideal of American cultural identity, many of the Tea Partyists' perspectives are understandable

This varied and conflicted outlook on the part of many Tea Partyists toward undocumented workers, primarily Latinos, for example, is summed up by a quote from Cheryl from the Revere County Tea Party:

There is an innate love for America and its culture. When we see it being co-opted by people that want to come to this country—not to become part of it, but to take the resources that we have . . . Nobody is against legal immigration. We encourage and want people to come to this country and love it like we do. We want to maintain our unique identity as a people, which of course is a mishmash, but with a common goal. But we see people come here illegally who have no desire to integrate in our culture. They're breaking our laws . . . coming into this country. They also have dramatic fiscal effects on grade schools and hospitals [and] most do not want to become American, but to just use the resources. If someone comes [illegally] from Canada I would be just as angry. [However], unless they come from Québec, I can at least understand them.

In this statement three perceptions, which were also voiced by other Tea Party consultants, are apparent. Each relates to the wider idea of a bounded, homogenous and ideal American cultural identity.

The first perception, which has been a recurring theme by Americans regarding Latino immigrants (Chavez 2013), regards immigrants' lack of desire to assimilate to American culture and norms. Many of my consultants believed, contrary to 2015 research showing that current immigrants assimilate as fast as previous ones (Preston 2015), that Latino immigrants actively refuse to assimilate to American culture. Furthermore, they also indicated that "progressives'" ideology of multiculturalism has allowed people to not *need* to assimilate.

The second perception was that the undocumented workers were gaining benefits—whether "food stamps" or public education—by breaking the law. This was the most common and most emotionally presented perception and was typically presented as stark either/or, de jure citizenship. I commonly heard, "What part of illegal don't you understand?" This was sometimes framed in relation to foundational belief in strict adherence to the Constitution. In short, the argument went: one shouldn't reap the benefits of the Constitution by violating the laws that emerged from it. Nonetheless, the actual contribution or qualities of the immigrant, regardless of how exemplary, are immaterial to what is strictly a legal determination.

The third perception was that undocumented immigrants are a drain on public finances. This concern was associated with some of the more outlandish claims, such as the belief that 25 percent of the Hawthorne County school budget is used to educate undocumented children or that immigrants often do not contribute taxes yet receive government benefits. This perspective in some cases reflected the argument that economic restructuring has fueled resentment toward immigrants by white Americans (Hardisty 1999; Hochschild 2016). Many white Americans are convinced that they have "played by the rules," while immigrants who have not are given, as one consultant described them, "freebies."

I was initially puzzled by her final sentence regarding language because it didn't seem to follow to the theme of legal citizenship she was articulating. Rather, she shifts the argument briefly and tellingly to the cultural citizenship, the socially negotiated, "ambivalent and contested relations with the state and its hegemonic forms that establish the criteria of belonging within a national population and territory" (Ong 1996). Language is arguably the most prominent marker of cultural citizenship, establishing a clear boundary of belonging.

However, there are conflicting criteria for cultural citizenship. Anti-immigrant furor must confront the foundational claim of America as a nation of immigrants and celebrate the immigrants that affirm the narrative of American exceptionalism (Honig 2001; HoSang 2010). An opposite interpretation of undocumented workers emerges from some Tea

Partyists' relating to the Tea Party figured world's ideal citizen, who is independent, successful, and conscientious.

Instead of resentment, some Tea Partyists express "xenophilia." Immigrants are viewed with conflicted admiration as super-citizens (Honig 2001, 77). Dale of the Pierce County Tea Party often used the term "Mexicans," meaning that Latino immigrants have a can-do attitude and work ethic that is no longer valued by white Americans. Mike, a member of the Hamilton County Tea Party and a restaurant manager, spoke with admiration of his dishwashers:

> I've got several Hispanics that work for me one of which has been with me for eleven years. I love this man to death. Is he here legally? No. He had to go home and bury his father several years ago which means he had to sneak back across the border to Mexico and three months later to sneak himself back over. He had to pay a mule to take him across the border and get them to Arizona. Then he had to get back to North Carolina. He's forty-three years old. And that border is worse than it's ever been. They work. You know why? Because they came from nothing.
>
> I had a guy washed dishes for me one time. He went to a university in Mexico. He graduated from the university with a degree as a public accountant. He was making more money washing dishes for me than he ever made in Mexico as an accountant. Washing dishes. He changed tires at a place down here during the day and washed dishes for me at night. . . . Look, I think we should secure the borders, but I think we need to have a better way for these people—my great grandfather came over here from Ireland. He was able to come over here by jumping through hoops. There has to be something. We need to control the borders. We have to stop the violence. Putting in the states' hands. Damn sure we will fix it then.

Even though his dishwasher was trained as a professional, he is in America starting at the bottom, one of the lowest status jobs in America, in order to provide for his family and to build a life in the United States. But you can see at the end of the quote, Mike is conflicted over legal and de jure citizenship. He then compares that outlook to other native-born Americans: "I have a guy whose stepson works for me. If one couldn't come in to work, the other one would. The work ethic—. They're not perfect, but I'm telling you, they do the jobs that Americans won't do. [Native-born Americans would say,] 'I'm not working for $7.25 an hour. I'm not working for eight dollars an hour. Hell no, I'm not doing that.' These people who have survived sneaking across the border, they appreciate what they got, and they appreciate the money they're making."

Tea Partyists' outlook toward undocumented immigrants is complex even when it is presented as cultural fundamentalism. One can interpret the recurring theme of the decline in the value of foundational principles of American citizenship, such as hard work, self-reliance, and achievement, in different ways when confronted with the immigrant. In one way the undocumented immigrant flaunts the founding principles while in others they embody them better than some native-born Americans.

The strongest areas of fundamentalism in the TPM are in political arrangements and economics. Tea Partyists express inflexible certainty on foundational principles such as low taxes and little or no budget deficit, as shown at the Stop Spending Now rally with their chant "Shut It Down!" Their fundamentalist outlook is most apparent in their approach to the Constitution. Adherence to the literal meanings of the Constitution itself becomes an interpretive frame against which policy and people are measured.

Dramatic social and economic change, such as in the political terrain in 2009 or the religious terrain in the early twentieth century, can lead to a sense of a loss of values and groundings. Though some see these changes as openings for new interpretations of the world, for others they lead to a desire for the reaffirming of traditional values, views, and frames (Crapanzano 2000). Christian fundamentalists turned to the literal interpretation of the Bible; Tea Partyists see the Constitution as part of tradition, as a guidebook for restoring American exceptionalism, and as a guarantor of personal liberty enumerating the rights of the individual and unambiguously circumscribing limits on federal power. In words written by anthropologist Vincent Crapanzano at the turn of the twenty-first century, but which could have been transcribed from a Tea Party meeting during my fieldwork, reinterpretation of such a sacred text, as liberals and RINOs attempt to do, "betrays the intention of the

Framers of the Constitution and mutilates the polity they created. It affronts nation, national pride, and tradition" (2000, 4).

Tea Partyists are not the first to fetishize the Constitution. Michael Kammen (1993) writes of an earlier era of danger and change when Americans also emulated the founding document. Beginning shortly after the First World War, there was a newfound concern over Americans' poor appreciation and understanding of the Constitution. That period of history was characterized by large numbers of immigrants coming to American shores and the first Red Scare. Consequently, knowledge of the Constitution was seen as a bulwark against radicalism. And like some of the LTPGs I will describe, grassroots organizations, such as Constitution League, emerged to increase public knowledge of the Constitution, and legislation was passed mandating public schools to specifically teach it. In 1919 the National Association for Constitutional Government printed and distributed fifty thousand pocket-size Constitutions to schools, factories, and various civic organizations.

In 2010 and 2011 it became widespread among Tea Party members and some Tea Party–aligned politicians to identify as "constitutional conservatives" (Berkowitz 2009). The label became popular because it easily allowed Tea Partyists and politicians to distinguish themselves from other Republicans who were seen as more likely to compromise on foundational principles. Michele Bachmann, founder and first chair of the Congressional Tea Party Caucus, built on the imagery of the constitutional conservative on her presidential campaign website in 2011. It read, "We have to recapture the founders' vision of a constitutionally conservative government if we are to secure the promise for the future. As a constitutional conservative, I believe in the founding fathers' vision of a limited government that trusts in and perceives the unlimited potential of you, the American people."

To practice constitutional conservatism, to use the Constitution as a set of principles to guide one's political and economic stances, one must know the Constitution. Classes on the Constitution were common among Tea Partyists and their groups. For example, a member of the Revere County Tea Party who was also a high school social studies teacher had a fifteen-minute block during regular meetings for his constitution lesson. Some members would take classes online, such as one offered by Christian, conservative

Hillsdale College and advertised on *The Rush Limbaugh Show*. There were even Tea Party–themed summer camps for children (Carbone 2011).

It was extremely important that the Constitution be understood as intended, which returns us back to Lepore's idea of historical fundamentalism. One of my Tea Party consultants entered the race for his county school board primarily to focus the curriculum on the original intent of the founding documents and to reinstitute mid-twentieth-century educational simplicity, such as multiplication tables and spelling bees. He thought that the Constitution should be taught in English class rather than social studies in order for students to understand the founders' true intent: "One thing I thought about doing is take the Declaration of Independence, the Constitution, and the Bill of Rights, the Federalist papers— they should all be taught in English class. The reason I say English is because the English teacher can sit down with the words [and] show you how these words have changed meaning." He felt very strongly that the words in the founding documents no longer were understood as they were written. In other words, even if students are taught the Constitution, they are not truly understanding it as it was written: "If you get an 1828 Webster's dictionary, I promise you that that thing will blow your mind. The words have changed. I mean there's tons of them. So, when this kid takes his vocabulary that he has today and he tries to read a document that was written over 200 years ago, those things aren't gonna mean what he thinks they mean."

Lepore writes that many Tea Partyists share the belief in a narrowly defined past in which the founding documents are "ageless and sacred. . . . These documents are to be read with the same spirit with which religious fundamentalists read for instance the Ten Commandments" (2010, 16). The most vivid illustration of this outlook was Rev. Wilson, who was connected to the Adams County Tea Party. He pastored a Baptist congregation and was working on an advanced degree from Liberty University, founded by Rev. Jerry Falwell. Rev. Wilson saw the need for the use of the same hermeneutic principles as used to interpret the Bible: "The same is true with the Constitution. And people like the Heritage Foundation use hermeneutic principles and criteria. When the Constitution says that individuals are endowed by their Creator, what did that mean to them at the time? If you go back in history, you see that those principles are derived from specific interpretations of individualism that come from the Bible in Judeo-Christian principles."

Rev. Wilson also directs our attention to the link between evangelical Christianity and the Tea Party movement. A discussion of fundamentalism in the Tea Party must also include the role of Christianity in everyday Tea Partyists' lives and in the figured world of the Tea Party. As I will discuss in later chapters, the role of Christianity in LTPGs is contested and varies among the groups with whom I participated. Yet regardless of the place of religion in the local groups, religion was a very powerful component of many of my consultants' lives and informed their political outlook. Nonetheless, I found the relationship between religion and the TPM to be complex and varied. For some Tea Partyists, politics may be subsumed by religion, for others the two may be combined as two discrete elements, and for others religion should be left out of politics. Many participants linked important aspects of their intimate (personal) religious identity to the broader symbols and discourses of the TPM.

Glenn Beck's programs and more obscure radio, internet, and print sources were important factors in Tea Party participants' politicoreligious connection. The substance of Glenn Beck's books and broadcasts often merged religious and historical references that he would outline on his famous blackboard. His response to the Obama administration's reckless increases in debt, entitlements, and spending was a renewed call for "faith, hope, and charity." Describing them as "essential teachings of Christ" (Beck 2009), Beck represented each word with an image and story of a founding father—Samuel Adams, George Washington, and Ben Franklin, respectively.

This link of faith to American cultural identity was circulated through other media as well but was best exemplified by the minister/author David Barton and his organization, WallBuilders. Through appearances on *The Glenn Beck Program*, religious broadcasters such as *The 700 Club*, the WallBuilders' website, published books such as *The Bullet Proof George Washington* (1993), and videos such as *America's Godly Heritage* (1995), Barton promoted a revisionist and often inaccurate (Schuessler 2012) portrayal of the links between the founding fathers and Christianity.

Glenn Beck also sparked renewed popularity for the 1981 book *The Five Thousand Year Leap: Twenty-Eight Ideas That Changed the World,* written by author and well-known anticommunist W. Cleon Skousen. Advocating the broad claim that the U.S. Constitution is based, not in the Enlightenment, but in the Bible (Wilentz 2010), Skousen outlined twenty-eight principles that he argued were collectively valued by the drafters of the Constitution. These principles are purported to be the basis of American exceptionalism and to have led to the success of the American Republic. Furthermore, because of the "freedom and prosperity which the American founders turned loose into the spillways of human progress" (Skousen 1981, 4), in just two hundred years, human society made a five-thousand-year leap, accomplishing the equivalent of all the human progress in the five millennia preceding 1776.

Skousen maintained these principles emerged from the common belief systems of the founders based on similar ideas of "religious principles, political precepts, economic fundamentals and long-range societal goals" (Skousen 1981, 32). Using selected quotes from the founders' writings and the record of the constitutional convention, the principles included themes such as "A Virtuous Moral People" (principle 2) and the "Role of the Creator" (principle 5). It also included classical liberal ideology of "Property Rights Essential to Liberty" (principle 14) and "Free-Market Economics" (principle 15) and even Cold War conservative foreign policy such as "Peace through Strength" (principle 24). The book had faded into obscurity by the time of the author's death in 2006. But Glenn Beck resurrected it in 2009, calling it "essential to understanding why our founding fathers built this Republic" (Wilentz 2010). The book provided a simple and easy-to-read diagnostic guide that traced current American ills to people and the government's rejection of those founding principles. Beck's endorsement boosted sales, briefly putting *The Five Thousand Year Leap* at the top of Amazon.com's best-seller list.

The book gained a popularity that had eluded its first printing. The messages and themes of the book lay dormant, waiting for the unique mix of assumptions, fears, and values promoted by the Tea Party movement to give it new life. If my research is indicative, the book was a popular resource for introducing newcomers to the Tea Party figured world, with its focus on the writings of the founding fathers and its strong linkage to faith, morality, history, and capitalism. The popularity of the book was not lost on politicians seeking Tea Party support. When asked about his "reading list" by the organizers of the Value Voters Summit, Texas governor Rick Perry replied, "'I find myself going back to a book called *The 5000 Year Leap*' leading to nods and sounds of approval from the audience" (Benen 2011).

Skousen's successor organization, the National Center for Constitutional Studies, took advantage of the book's newfound success by selling seminars based on the book led by the organization's members and even marketing a do-it-yourself curriculum whereby facilitators could purchase a text, simple lectures, a course plan, and quizzes to organize their own classes teaching the twenty-eight principles. Several of my consultants bought multiple copies of the book at a volume discount in the hopes of selling them to other members of their Tea Party groups, but often they simply gave the books away because of the truths they saw the book containing. One of my consultants who was unsuccessful in establishing an LTPG reported spending forty-nine dollars for the course, ninety-nine dollars for the textbook, and six dollars for each of the ten copies of *The Five Thousand Year Leap* she purchased.[6]

The preceding discussion of patriotism, cultural fundamentalism, and religion draws attention to the oft-cited similarities between the Tea Party and the Christian Right. These connections became apparent early on, when a respected survey showed that nearly 50 percent of Tea Party supporters considered themselves Christian conservatives (Cox and Jones 2010). In another poll 81 percent of Tea Party participants identified as Christian, and a third survey (Liu 2011) found that 46 percent of Tea Party participants had not heard of or did not support the "conservative Christian movement."[7] Describing the relationship between these movements, one must resist the urge to incorrectly combine the discourse and symbols of the Tea Party and the religious Right into a hybridized singular ideology—what Brody (2012) terms "Teavangelicals" (see also Sharlet 2010). The situation is more complex. Indeed, moral claims lie at the heart of the Tea Party's and Christian Right's figured worlds. However, these moral claims have different foundations and lead to different actions. Accordingly, employing the figured worlds concept helps describe the connection and distance between these two social movements.

As discussed earlier, figured worlds are systems of interpretation that are forged socially in practice, in historically particular times and places. Individuals manage memberships in several different figured worlds simultaneously and throughout their lives. One may be a participant in the figured world of a commodity trader and then later in the figured world of Catholic religion. These two figured worlds in many ways exist as separate spheres of life with points where the discourses and practices of the two worlds, if brought together, would conflict. In this example the figured world of the commodity trader may favor unrelenting pursuit of profit, which may conflict with works of charity she does with the church. Contradictions within political identities and outlooks are not uncommon (Converse 1964) and are often managed (Strauss 1997).[8]

Although my fictional commodity trader who is a Catholic poses conflicts, people often occupy figured worlds that do not contradict each other but rather have points of connection. In other words, two distinct worlds like the one of a Christian conservative and the one of the Tea Party may have multiple points of coherence, such as Rev. Wilson's hermeneutic principles. For example, many American Christian fundamentalists ascribe to the belief in economic and social individualism and a distrust of government (Barker and Carman 2000; Bean 2014; Emerson and Smith 2000). Emerson and Smith write that white conservative Protestants are often "accountable free will individualists" who believe individuals are accountable for their own actions regardless of social structures, such as gender and class, that burden some more than others. Barker and Carman write that though some Christian conservatives express a responsibility to the poor, they do not favor government efforts to help the poor because of government promotion of secularization, LGBT rights, and abortion, which have been corrosive to traditional morality. Other Christian conservatives adhere to the doctrine of "millennial dispensationalism," the belief taken from the Book of Revelation that end times are approaching and that before Christ's return the conditions of life on earth will deteriorate. Thus, any aim at improving the world now is futile. In each of these cases, respondents would oppose government social programs and spending, yet they would come to those decisions for different reasons.

From these examples, Christian conservatives and Tea Partyists do have similarities in their themes, yet these themes are based in different cultural understandings. Both groups trace their moral discomfort to the breakdown of American values, though the nature and foundation of those values are distinctly different. From the rise of the current religious Right in the 1970s, its grievances are traced to secularization, such as removal of prayer in school and "family issues" of abortion and LGBT rights. As discussed earlier, Tea Partyists trace the decline to government and individuals forsaking foundational values, which although also based in a "Judeo-Christian tradition," are legacies of the founding fathers. Nonetheless, one can easily find evangelical Christians who practice accountable individualism and who have been disappointed by the Republican Party for decades yet who support the insurgent Tea Party.

How do Tea Party activists—those regularly performing in the Tea Party figured world—manage the similarities and the occasions when some participants try to make the two worlds intersect? Religious Right issues were rarely raised in the LTPGs with which I participated because those issues were not the cultural themes stimulating the forging of the Tea Party figured world. Rick Santelli's "losers" were not, according to him, rejecting Christian values. They were rejecting American values of responsibility and self-reliance. In her study of women Tea Partyists, Melissa Deckman (2016) found the women held outlooks on social issues similar to those of Christian Right women of past decades. However, "most Tea Party women place economic issues far ahead of social concerns in their [Tea Party] advocacy" (Deckman 2016, 26). This was primarily due to the acceptance that issues such as abortion are fault lines in American political culture that would interfere with building Tea Party support. In my research, as will be discussed in chapter 4, some Tea Party individuals' attempts to foreground religiously based issues, such as opposition to the teaching of evolution, were strongly discouraged in groups because it was seen as alienating potential Tea Party members.[9] Similarly, other components of the Tea Party network, namely, NTPOs such as FreedomWorks, Tea Party Patriots, and Americans for Prosperity, took pains to avoid social issues (Armey and Kibbe 2010) and, in the case of Tea Party Patriots, to specifically discourage talking about these issues (Meckler and Martin 2012).[10]

Of course, as noted with Glenn Beck and David Barton, others are working at the organizational level to meld the two worlds by forging a closer link between the Tea Party and the Christian Right. Christian conservatives have attempted to produce connections with fiscal policies for some time, most specifically through Ralph Reed's organizing of the Christian Coalition in the 1990s (D. Williams 2012; R. Reed 1993). More recently, during my research there were new concerted efforts by Christian conservative organizations to build common links with the TPM through emphasizing the connections between conservative religious values and fiscal policy (Bean 2014; Montgomery 2012; Wilson and Burack 2012), most vividly in Ralph Reed's latest effort, the Faith and Freedom Coalition.

Many of my Tea Party consultants did wholeheartedly agree with banning abortion and gay marriage and reintroducing prayer in public schools. Nevertheless, the cultural world of the Tea Party was formed on a generally secular foundation of American exceptionalism based in neoliberal values of individualism and responsibility framed as an American *and* Judeo-Christian legacy.

EMOTIONAL EXPRESSION

The third characteristic of the Tea Party figured world is an emotional tenor that circulates among the different components of the movement. The prior two components of the Tea Party figured world are permeated by emotions of anxiety, self-sacrifice, and resentment. Lutz and Abu-Lughod (1990) argue that emotion is a discursive component of culture, which should be interpreted as in and about social life—a form of social action read and understood by participants. Satterfield shows how emotion in the northwest logging dispute acts as a "lens through which one can view everyday moral discourse about what constitutes appropriate human behavior" (2002, 136). Much of the previous discussion of patriotism was based on how it is anchored in emotional conviction, but I want to develop the concept further in this section.

There is now a vast literature pertaining to emotion in social movement studies, which is heavily informed by sociology. Since the "cultural turn" in social movement studies, scholars now approach emotion as crucial to understanding social movement mobilization. For instance, in framing theory, "injustice frames" (Gamson 1992) channel grievances into specific interpretations of problems and solutions relying on emotions to drive the process.

To a large degree, work on the relationship of social movements to emotions emerging from sociology is focused on the strategic uses of emotion, such as how leaders use, cultivate, discourage, and maintain emotional registers (Jasper 2011; Goodwin, Jasper, and Polletta 2001). Cultivating and maintaining emotion has been crucial to the rise of the Tea Party movement. Fear, anger, and indignation are prominent and ongoing emotional registers continually circulating through and between the different components of the TPM. They are employed in anger-inducing communication from Tea Party Patriots or the conservative think tank / advocacy organization Heritage Action, drawing attention to the latest betrayal by government, such as the alleged targeting of Tea Party groups by the Internal Revenue Service. And of course, today's twenty-four-hour cable news and talk radio are typically characterized by a consistent repertoire of current political outrages. Much of the writing about the sociopolitical Right focuses on a politics of resentment directed toward the rising influence of ethnic and racial minorities, feminism, greater acceptance of LGBT persons, and undeserving "welfare" recipients (e.g., Diamond 1995; Hardisty 1999; Berlet and Lyons 2000; Stein 2001).

The emotion of fear and sense of betrayal within the Tea Party are accompanied by a strong emotion of indignation or righteous anger. Though other social movements have certainly been characterized by this emotion, it is central to the Tea Party. Tea Partyists understand themselves to be authentic patriots in the face of an increasingly unpatriotic and misguided nation. Moreover, as McVeigh (2014) describes, their access to institutional power has been diminished. Whereas many of the "new social movements" were attempting to gain rights that they never had, the Tea Party is trying to retain or regain power members feel they have lost. Accordingly, circulating Tea Party discourses are often characterized by messages such as "Take the Country Back!" and "They [politicians] Work for Us!" However, as noted by social movement scholars (e.g., Goodwin, Jasper, and Polletta 2004; Rohlinger and Klein 2014), anger and resentment are typically not enough to maintain a social movement over an extended period. Inspiration is also necessary to keep individuals involved (Rohlinger and Klein 2014).

Following Juris (2008b), I am less interested in the strategic or managed applications of emotions in social movements and more in how they model a vision of the world and provide a space for those visions to be realized. Juris quotes from Guobin Yang's focus on the empowering, experiential dynamics of activism and mass actions, which allow activists to produce "affective solidarity" by pursuing "emotional achievement" or "the attainment of self-validating emotional experiences and expressions through active and creative pursuits" (Yang 2000, 596). For example, in some ethnographies of the alter-globalization movement (Juris 2008a, b; Graeber 2002, 2009), large-scale protests were often organized into different blocs characterized by different emotional tempos. One section of protests was the Revolutionary Anarchist Clown Army, which focused on playfulness; another section, called black blocs, was characterized by anarchism, physical defense of protesters, and the defacement of symbols of capitalism; pink and silver blocs were characterized by festiveness and song. Juris argues, "Identities are expressed through distinct bodily techniques and emotions that are generated through ritualized conflict and the lived experience of prefigured utopias" (2008a, 62). These "affinity groups" provided spaces where the people who wanted to engage in different degrees of protest, or shared similar visions, could act together. And these blocs were not spontaneous but were ongoing and collectively understood whether the protest was in Genoa, Prague, or Barcelona. Hence, emotion in this context was a desired style of life that was practiced within social spaces given over to the performance of particular figured worlds.

Returning to Cain and her discussion of the figured world of Alcoholics Anonymous, emotions are considered cultural resources. Though she does not elaborate on the point, Cain argues that since alcoholism dominates all aspects of the person's life, sobriety must also, including "spiritual aspects of . . . humility, trust, honesty" (Holland et al. 1998, 70). These feelings, to which I would add "gratitude," constantly circulate through AA meetings, are emphasized as crucial to succeeding at long-term sobriety, and become an important indicator of how one is to act as a sober alcoholic.

For many Tea Partyists, participation in Tea Party activities allows them to perform the emotional dispositions that characterize the type of citizenship they value. As noted previously, a key factor in American decline according to my consultants is a rejection of people's expression of patriotism. Several consultants mentioned that one of their visions for the future is that people will display the flag and readily express their patriotism freely. In my research the TPM provided a space where patriotism was freely expressed. This patriotism was often circulated through social and mass media, for example, in the emotional displays of Glenn Beck. On one episode of his program, Beck said, "Let us find ourselves and our solutions together again." His eyes welled up with tears; he paused and looked down. He then looked back up with a slightly wrenched face and said, "I'm sorry. I just love my country and I fear for it." Of course, Glenn Beck is much too savvy a media personality for us to believe that this utterance was anything but scripted, yet his emotional expression opened a space where the emotional aspects of patriotism can be freely displayed. In other words, it's appropriate to be emotional about America because to Tea Partyists America is in peril. It is appropriate to pledge your "sacred honor" to America. On two occasions when I asked my semi-structured interview question about the interviewee's sense of patriotism, the consultants (both male) paused and briefly choked up with damp eyes. Neither verbally acknowledged the episode, but I took their damp eyes to indicate a strong emotional connection to patriotic feelings about the country lying just below the surface and an intensity not necessarily appropriate outside the Tea Party in a conversation with a non–Tea Partyists like myself.[11]

Though displays of resentment, indignation, anger, and fear are common recurring, meaningful aspects of the TPM's figured world, I maintain and will further illustrate that the success of the movement was based less on these emotions of anger per se and more on participants' possibilities for sharing and expressing patriotism socially, and so, to create a positive emotional bond. Tea Partyists see a world in which America is losing claims to a cultural identity they cherish, yet they are not able to express the emotions they have about this loss to others in everyday life. Yet as I will show in chapter 4, with the Tea Party, they not only can express those emotions, but the experiences are personally transformative.

Santelli's rant set in motion the construction of an interpretive frame that ordered people's sense of fear, anger, and resentment. However, much deeper culture work was going on in those early months. Through practices, emotions, and symbols circulated through different media, the Tea Party had concreteness or materiality to the active participants.

Through social media and mass media networks, different components—both elites such as Fox News and FreedomWorks and grassroots everyday citizens—were able to fill in and expand the interpretive frame into a figured world that allowed people to experience and practice their now cohesive political outlook. And while figured worlds provide the interpretive frame to evaluate issues, history, themselves, and others, they also allow people to fashion shared bodily dispositions, such as uncompromising firmness, patriotism, indignation, and as we will see, activism.

However, the processes by which the Tea Party figured world becomes a lived world and an embodied practice have not yet been fully developed. As will be discussed in the following chapter, everyday citizens, in the context of the movement, begin to articulate their lives with the figured world and vice versa.

2 Troubles

In the early months of 2009, the three components of the TPM circulated a consistent and compelling narrative about the ills America faced and the actions to set the country right. The narrative was supported by emblematic practices, metaphors, historical images, and emotional registers. However, it is important to stress that people are not simply seized, in a Foucauldian sense, by a movement's messages, practices, and symbols as a docile subject or as some political rag doll. I don't think the Tea Party would have been as successful were that the case. People exist in a social world where they watch and often face small and large political struggles and decisions almost daily. People grasp the compelling messages of a movement and then work through finding individual meaning in the movement. From meaning making, one may forge an identity at the intersection of the self and the movement (Strauss and Friedman 2018). This identity work intensified people's commitment to the TPM by making it personally meaningful. Simply, participants were able to establish significant connections between their lives and aspects of the figured world of the Tea Party.

Anthropologist Charles Price (2007, 132) writes that the first step of collective identity formation is establishing a connection between the personal and the sociohistorical. In his book on the formation of the Rastafarian movement in Jamaica (Price 2007, 2018), he builds on the concept of personal "encounters" (Cross 1971), dramatic personal experiences that help crystallize one's sense of blackness and injustice. These encounters, he argues, drive the fashioning of black collective identities. Of course, my Tea Party consultants were not suffering violence, oppression, and stigma as Price's interlocuters were. Yet Price's focus on the connections between the intimate self and social movement participation is central to understanding why movements are successful. Simply, Tea Partyists bring their experiences together with meanings from the movement to interpret and react to wider sociohistorical processes (Holland and Lave 2001).

Social movement participation is often a highly personal journey (Teske 1997) in which different aspects of a person's intimate identity will motivate political participation. As political scientist Edward Schatz writes on the importance of political ethnography, "If the study of justice, freedom, democracy and order are to mean anything, it must take into account individuals' lived experiences and how they perceive these abstractions" (2009, 10). Sociologist Rebecca Klatch (1987) found female conservative activists in the 1980s to be characterized by two distinct conservative identities relative to the primary, historical conservative cleavage of "economic conservative" and "social conservative." These perspectives were influenced by how the women shaped their conservative identity in light of their own personal histories and beliefs about the role of women in American society. An even more intimate conception of mobilization emerges through the "procreation stories" told to Faye Ginsburg (1998) in her study of female activists on both sides of a local abortion debate. Women who joined the pro-life movement not only were often reacting to their impressions of a changing society that glorified permissiveness, materialism, and narcissism, but many were undergoing transitions in their personal lives as women and parents, what Ginsburg terms "life crises." Abortion became an important component of the historically particular explanatory frames through which activists made sense of different transitions in the female life cycle. The stories "illuminate how . . . dimensions of experience considered private—particularly to the self—intersect with particular social and historical conditions that distinguish the membership of each group" (Ginsburg 1998, 134).

The figured world produced and circulated by the wider Tea Party movement—patriotism, fundamentalism, and the attendant emotions centered on a perceived decline in American exceptionalism—served as a resource that people learned from and about and conferred personal meaning on. They then "joined" that figured world when they found resonance between it and personal experiences and beliefs. In short, people were able to experience a sense of belonging by finding coherence between their own intimate identity and the cultural resources integral to the Tea Party figured world.

Ernesto Laclau (2005) sees the essence of populism, such as Tea Party conservatism, as structuring personal experiences such that individuals see them as "equivalent" to the wider grievances of the movement. In some cases consultants evoked memories of their local communities, where many lived on "welfare" and "food stamps," or of personal triumphs of surviving broken homes and finding new lives through perseverance or faith or of family histories of honor and sacrifice, some passed down from the Civil War. For most of my consultants, the Tea Party allowed for the establishment of equivalences among emotionally significant memories, unresolved discontents and disharmonies, and wider sociohistorical developments.

The method then is to trace out the places and processes of identification that link the movement to the intimate, on the one hand, and the wider political processes, on the other (Holland and Lave 2001). In their study of activists and political engagement by North Carolinians, Holland et al. (2007) sought "political autobiographies," semi-structured interviews that asked people to trace their history of political participation. The authors used the concept popularized by C. Wright Mills (2000) in the *Sociological Imagination*, which highlights the importance of how "people . . . see their problems as having public solutions" (Holland et al. 2007, 37). Mills employed the concepts of "troubles" and "issues." Troubles are "values cherished to an individual that are threatened." An issue transcends these local, personal spheres; it is a "value cherished by publics [that] is felt to be threatened" (Mills 2000, 8). Holland et al. (2007) found many people who made the connection between troubles and issues in turn formed or joined activist groups (and many who did not). By drawing on Mills, the authors theorize a chain of participation. Mills discusses the connection of the biographical to wider political processes, while Holland et al. add the important aspect of mobilization that sometimes emerges from such connections.

The political autobiography proves useful for analyzing the Tea Party movement and tracing out the lines of identification. In some cases Tea

Party participants voiced simple ideological connections between their conservative identity and their concerns regarding declining values, government debt, expanded government intervention in the economy, and the direction that Barack Obama was taking the country. As the following examples will show, many of the interviews with Tea Party participants revealed the movement as a moment of personal meaning making, during which participants made complex connections between personal and family history, long-held social concerns, their understood goals and meanings of America, and the concerns of the movement.

For example, Trey, a web designer in his late thirties and a co-founder of the Hawthorne County Tea Party, linked the moral claims made by the Tea Party to his upbringing in northern Kentucky and his current life as a youth soccer coach:

> My family members are Kennedy Democrats. And I've seen them sucking on the nipple of government. I've seen what it does to people—not just financially but what it does to people spiritually. No motivation or inspiration. Absolutely—you have to live in a society like that where it is all around you. The people down the street live like you do. The people across the tracks live like you do. Everybody in your little world lives like you do. You see people you know when you go down to sign up for your WIC card, and everybody's waiting on a check at the beginning of the month . . . It creates the kind of society . . . I just hate everything about it. I really do. That's an economic picture of it. The social aspect of liberalism is . . . A lot of it is detached from morality to some standpoint. I think too much liberalism is a detachment from morality. When I talked earlier about things we need to stay tethered to, morality is one of them. I don't believe in perfect people; I'm not one. But I keep reaching for the bar. I probably will never reach it. But don't lower it. I believe liberalism is the lowering of the bar so that everybody can reach it. Liberalism socially promotes things like—I'm a soccer coach and we give out the same medals to the winners as the losers because we cannot promote a competitive environment. But that is why you do sports to begin with; it is to instill competitive nature in children.

Trey illustrates the deeper moral meaning, discussed in chapter 1, of how the spending and debt concerns of Tea Partyists lie on the surface of what is truly deep-seated cultural concerns regarding the way government has eroded the moral framework of American greatness. Trey's conservatism is firmly connected to his experiences.

In the following three sections, I will describe some of the connections my consultants drew between their personal experiences and the meaning they assign to the Tea Party movement. The first will address how personal memories and life history are used to construct a moral-political justification for participating in the Tea Party. The second section will include the more instrumental motivations stemming from a sense of alienation from formal politics. Finally, I will continue with last chapter's discussion of Christianity, describing how one evangelical clearly connected the Tea Party to her own complex spiritual life history. Drawing on the experiences of people from most of the groups I participated with, the variation present across groups also begins to emerge.

Explaining Engagement with the Tea Party Movement
by Drawing on One's Life History

As I scheduled interviews with my consultants, I typically mentioned that I was interested in learning how and why they became involved in the Tea Party movement. I expected people to begin with the widely understood Tea Party discourse of debt, patriotism, and the dangers of the Obama administration. However, in many instances I was surprised when people, before my first question, initiated the conversation with stories of their upbringing or family history, laying out quite vividly how they linked their senses of self to the Tea Party.

Like my approach to history, I see the memories (both individual and collective) as a resource for and a product of the construction of the selves. Memory is typically evaluated and used according to its accuracy in portraying actual events (Thelen 1990). Yet memories are not reproduced but constantly reconstructed in the context of community and social dynamics (Carbonella 1996; Thelen 1990). "People recollect and rework the past through social practice that links meanings of the past to conditions in the present" (Gregory 1998, 13). In some cases these reconstructed stories, when shared by a group or community, can construct or reproduce a collective "we" (Doukas 2003). Relatedly, in what Sandra Morgen (2002) terms "foundational stories," people joining social movements may identify similar feelings and emotions in their own stories and those of other movement participants. The Tea Party cultural world laments the loss of a certain past, whether it is the Revolutionary era characterized by the values of the nation's founding generation or the idealized mid-twentieth-century communities against which many evaluate contemporary American society. This sense of loss emerges in many of the foundational stories Tea Party activists told.

I met JoAnn on a chartered bus traveling from Winston-Salem to the state capitol in Raleigh for a rally and a day of grassroots lobbying of the legislature. This was a yearly event for statewide FreedomWorks activists that was organized by the national organization and included a speech by its president and CEO, Matt Kibbe; an award ceremony for individuals who were particularly active with FreedomWorks; and a catered lunch of Carolina barbecue. A slight yet intense woman in her early sixties, JoAnn, in her younger years, had been an especially fast tobacco "stringer," a person who strings recently harvested tobacco leaves together in bunches in order to flue-cure or dry them in flame-heated barns. Because many of the people who raised tobacco in this region did so on small holdings, most tobacco farmers relied on informal labor from neighbors in order to prepare tobacco for auction. When JoAnn was raising her children at home, she would often help neighbors to string tobacco in exchange for small payments. She related to me one occasion when, after she had helped a neighbor in exchange for payment, a county employee asked her whether, since she was doing small jobs and had children, she would like to "go on welfare." JoAnn related this story to me as the way that government "captures" people, creating cycles of dependency that undermine individualism and self-responsibility, and ultimately the greatness of America.

JoAnn's experience with the tobacco economy in western North Carolina greatly informs the motivations for her involvement in the Tea Party movement by filling in abstract conservative discourses with personal experience. Another of those discourses is "onerous government regulation" such as initiated by the Environmental Protection Agency

(EPA). As JoAnn sees it, "Farmers have been here long before the EPA and they didn't need the government to tell them what needed to be done [to protect the environment]." In light of both global and national politics, JoAnn's political position in opposition to government makes sense. The 1990s tobacco settlement and the 2004 end to tobacco price supports—called the "buyout" in tobacco-producing states—brought a severe disruption to an already declining industry as the result of government action.[1] The appropriation of some settlement funds for anti-smoking campaigns acted as another example of how the government undermines personal responsibility. "I don't see why the government should be helping those people who can't quit smoking," she states, punctuating her statement with a caustic, "Boohoo."

JoAnn articulates how larger national and international processes are made real at the local level and how individuals draw on these connections in the construction of their political identities. JoAnn is articulating fundamental conservative beliefs regarding the role of government vis-à-vis the individual. I was disappointed when JoAnn canceled our scheduled later interview, which was to be more comprehensive than our brief discussion across the aisle of a chartered bus. A longer interview would have helped me understand specifically how the TPM played a role in her personal history, but our brief interaction provided an important juxtaposition in which to evaluate the importance of political autobiography in tracing the development of political identities. Through the longer semi-structured interviews, I was able to identify how a Tea Party identity goes beyond the simple conservative identities of many Americans.

The primary difference was how Tea Party members combined conservative discourse and specific themes from the cultural world produced by the Tea Party network. As was the case with JoAnn, motivations were driven by personal experiences of family, place, and previous political involvement. Yet Tea Party participants were actively "working" their identity to make connections between those conservative themes and Tea Party motifs with their emphasis on history and patriotism, political dispossession, and political fundamentalism.

David was an active member of the Greene County Tea Party, which while a different rural county than JoAnn's, was still near the city of

Winston-Salem. Many counties in the region once supplied bright-leaf tobacco to the city's then-flagship employer, R.J. Reynolds. David, age sixty-four, grew up in a small house in an agricultural area of the county. After high school he took an entry-level job at Reynolds Tobacco, where the company recognized his potential and subsidized his college education. After many years at Reynolds, David was hired by a major national trucking company, where he eventually rose to CEO. When I met David, he had recently retired, returned to Greene County, and taken over the farm he grew up on as his father's health declined.

I asked him how his community had changed since he had left it and whether he remembered any aspects of the political culture from his earlier residence in the county. He began by saying to me, "Bill, in the community I grew up in, we had a lot of barn-raisings. You're going to have a lot of barn-raisings when you live in a place where wooden barns are used to cure tobacco." In hindsight his response should seem puzzling coming from a Tea Party conservative. Instead of praising the moral value of individualism and responsibility, he begins by expressing the value of collaboration and strong communities. He continued, "When I was growing up the three most respected people in the community were the preacher, the schoolteacher, and the sheriff." He then raised his eyebrows and looked over the rims of his glasses in a nonverbal invitation for me to consider how those occupations are valued today. David's father was the county's representative on the Agricultural Adjustment Commission, the Depression era government entity that set production levels for tobacco. As the county "community committeeman," he was responsible for allocating additional tobacco acreage to be under cultivation each year, an important position that not only influenced the income of many in the community but also carried immense incentives for graft. David proudly said that in the years that his father was in the position, he never allotted himself any extra acreage: "My father would give you a dollar before he would take a dime."

Along with taking over the farm, David had a strong interest in giving back to the county in which he was born and raised. He began to sit on community boards and even organized a farmers' market for the county. In the process he became disillusioned with politics. He began to resist taking on leadership roles in the county because, "once you take a leadership role, they paint a big bull's-eye on your back. They want to tear you down for personal reasons." From that experience, the seemingly corrupt, self-centered, and invisible horse trading going on in North Carolina's capital began to make a lot more sense to him. The government was not the problem per se, but rather the people in the government. When he encountered the Tea Party, he realized it was something completely different. "The politicians were more supportive of the ones that were doing nothing, drawing a welfare check, than they were for me who was the taxpayer, paying for it. For the first time it wasn't somebody promising something. That's what really drew me to [the Tea Party]. It was nobody saying that if you vote for me, I will give you something."

The Tea Party to him was not "political" because it did not involve itself in the deal-making aspects of politics but rather it stood on the outside, in the "grassroots," holding politicians accountable.[2] But more significant, David is living by a type of conservatism less often seen today, commonly called "traditional conservatism" or "social tradition-alism." Traditionalism rejects the hyper-individualism of current conservatism, faulting America "for failing to recognize the fragile bonds of social order and for neglecting to defend the authority of ancestral institutions" (Deutsch and Fishman 2010). In her study of the emergent New Right in Southern California in the 1950s and 1960s, Lisa McGirr (2001, 149–50) writes that in the shadow of the New Deal and the further expansion of state power during and after the Second World War, the state reduced "civic autonomy" and intervened in social and economic problems with centralized and bureaucratic solutions. David was valuing a type of government he thinks has all but disappeared, even in small communities like his. If Tea Party members hark back to earlier times, this includes the loss of earlier forms of government that were personal, local, and wrapped up in the moral economy of the community. This distinction is not often made by popular media–generated conservative discourse.[3] But if someone like David was trying to make sense of the moral and social decline in America and especially American politics, he needed look no further than the ways in which government and the priorities of political leaders had changed since the early 1960s, especially when compared to a lionized figure like his father.[4] The TPM's symbols of revitalization enabled David to connect the meanings in these experiences with a suitable avenue for political expression. During the 2010 election he chose his candidates carefully and volunteered for those he supported. "The ones that I supported are ones I am in constant contact with. There is not a week that goes by that I don't talk to the people that I worked for . . . I'm now a better citizen. People come up to me and ask me about things because of my involvement."

Others drew on memories that related to different themes of the Tea Party figured world. Sandra, a retired elementary school teacher, found motivation in her memories around patriotism and corrosive government priorities. Also, like David, she traced her path to the TPM as not beginning in 2009 but much earlier, through significant memories of her upbringing. She began her interview with an explanation:

> I'm going to give you some background first of all. I am an expatriate. I wasn't born in the United States, and I wasn't raised here. I was born overseas [in the Panama Canal Zone]. We worked for the U.S. government. And when you live overseas, your patriotism, to me, is stronger than when you live in the United States . . . We had a lot of military bases around us, and we were engulfed in the ritual. So even when we were growing up in high school, we were involved in patriotism. The Pledge [of Allegiance] meant so much to us, and the flag meant so much to us.

Because of the unique place where Sandra was raised, on U.S. territory outside the borders of the country and within another nation's territory, her national identity carried special significance. She embedded her family history into the history of the Panama Canal. As part of the American community in a strategically significant territory, where military and civilian roles were interwoven, patriotism was instilled in her by way of rituals more customary of military service.

> When you go to a movie theater and you stand up and hear the "Star-Spangled Banner" before the movie starts, we didn't even think about these things. Things just happened. The whole theater stood up. When you are in school, you gave the Pledge of Allegiance. It was something to be respected . . . We had a ceremony for raising the flag every morning and taking it down every evening. When you could drive and you

were on the military base at five o'clock, you stopped your car and you got out and you stood at attention wherever you were and watched that flag come down.

As mentioned, part of the significance of patriotism in the Tea Party figured world was the sense that patriotic performance and sentiment by Americans was waning. What Tea Partyists saw as defining features of American identity and exceptionalism had fallen away in ways similar to the falling away of traditions and small community life discussed by David. In a twist on this concept, Sandra then compares that patriotism to both those back in the United States and younger generations—those complacent with their freedom—who lack the patriotism inculcated as an American living abroad.

When I came to the states and I see how [the American flag] is treated, it just kills me. They leave it up all night. They are tattered. When they get rid of one, they throw it away. You are not supposed to *do* that. There is a protocol on how you treat the American flag and how you fold it. Kids aren't taught that anymore. Now I understand there's something out now where they're going to ban flying the American flag in front of schools because it is offensive to foreign students. That came along the internet. I hope it's a hoax. We were engulfed in patriotism. If I grew up here, I wouldn't know. My kids don't even think much about it. When I talk about it, they say I'm an old fogey. No, this is the way we were raised. This is my environment.

As David was mourning the demise of moral economies and traditional social relationships, Sandra relates with sadness the demise of the rituals of patriotism and American cultural identity. Rituals maintain a social order by symbolically reaffirming the values, myths, and institutions of a group. Rituals may lose significance as societies change, removing a significant marker of the group's identity and solidarity and leaving group members with a sense of dislocation. Sandra also mentions a rumor that American flags may be removed from in front of schools because they may be offensive to foreign students. Though Sandra seems to consider the rumor a hoax, it nonetheless supports a belief not simply that the importance of the American flag is fading, but also that government has become overly concerned with "political correctness" and promoting multiculturalism.

She returned to this theme later in the interview when she described her participation in the "flagpole incident" at Balboa High School in the Panama Canal Zone. The incident sparked the 1964 Panama riots, which left twenty Panamanians and three U.S. soldiers dead. Oddly, however, the way she presents the story omits the riot, which some argue was the defining event in the decision to return the canal to the Panamanians in 1979.

> We had the 1964 flag thing where the Panamanians wanted to take the U.S. flag down and raise their own. The school kids, one of which was me, said no. We drew a line in the sand and said, no, the United States flag will fly over our high school. We didn't care if the Panama flag flew next to it, but it would not fly alone . . . Balboa High school. That's where the first beginnings of this started, when we took a stand against the United States government. There are two flagpoles in front of that high school. We took twenty-four-hour shifts around the flagpole so that no one would take that flag down. And we stood them down. In that regard, the U.S. government was putting something against us that we did not want. That we did not think was fair or right.

I asked her to explain.

ww: So the U.S. government wanted to put up the Panamanian flag?
SANDRA: The U.S. government, Lyndon B. Johnson wanted to do that.
ww: Do you know why?
SANDRA: He wanted to appease Panama, like Carter always said. Let's appease the foreign nation and give it to them. And the Americans down there felt that it was a sign of weakness. It was a sign of weakness. It was a sign that we were watering down everything. That's basically why all of us in the military took a stand.

Sandra's recollection of the events of January 9, 1964, centers the conflict on the U.S. government prohibiting the flying of the American flag at civilian installations in the Canal Zone. While accurate, the real drama of the event, immortalized to this day as Martyrs' Day in Panama, was the march by Panamanian students to the flagpole surrounded by the

American students and the scuffle that ensued among Panamanian students, American students, and Canal Zone police that led to the two days of rioting in the Canal Zone. In Sandra's recollection of the events, it was not the students protecting American sovereignty from the Panamanians, it was protecting American sovereignty from the U.S. government bent on appeasing the Panamanians—"watering everything down"—in a similar fashion to the erosion of respect for flag and country today. In Sandra's telling, the decline of patriotic values has been a long process lead by a government that no longer values American identity. Her beliefs were so strong that she stood up to the U.S. government to uphold those values. Fifty years later, that struggle continues to inform her sense of political identity.

David's and Sandra's stories provide an apt illustration of how Tea Party participants actively connect their experiences and subjective senses of self to the Tea Party movement's emphasis on the past and its idealized political and moral underpinnings. Sandra's and David's stories are similar to the "remembered village" constructed by dispossessed Malaysian laborers discussed by James Scott (1985). Because of dramatic social change, past arrangements are cast in a positive light. "The past becomes an effective ideological backdrop against which to deplore the present" (Scott 1985, 179). Yet what Scott refers to as "past in the service of the present" is selective; it focuses on specific things that have been eroded while omitting others.

In chapter 1, I referenced Jill Lepore (2010) and her term "anti-history" to describe the way the TPM claims ownership over historical persons and events. To many Tea Partyists, historical themes and images, such as the founders and the Boston Tea Party, are not seen as past events with vague similarities to the present, but as "more literal than an analogy." She writes, "It wasn't that the struggle was like theirs. It was 'we are there' or 'they are here'" (Lepore 2010, 15). No historical event is a direct analog to the present because of the unique forces and circumstances present in each. This direct connection to the past was dramatically illustrated to me by Jack, a hard-edged, retired machinist with a visible anger toward politicians, especially Democrats, his demeanor punctuated with a loaded shotgun propped behind the front door. Jack and his ancestors had lived in the same general vicinity since before the

Civil War. According to Jack, his great uncles were both Republicans—that is, opposed to the Confederacy—yet remained in central North Carolina during the Civil War.[5] Because of their political beliefs, both of these relatives were hanged by the Home Guard, the local paramilitary Confederate constabulary, in 1864 at a spot within fifty miles of Jack's current home. With palpable bitterness he related the story to me and described those who executed his relatives as "Democrats," seemingly drawing a direct line to the Democratic Party of today. Owing to the passage of time and other historical processes that have changed both parties, few would draw those similarities. But Jack, with what seemed to be anger toward liberals just below the surface waiting to explode, had relied on this connection as a major factor in his conservative identity.[6]

Woody, of the Pierce County Tea Party, drew on historical events predating the Revolutionary War that gave personal texture to his participation in the Tea Party. Like Jack, he made a direct personal connection to defining periods of American history. As I sat down with Woody for an interview in a small-town diner over breakfast, he told me that he wanted to show me something after the interview. During the interview he told me that his family had settled here before the Revolutionary War and that he was "kin with half the county." After the interview we walked out to the town square, where a plaque was set in stone. The plaque commemorated the capture on that spot of Benjamin Merrell, a leader of the Regulators, one of several pre–Revolutionary War uprisings against the colonial government; this one fought between 1766 and 1772 (Stock 1996; Whittenburg 1977). The leaders captured at that spot were eventually hanged by the colonial government in Hillsborough, North Carolina, in 1772 (Fitch 1989). Woody told me that the story of the Regulators moved him, and he believed that over two hundred years before, his ancestors might have helped launch this early revolt against tyranny. He also saw a significant connection to the Tea Party movement that emerged over two centuries later. Few besides history buffs or long-term North Carolinians are familiar with the Regulators, but Woody, who likely passed that plaque a hundred times, had appropriated it as a local manifestation of his political outlook. His outlook gives the TPM historical weight, making the struggle timeless and personal. The concerns and sacrifices of the Regulators were actual demands by patriots fighting for liberty from an unresponsive government. To Woody, he is following in the footsteps of his ancestors who took previous stands against tyranny.

Connecting the Movement with Feelings of
Political Dislocation and Disempowerment

Like David, many Tea Party participants see the movement as restoring a lost style of politics characterized by closer relationships between leaders and citizens. Many considered, even before the 2008 election, representative democracy to have failed because of politicians' distance from the voters. Though many Tea Party participants partially blamed themselves for being complacent or uninformed in prior years, for many the return to a more responsive politics seemed a fitting solution to their own experiences of observing or attempting to participate in formal politics. Though the Tea Party movement emerged as a response to the policies of the Bush and Obama administrations, there was nonetheless a deep sense of political dissatisfaction among Tea Party participants toward politics in general. Furthermore, the Tea Party's sense of the movement as an insurgency is directed as much toward politics in general as politicians. Early in the interview with Woody, I asked him what the Tea Party was, expecting to hear about the national debt, President Obama, and taxes. Instead he replied, "It's a group of people that has decided that representatives—our elected representatives—have went off on their own course instead of representing the people, and they are trying to rein them back in. Get them to follow what the people elected them for and what they campaigned on. It's like Barry Goldwater said,—I didn't understand it when I first heard it the first couple years—but he said of Republicans and Democrats that there's not a dime's bit of difference between them." Tea Party participants commonly assert resentment toward the lack of ideological purity on the part of officeholders, including George W. Bush (Formisano 2012; Dionne 2016; Hirsh 2010; Zernike 2010). To Woody, Goldwater's quote took on significance for himself and other conservatives as frustrations with the Bush administration grew and the GOP temporarily collapsed after the 2008 election. President Bush's policies concerned nascent Tea Partyists. Eileen, a young army veteran trying to form a local Tea Party group in a small Piedmont town, related her motivation for participation back to George W. Bush:

> It goes back to the last or the second term of Bush, President Bush, when I started to see him veer off, I mean completely veer off the track as far as . . . he went with Medicare part D, and things like that. I was sitting back going, "Wait a minute, what are you doing, that's not—. The Republicans don't stand for that." I'm not a die-hard Republican. I'd characterize myself as a conservative, very conservative and not always on social issues, just conservative across the board, and um, when I saw him taking a track to the left as far as economics went, that really concerned me.

Though Tea Party participants would most likely vote for the Republican candidate in a general election, and in fact many volunteered on Republican campaigns, they were nonetheless on guard for the RINO, those GOP politicians that support increasing the size of government or are more likely to compromise with Democrats.

This deep mistrust of politicians and politics in general led to new evaluative political categories apart from the typical Right-Left dichotomy. David's description of his father juxtaposed with his sense of having a bull's-eye painted on his back illustrates a common Tea Party grievance that goes beyond customary Left and Right political divisions, but rather to the perceived nature of politics. David was remembering a much different relationship between the state and the citizen. Similarly, other Tea Party members articulated a feeling of resentment and exclusion from institutional politics. They referred to the "ruling class" or "governing class," a separate group of people, both politicians and bureaucrats, cut off from the people that they represent and serve. These politicians act on the whims of power and the preferences of economic, social, and cultural elites. Mark Meckler and Jenny Beth Martin, founders of Tea Party Patriots, claim Tea Party supporters' vision of American greatness "was missing from the values of the political class, who had abandoned the principles that allowed America to create more wealth and freedom than any nation the world had ever seen before" (2012, 14).

During an interview I asked a member of the Hamilton County Tea Party, a well-educated and financially prosperous male business consultant, what "governing class" meant and why a group of privileged, upper-middle-class professionals should feel so dislocated from government. He responded that politicians have never worked, made payroll, or generated jobs and as a result want people to stay "in their place and be dictated to." Oddly, despite his advantages in wealth, education, and social capital, he nonetheless considered government to be a separate, insular class made up of powerful people with different and corrosive values.

His position reflects historian Michael Kazin's populist theme of producerism regarding the distinction between those who produce and those who do not. In Kazin's (1995) account, populists construct enemies of those whom they see as "not producing anything," such as the nineteenth century banking and railroad elites. Yet in this case, it is the political class that is unproductive—politicians do nothing that is valuable (see also Berlet 2012b). In Kazin's cases from the nineteenth century, the producers were not necessarily workers and farmers, but the petty bourgeoisie who were also present in such groups as the Knights of Labor in the 1880s. Populism didn't necessarily adhere to strict class categories; professionals and small business owners were often welcome as part of a "moral community of self-governing citizens" against monopolies and elites (Kazin 1995, 35). In that world a Marxian conception of class was not what determined being a "producer" but rather where one's politics came down on the topic of plutocracy.

Correspondingly, Stanley Aronowitz (2003) argues that class divisions today are separated by formations of power that are not necessarily tied to relations of production. He writes that class should be more broadly considered as the "ownership and control of key means of material and *immaterial* production" (Aronowitz 2003, 10; emphasis added). Separating himself from those who would use Marxist theory in a deterministic way, he argues class divisions have "historicity," meaning they emerge and change under specific historical conditions. If class is considered as a relation to the "ownership" of politics instead of solely to the means of material production, a different sort of alienation emerges creating a cross-cutting cleavage transversely to Marxian class divisions. I argue that this alienation has coalesced into a sense of political disempowerment or dislocation on the parts of those in the Tea Party.

Consistent with the usual assumption that local politics are closest to people's immediate concerns, the local arena is where the remoteness of politicians from the people was most apparent to many Tea Partyists. County-level GOP organizations have historically been the entry points for conservative citizens to first get involved with politics (Crowder-Meyer 2010). But according to many of my consultants, those organizations had become bureaucratic and hierarchical. In many counties Tea Party members looked on county GOP committees with disdain as "good old boy networks" whose main activity was the local Lincoln-Reagan fund-raising dinners held by GOP committees nationwide. Gone were the days when county-level party organizations had a fully operating pyramid of local functionaries down to the neighborhood level. In many of the counties I visited, there were few permanent precinct captains at the grassroots level. This left the county party organization in the hands of a small group usually thought of as the local establishment, such as elected officeholders and local businessmen, who were likely to resist change and controversy.

More often this sense of political dislocation was expressed through anger at the perception of being ignored or taken for granted by elected officials. Mike, co-founder of the Hawthorne Tea Party, discussed his motivation for co-founding the group: "You're telling me that I helped put you in office and that I want to talk to you on the phone and I have to jump through hoops? I have to go through thirty-seven assistants and aides? To only leave a message? For you to not call me back? Because he's busy? . . . Okay."

The themes of dislocation were also strongly linked to political fundamentalism and uncompromising ideological firmness that emerged from Tea Party members' idealizing of American history and their idolization of the founding fathers. The interviews showed constructions of politicians differentiated between inauthentic politicians or RINOS and the ideal, ethical politician who acts sincerely according to conservative values. People's stories of engagement with politics illuminated how North Carolina Tea Party activists referenced ideal politicians as straightforward citizens who do the work of a leader. This became apparent through conversations with Tea Party participants in which they lamented how today's politicians lacked authenticity and candor. Mike continued, "They're not like me. I want to meet the guy like me. Sarah Palin? She might not be electable as a president, but she so impressed me. Because I believe she is absolutely who she says she is. She doesn't care. 'This is how I see it, folks. This is how I see it.' She went out there and helped get people elected. The Left can talk trash about her all they want, and the Right can be scared of her all they want; I like her. Because I think she's genuine." This example gives a hint regarding the later attraction of Donald Trump to my Tea Party consultants. Donald Trump took the authenticity to a new height by directly confronting what many consider the "unsayable," from personally insulting campaign opponents to racist comments about undocumented Latin American immigrants.

Others further demonstrated that the attractiveness of "authenticity" was nothing particularly new in American politics. They had clear memories of other idealized politicians and specific instances of their deeds. Many participants referenced Jesse Helms, the late five-term, conservative Republican senator from North Carolina, as such an ideal.[7] Diane, whom we will meet in the next section, said, "I really don't think that our congressman and our senators have really cared for the most part. I will have to say one thing about Jesse Helms. That man, if he ever told you he was going to do something or wouldn't do something, he was true to his word. Absolutely true to his word . . . And we need that. Yes, we do need that."[8] Woody also evoked Jesse Helms about being direct and true to his word, referencing a candidate forum Helms attended while Woody was in secondary school:

> They asked [Helms] questions . . . they were asking very pointed political questions. He would just say yes or no and not beat around the bush. He told the truth. He told what he wanted. It wasn't put out in grandiose terms making people take a mental jump as to what it meant. Like "conservative values." What does that mean? Family values. That can mean a whole lot of things to a lot of people and a lot of the progressives use those terms—both sides of the aisle do. It's as vague and nonspecific as possible. It sounds good. "Family values and conservative principles." Jesse Helms would say that that means this.

Woody also idolized another manner of Jesse Helms's directness: his willingness to directly confront racial divisions at that same event.

There was a small group, maybe fifty people, mostly whites. The older blacks always made the rest of [the black students] sit together in a group up front on the side. If somebody tried to sit over there, they would run them off. "That is our area." There were a few blacks that didn't want to sit with the rest of the blacks, but there wasn't very many. And it wasn't animosity. We were not going over there; and they were not coming over here and they didn't want it to be for mixing. The first thing that Jesse Helms said was that we can't have this segregation. And he said, "You get up here and go sit over there, and you folks come over and sit over here and mix this thing up a little bit. You've got to get how society is supposed to be." He made everybody get up and move around and sit down in different places.

As will be discussed in the next chapter, race is a difficult terrain to navigate for many Americans and especially for Tea Party participants. Conservative concepts of colorblindness and personal responsibility have led to charges that Tea Partyists are racist. Owing to this, Tea Party participants I observed had a preoccupation with race because they felt unfairly labeled as racist. Yet Woody, by evoking and articulating this memory, paints Jesse Helms as an agent directly confronting and refusing to ignore racial divisions, forcing groups together like "society is supposed to be."[9] Woody's memory was of seeing a true conservative and an ideal politician act in a manner that many politicians would fear: directly confronting and intervening in one of the defining social divisions of the American South.

Declining America and the Rejection of Christianity

In the prior chapter, I drew a comparison between the figured worlds of the TPM and of white evangelical Christians and noted how there are often what I termed points of contact between the two figured worlds. The question then is, How do these points of contact appear in the data? The semi-structured interviews, by allowing my consultants to expand on their lives and paths to the TPM, indicated how these two worlds support each other. For many individual Tea Party participants, the movement acquires meaning through their own religious background. Conversely, their religious identity is sometimes given new meaning by Tea Party participation.

To some this new Tea Party conservatism gave new meaning to the "culture wars" issues of the 1980s that continue to this day. Paul, a forty-six-year-old web consultant and part of the Greene County Tea Party, began his interview with the declaration, "I am a believer. And as a believer, I believe we have an enemy, an adversary." Paul connected the Tea Party movement to his Christian upbringing and memories of his early initiation into politics in the 1980s. He saw the importance of moral truth through its articulation by Ronald Reagan, the Moral Majority, and their goal of pursuing these moral truths as public policy. He repeats the theme of normative truths that are apparent in the political fundamentalism of the Tea Party by saying that in the 1980s he began to understand the idea of right and wrong and the dangers of moral relativism. "I don't believe in gray areas. Satan lives in gray areas, and those gray areas do a great deal of harm to people."

He thinks that the drive for morally guided public policy, such as what he saw articulated by Jerry Falwell, is even more important today. To Paul, liberals have become more liberal, and conservatives have also become more liberal. As a result, he was shocked by a society that values the early sexualization of children and what he calls the "culture of death," characterized by euthanasia and abortion. He strongly believes that John McCain provided the initial impetus for the rise the Tea Party. Paul claims a low point of morality was illustrated by the candidacy of John McCain. "His values were all over the place. We didn't know whether he was with us [Christian evangelicals] or against us. It was a gray area."

With other Tea Party members, the connection between Christian principles and classical liberalism emerged from their newfound political activism, as was the case with Sandy, an upper-middle-class stay-at-home mother and co-founder of the Hamilton County Tea Party whom we met in the introduction. Sandy's Christian faith predated her political awakening with the Tea Party movement. Yet she established connections between her identity as a Christian and as a new conservative activist. Sandy, when asked why she was conservative, answered that (left-wing) liberalism did not line up with her religious beliefs. "Christianity is the foundation of decision-making and principles I live by. My conservative beliefs of freedom and personal responsibility align with that."

She continues,

I think when you look at Christ's coming. He came for the individual. He came to set them free. And there is personal responsibility in making those decisions as to who you are as a person; what your life looks like; where you're going; and his plan for you . . . I enjoy my freedom. I want to make decisions as to where I am going. I want to go where the sky is the limit . . . With Christ, you're free and as an American you are free . . . America is the last and greatest place to practice Christianity because of the freedom. As those freedoms get chipped away, the prevalence of Christianity, you can kind of see—. There's something going on where they are diminishing.

Many attempted to make similar connections between the moral claims of Christianity and conservatism. I mentioned Rev. Wilson in the previous chapter and his hermeneutic reading of the Constitution. He also spoke strongly about the connection between morality in one's personal life and morality in fiscally responsible public policy. Rev. Wilson, at the time of our first meeting, was trying to determine whether to become affiliated with the Adams County Tea Party group. He later became a regular participant and a speaker at regional Tea Party events, and in 2012 he was elected by a Tea Party constituency to the county's board of commissioners. Rev. Wilson had apparently given a lot of thought to the relationships among faith, secularization, and fiscal policy in the manner that many Christian advocacy organizations were trying to highlight at the time (Deckman 2016; Wilson and Burack 2012; Montgomery 2012).

Rev. Wilson, like others, volunteered his family history before I asked my first question, linking his political autobiography to his upbringing among poor, rural Southerners. He made sure to mention that he had black and white playmates as a child and that his family often shared food with equally poor black families. He stressed the importance of standing on principles. This was demonstrated by his father, grandfather, and even a great-grandfather and great uncle who both fought for the Union during the Civil War despite the threats to the family. To him, the moral decline of America had direct effect not simply on societal well-being, but on the nation's finances. He saw the breakdown of the family, substance abuse, and teenage pregnancy as drains on the nation's finances, which in turn drove excessive government spending and debt. "When you have a moral breakdown in society and in the family, somebody's going to pick up the tab. We're not going to let kids fall through the cracks; we're going to help a single mother." Government intervention to address these issues through social services was hugely expensive. Yet these social problems are a result of the rejection of faith. Restore faith and we eliminate a large amount of government spending. To him, a dichotomy between fiscal and social conservatives makes no sense; the perspectives are linked.

The Pierce County Tea Party, which is discussed further in chapter 5, was unique among the eight LTPGs I studied. This group was characterized by strong Christian fundamentalist themes and attracted many devout Christians who might not have otherwise gotten involved with a typical Tea Party group. Some found the group an attractive venue where they could express their own type of faith-based conservatism. Diane was such a person. A tall, sixty-eight-year-old Pentecostal, she grew up as the daughter of a sharecropper in the South Carolina low country. Her family moved to Pierce County in the 1950s seeking employment in the furniture industry. As discussed earlier, Ernesto Laclau writes that populism is driven by equivalences between personal experiences and movement grievances. He maintains this coherence is strongest when individuals forge "equivalent chains" of multiple experiences. Diane's political autobiography is a long chain of conflicts she witnessed among church, state, and capitalism, such as *Roe v. Wade*, the 1963 ban on school prayer, and the decline of North Carolina's textile and furniture industry. Diane's political identity is reflective of a fascinating ideological heteroglossia (Strauss 1990, 1997) that integrates faith, class, and the influence of mainstream conservative media and obscure eschatological, charismatic preachers and authors. Like many others, Diane stresses the moral decline of the nation, situating its origin in the political developments in the 1960s and 1970s. She became a Republican because of abortion: "Whenever you are for abortion, you are against the country . . . period. [God] says we have to do the right thing. That's what he expects us to do. To do the right thing. He tells us 'innocent blood defileth the earth' and defileth means he will push you off his land. I knew that in 1973 or whenever they passed that bill of *Roe versus Wade*. We were in big trouble. I was young, but I knew we were in big trouble."

Among the memories that were clear to her was when "Madalyn Murray O'Hair took the prayer out of school." Attending public school before the 1963 *Abington School District v. Schempp* decision, which prohibited school-sponsored Bible reading in public schools, she remembered those readings and the strong effect they had on her life. "Saying that a child can't hear somebody pray in school is beyond me. When our tax dollars go to fund this stuff. Tax dollars pay for it, yet they say you can't pray to God Almighty? . . . That made this land? That made the wood that built this building and the products that made the bricks? And the person, that God made the person themselves? Then you tell me that you can't pray in school and you can't have Bible reading in school? Now, that bothers me." To her, the government's authority over education had far-reaching effects on the shaping of moral and responsible citizens.

Diane makes a wonderfully concise and culturally specific connections among government tyranny, moral education, the Constitution, and her frustration with politicians:

The reason we are losing [our country] is because of what our federal government has implemented into our schools and the authority they have taken away from parents. Parents are scared to death to switch [whip] their kids anymore. [They are] scared [the government] will come and take their kids away. The government says these kids don't belong to you; they are ours. The things they have implemented runs contrary to the Constitution, so there's not a whole lot of defense that you can do against it, unless we get some leaders that will stand up and defend the Constitution. They think that when we do not know our Constitution, they can write anything over on us. You can't do it and expect things to be right and above board and have a good nation because it ain't gonna happen.

The paramount importance of reincorporating prayer in school is part of a wider connection among faith, history, and politics that animates her participation with the TPM. To her the Tea Party is an important new agent to reestablish the Christian basis of America. "[The Tea Party aims] to bring our country back to what it used to be. To-Bring-Our-Country-Back [rapping her hand on the table with each word] to a realization of God and what our forefathers set forth in this country when they wrote the Constitution."

As a Pentecostal, Diane follows premillennialism, the belief that an Antichrist will emerge after the condition of the world dramatically worsens. After that point Christ will return to summon the faithful (Wilcox and Robinson 2011). Diane applied current politics to different aspects of this thinking. She believes that there are forces striving for one world government, which according to the premillennial interpretation of the Bible's Book of Revelation is established by the Antichrist before the return of Christ (Rev. 13–21). Many premillennialists, including Diane, believe the United Nations is an effort to bring about one world government. Diane saw the North American Free Trade Agreement (NAFTA) as another such example but with a personal and painful meaning. NAFTA, which hastened the demise of textile and furniture manufacturing industries in North Carolina, uprooted her life and the lives of many of her relatives, friends, and coworkers. Asked why President Bill Clinton would sign NAFTA, she replied, "One world government. One world government . . ." She then adds, "And money—money for the big man." When asked why politicians act in their own interest as opposed to the country's, she states with certainty, "Because they think they can do it and get away. They do it for political purposes and money. God says the love of money—not money, but the love of money—is the root of all evil. Follow the money trail and you will know."

This last utterance, cloaking end times prophecy in class-based grievances, discloses a resentment of not just politicians, but capitalism as well. As argued in this chapter, people rely on experiences to fashion their political subjectivity. However, in many cases these experiences lead to subjectivities that may not necessarily adhere to typical American Left-Right categories (Strauss 1990). For many, ideologies are not acquired through learning theories but through making associations between concepts experienced in daily life (Strauss 1990, 314). Some, like Diane, must work through the obvious contradictions of American conservatism, namely, the conflict between Christ's teachings and advocacy for free-market capitalism. Diane spent thirty-one years working at a furniture mill under demanding physical and often uncomfortable conditions. Though believing herself to be strongly conservative, she has worked out some of the contradictions of capitalism. She found the answer to the contradictions in the moral economy that connects with her own experience of the furniture plant closing and transferring its manufacturing overseas. Diane's experiences with a transitioning economy, political dispossession, and strong Christian faith translate into views on capitalism that run counter to typical evangelical conservatives and those associated with much of the Tea Party movement.

When asked to define capitalism, Diane responded that it is a person's ability to "start their own business and that government has no right in the business of private enterprise." But in the next sentence she states that a businessperson must run the business "righteously." "You must pay people a fair wage. They need to remember that the people that are working in the plant are as important as the CEO. That person that is out there pushing and shoving at a machine or sewing material is just as important as the CEO, and they need to share equally." This, however, is not to say that Diane believes in government intervention. "It has to come from the heart, their heart. They have to decide that they are going to do the right thing because it is what God expects of them." Regarding the furniture manufacturer that eliminated her job in North Carolina in favor of creating one overseas, she states, "The company left because they could make more money overseas and that is because of greed. When people say they had to move overseas because of this and this and this . . . no, no, no. The Bible says in the last days it's greed and greedy men."

Diane provides a vivid illustration of how a life of experiences creates the foundation for political identities. Yet she also linked her political and religious outlooks to a particular interpretation of the Tea Party movement. This interpretation argued that the words of the Constitution called for a biblical foundation for public policy. And though this interpretation was accepted in the Pierce County LTPG, such an outlook would not be embraced by national Tea Party groups such as Freedom-Works or many everyday Tea Party members. However, I would also argue that hitching her hopes to the Tea Party movement is a reasonable choice given how the Republican Party has consistently disappointed its evangelical Christian base.

Political scientist Katherine Cramer Walsh has written extensively on how close engagement with individuals provides important information about political outlooks that often do not emerge from polling and surveys (Cramer 2016; Walsh 2004, 2009). She critiques Thomas Frank's argument in *What's the Matter with Kansas?* (2004) that working-class conservatives act contrary to their own best interests. She writes, "If we listen to the way people understand their votes or policy preferences we might conclude otherwise. Are they really not making sensible choices? Or are they just making choices that do not make sense to the perspectives that we assume are appropriate?" (Walsh 2009, 180).

In the prior chapter, I described how the different components of the Tea Party create a figured world that provides a meaning system and an interpretive frame for evaluating people, issues, and selves. The interpretive frames typically lead to mobilization by helping people make connections between the social movement and broader cultural understandings. These cultural understandings are infused with intimate, subjective experiences. Political autobiographies help us understand the different perspectives through which people assign meaning to politics, issues, and political participation. The figured world constructed by the Tea Party network, with its symbols, discourses, and practices, allows individuals to personalize the meanings for a variety of different concerns and discontents that lie much deeper than the generally understood position of the Tea Party as advocating simply for constitutional literalism and fiscal austerity. The ability of people to easily reorient significant parts of their lives to the meaning of the Tea Party is a major factor in the movement's success.[10]

The outlooks from my Tea Party consultants expressed in this and the prior chapter begin to also open a window into the more recent form of right-wing populism, support for Donald Trump. Several of the themes Trump drew on are present: undocumented workers, wishy-washy establishment politicians, and the outsourcing of jobs. This begins to provide an answer to a later discussion how most of my Tea Party consultants became strong Trump supporters. Moreover, from my conversation with Diane, Trump's more puzzling sources of support—such as from evangelical Christians—begin to make some sense.

This chapter also begins the description of the agency of social movement participants and the personal transformations that may occur. Here, grievances contextualized by the Tea Party movement motivate the active reworking and repurposing of participants' personal histories. As will be discussed in chapter 5, this repurposing and reworking is even more active and effective in the local Tea Party groups, which provide the space for them to fashion activist identities as Tea Party members. But first, in the next chapter, it is important to demonstrate how the Tea Party figured world is a model that helps us understand Tea Partyists' positions on issues outside of the TPM's initial grievances.

3 Plantation Politics

RACE IN THE FIGURED

WORLD OF THE TEA PARTY

The success of the TPM, I've argued, lies to a large degree in the figured world that the movement constructed and that people subsequently joined. The figured world acted as a cultural lens through which Tea Partyists named fears, concerns, and visions regarding America. They also, as shown in the previous chapter, imbued these frames and narratives with personal meanings from their own lives. I have maintained more broadly that the TPM helped citizens not only interpret the changing terrain of American politics, but also act within it. Yet the figured world of the Tea Party also helps us better understand actions and beliefs of everyday Tea Partyists. We have seen that in, for example, Santelli's first words decrying sociocultural change. Yet the figured world as an analytic also helps explain Tea Partyists' positions on other issues that were not initially connected with the movement or that may have been misinterpreted by some observers of the movement. The same interpretive frames used to explain government fiscal profligacy were also eventually applied to other issues, such as the environment and questions of American racial inequality. This chapter takes up my Tea Party consultants' stance toward race.[1]

Racism was one of the most frequent charges leveled against the Tea Party, a charge that leaves many Tea Partyists resentful. On a crisp afternoon three weeks before Christmas in 2010, I was sitting in the bed of a large pickup truck with Mike, co-founder of the Hawthorne County Tea Party. We were participating in the central North Carolina town of Reston's Christmas parade. Towed behind us on a flatbed trailer was the homemade parade float Darrell was building in chapter 1. Members had made a plywood silhouette of a teapot-shaped sleigh and reindeer along with the Hawthorne Tea Party logo and placed them on top of the trailer. Three members of the group were standing on the float dressed in colonial-style costumes waving to the bystanders. As we proceeded slowly up the town's main street, Mike, his children, and I handed out small American flags to people in the audience lining the street. At one point we passed a young black woman who did not reach for a flag. She looked at Mike and said, "I don't like the Tea Party because *I'm black.*" Mike looked at me and in a mix of indignation and amusement said, "Did you hear that? She thinks we're a bunch of freakin' racists!"

This was not the first—nor was it the last—time I heard a Tea Partyist express indignation about being labeled as racist. Many of the Tea Party movement's detractors believe the TPM is driven at its very core by racist beliefs, sentiments, and motivations. Some have argued that racist individuals have joined the Tea Party specifically because of the election of a black man as president of the country (Parker and Barreto 2013). Others have seen the Tea Party movement as a reaction to the loss of status on the part of whites as ethnic and racial minorities gain social, political, and economic benefits in a multicultural America (Street and DiMaggio 2011; Hochschild 2016). Others have argued that while the Tea Party may not have been formed specifically for racist purposes, it nonetheless is populated by racist organizers, providing a new political space for militia members and white supremacists (Burghart and Zeskind 2010). My research suggests that while the antipathy toward Obama is a common rallying theme of the TPM and the current American Right in general, portraying the movement as driven by those who champion white supremacy misses an important aspect of how racial difference is talked about by Tea Party participants. My research with Tea Partyists discloses instead how racialized discourses are actually incorporated into the frames and practices that constitute Tea Partyists' political identity. In LTPGs where racialized discourses did circulate, my purpose was to trace out those discourses and see how they were processed, used, and translated into action in the spaces where Tea Partyists interact.

The Inconsistent Appearance of the Tea Party and Race

My early observations of Tea Partyists showed a conflicted relationship with race. Tea Partyists often ruminated in their meetings about how to attract more blacks to the movement.[2] Many also actively supported and volunteered for black conservative political candidates. Media personality Glenn Beck, while continually highlighting the unimpeachable values of the nation's founders, did not restrict these qualities to white founders. Throughout 2010 he spoke of the contributions of black Americans to American history often through the promotion of the book *Setting the Record Straight: American History in Black and White* by Christian fundamentalist and author David Barton (2001). Beck also organized the Restoring Honor rally held on the steps of the Lincoln Memorial on the forty-seventh anniversary of Dr. Martin Luther King Jr.'s "I Have a Dream" speech.[3] At the same time, many Tea Partyists rejected claims that institutional and individual racism persist in America. They often attributed the rejection of the TPM by most black Americans to longstanding apologetic conservative discourses that link government dependency, dysfunctional black culture, and black identity politics.

To illustrate these distinctive and sometimes contradictory views, I relate a conversation with James. James is a fifty-two-year-old digital applications technician who views his path to the Tea Party as beginning long before its inception, during the second term of George W. Bush. James views government as a "pathological packrat," constantly accumulating more power for itself at the expense of individual liberty. As he saw the Bush administration continuing that tradition, he registered to vote as "nonaffiliated" before the election of Barack Obama. As the Tea Party emerged, James found his political beliefs represented in the nascent movement: "We have generated problems in this country, and we've done it from the original founding. For instance, slavery. If I could do one thing, I would sink every slave ship . . . I don't want to kill the people that were being kidnapped but destroy the whole premise that we needed people here to do the work. Think of what that would've done to this country today with all the divisions that we have with blacks now." James, like most Americans, rejects slavery. However, I was puzzled by how he was framing slavery more as a misguided means of procuring labor than as a human tragedy. His perspective is clarified as he articulates what he sees as the source of needless racial divisions:

> If blacks had come here through voluntary immigration, we would probably still have a little racism going on, but we wouldn't have all this crap about the never-ending "we've been victimized" thing going on . . . It [racism] will never be gone until there is some complete intermixing of the races where no one will be able to say they were victimized any more than anyone else. That problem has been propagated. I've never had slaves. And I'm not aware that I have ever repressed anybody who is black. But I am still suffering for something like that while we are trying to deal with broader issues.

Though never actually saying that slavery was morally and ethically wrong, James sees the episode as passed. The divisions he sees are the results of the no-longer-valid resentment on the part of blacks to historic wrongs. But in stark contrast to the sensibilities of a white supremacist, he saw the mixing of the races as a desirable, if not inevitable, process of history.

While I did experience instances of unvarnished bigoted statements regarding blacks, such statements were more commonly made about Latinos and Muslims. In most cases I observed Tea Party participants attempting to understand racial difference in the contemporary United States using the frames and narratives of modern conservatism. James was showing a disregard—whether willful or a product of ignorance I don't know—of a racialized system of inequality and instead applying the foundational conservative discourse of individualism. He articulated an underlying assumption that the troubled race relations in America are more the result of group-based identity politics, which subverts the individualism associated with an *American* cultural identity. In his thought experiment, by "intermixing" races, those born in the United States become phenotypically the same and, by extension, make plain for all to see that it is one's individual talents and resourcefulness that determine success in America.

James illustrates this perspective further when he shifts to discussing immigration:

The main reason that I think we're having all these clashes is because people aren't really connected with the idea of the United States as being a free people—everyone is created equal. I don't know when this started, but all this stuff about dividing people into smaller groups and getting the groups to try to vie for their own group grievance. That's the worst thing that happened to this country . . . We are no longer a melting pot, we are a freaking tossed salad, and the lettuce is kicking the carrot's ass or whatever. It's a nightmare and I don't see how it's going to end. Especially since we're bringing in 1 million new immigrants a year and another million illegally. I see that as a train wreck because the people that are coming in are bringing in their own little ethnic differences with them. We are not melting them into the pot anymore. They're just becoming another little group.

This outlook signals a shift in discourses that is distinct from the discourses and symbols of racial resentment regarding crime and social unrest tapped into by Richard Nixon (Lowndes 2008) or regarding affirmative action tapped into by Jesse Helms's "white hands" ad or regarding the inherent danger of blacks tapped into by the Willie Horton television advertisements aired during George H. W. Bush's presidential campaign. The Tea Party rhetoric indexes an identity of whiteness and a contemporary "color-blind" race ideology more attuned to neoliberalism (Omi and Winant 2015).

I observed a dual relationship between Tea Partyists and race that reflects the Tea Partyists' political identity. On one hand, the Tea Party figured world rests on taken-for-granted, unrecognized whiteness, a core set of racial interests often obscured by race-neutral words, actions, and policies (Hartigan 1997). This is displayed primarily through the Tea Party's vision of American exceptionalism and patriotism and in the contemporary white hegemony discourse of color blindness. Simply, Tea Partyists ignore enduring institutional and interpersonal discrimination in American life while asserting American nationalism and unity across the supposedly disappearing boundaries of race (Omi and Winant 2015). On the other hand, Tea Partyists frame the problems of the black underclass as the tragic result of dependency created and nurtured by government action such as Great Society social programs. These concepts are all meaningful within the core frames of Tea Party members' collective identity, which places significance in the insidious effects of too much government, the moral foundation of individualism and personal achievement, and the importance of America's dominant founding narratives. Moreover, this outlook provides for Tea Party participants an explanation of blacks' unwillingness to join the TPM. Many believe this government-spawned dependency, what some termed modern-day "plantation dependency," creates strong loyalty to the Democratic Party and strong social pressure for conservative blacks to hide their true feelings. Combining theories of whiteness, color-blind racism, and collective identity, a picture develops illustrating the relationship between the TPM and racial difference in the United States.

Descriptions of Tea Party Racism in the Literature

My argument differs from some scholars' interpretation of the Tea Partyists' relationship with racial difference. Parker and Barreto (2013; see also Parker 2010) and Burghart and Zeskind (2010) are two primary sources that are often used to parse racism in the Tea Party movement. I argue that both works have methodological shortcomings that fail to capture how Tea Partyists assign meaning to race relations and give an oversimplified description of how race pertains to the TPM.

Burghart and Zeskind (2010), relying on a survey of websites and media sources, argue that NTPOs such as FreedomWorks, Tea Party Patriots, and Tea Party Express are populated by numerous people with histories of racist leanings. Further they argue that even if the TPM does not focus on race, it offers an attractive target for cooptation by white supremacists and nativist militia members.

The authors' analysis overlooks several important points regarding the Tea Party movement. First, the analysis implies that the NTPOs are the predominant and prevailing component of the Tea Party movement, which, as I have argued, is an oversimplified description. For example, along with Tea Party Patriots and FreedomWorks, which have vast memberships and grassroots presence, they also include Tea Party Express, a political action committee (PAC) formed by two Republican political consultants based in California. The organization, which did run several national bus tours with Tea Party–aligned candidates, is little more than a fund-raising operation and cash cow for the founders' political consulting firm (Roth 2009). Burghart and Zeskind themselves described it as having no desire to build up a membership or have a grassroots presence. Yet they focus on the Tea Party Express as a site of an early racial controversy indicative of grassroots sentiment. In 2010 Mark Williams, a spokesman for the organization, was ousted after he refused to recant an offensive, racially charged blog post. Second, the report completely ignores the influence of Americans for Prosperity, the Charles and David Koch–sponsored organization, which the authors describe as "ancillary" to the movement. Far from ancillary, AFP has been, along with FreedomWorks and Tea Party Patriots, the most engaged and effective NTPO in the Tea Party movement. Aside from AFP's support for voter identification laws, which many outside the group regard as voter suppression laws, the professionally run organization has been relatively successful in remaining free of racial controversy. Finally, Tea Party Express was viewed negatively by my consultants. My consultants generally made it clear that their LTPGs were not directly affiliated with any NTPO. Moreover, on the few occasions when Tea Party Express came up in interviews, the consultant stated that the organization lacked bone fides as a true part of the movement.

Parker and Barreto (2013) and Parker (2010), using quantitative methods, present results from surveys of Tea Party supporters' inclinations toward racism, as measured by existing scales, and toward "authoritarianism," as defined by social psychological models (Hetherington and Weiler 2009; Stenner 2005) and social dominance orientation (Pratto et al. 1994). Parker and Barreto (2013, 34), which argues that the TPM is motivated by animus toward Barak Obama primarily because of his race, is often cited as the primary support for racism in the Tea Party movement. Among their findings, Parker and Barreto show that Tea Partyists, more so than Republicans in general, believe that the problems of black Americans are rooted in personal and moral failings, such as individual responsibility and motivation. My research complicates the picture, as I found that my consultants attributed the roots of the crisis in America to the decline of personal and moral qualities in Americans as a whole, not just black Americans. Along these same lines, Skocpol and Williamson (2012, 68) point out that Parker's data in fact show findings similar to mine: Tea Partyists hold a negative view of the personal and moral qualities of *most* Americans, whites included.[4]

More significant, a clear picture of the racial sensibilities of Tea Partyists is clouded by how Parker and Barreto characterize a Tea Party supporter. As noted earlier, differences in how researchers define a Tea Party "member" influence the conclusions drawn regarding the movement. In Parker and Barreto's wording of the survey questions, anyone with a positive impression of the TPM is considered representative of the Tea Party and is given the unsupported label of "true believer." Such a vague data set raises two serious concerns. First, the authors are generally gauging an audience or "issue public" (Converse 1964; Warner 2005), rather than the engaged members of a social movement. The surveys included people who had had no actual engagement with people directly involved in the movement. Such general criteria for "true believers" are likely to be highly contingent on the political atmosphere at the moment of the survey. Most prominently, Parker and Barreto's second survey was conducted in the first three months of 2011, a period directly after dozens of Tea Party–supported candidates who won election in the Tea Party wave election of 2010 entered Congress—arguably, the high-water mark of Tea Party support. The survey concluded before the 2011 Tea Party–inspired threat of government shutdown in April of that year, which eroded much of the Tea Party's support (Zernike 2010). These methodological decisions make it difficult to grasp accurately what Tea Party activists of the degree of engagement I was interviewing espoused. Parker and Barreto's work provides extensive and valuable data regarding conservative reactions to early twenty-first-century cultural and social change in America. However, our divergent conclusions regarding race and the TPM likely reflect our different data sets.

I maintain that the LTPG component of the Tea Party movement at the time of my research was not driven by what Etienne Balibar (1991) terms "auto-referential" racism, in which Tea Partyists see themselves as representatives of a superior race; neither did they express "hetero-referential" racism, in which Tea Partyists see blacks as evil or inferior. Rather the collective identity of Tea Partyists valued a narrative of America that was unremarked by them as distinctly white. This perspective favors a classical liberal ideology and ignores the enduring structural and individual racial bias in America.

Political scientist Joseph Lowndes (2012) remarks on changes in the contemporary conservative movement regarding race in the post–civil rights movement era.[5] His primary argument is that the conservative movement of the 1960s was forged in partial opposition to the civil rights movement. Barry Goldwater, the Republican presidential candidate in 1964, and Richard Nixon in 1968 and 1972 each attempted to exploit white resentment of the extension of rights to blacks for political gain, as did Ronald Reagan with his reference to "states' rights" in his 1980 speech in Philadelphia, Mississippi (Black and Black 2002, 216).[6] However, Lowndes believes that white populist anger is now directed at the state. During the time of my research, there was no large-scale, organized black social movement against which conservatives might rally. Also, open and coded racial appeals across issues of employment, crime, housing, and education have less affective appeal in the post–civil rights era. Lowndes believes this is partly due to the presence in popular culture of popular black athletes, politicians, and other celebrities who have prominent roles in American culture. Finally, although my data do not fully support this claim as they did his first point, Lowndes writes that welfare reform and the full realization of the prison-industrial complex have reduced the potency of welfare and crime as raced discourses animating conservative action.

Supportive of my critique is Meghan Burke's (2015) more recent yet rarely cited research among Illinois Tea Party leaders. She reaches similar conclusions as mine and Skocpol and Williamson's regarding race yet goes one step further. She makes a compelling argument that Tea Party racism is really just "American racism . . . not fundamentally different from the mainstream, including on the left" (Burke 2015, 37). This argument is based on her research regarding racial attitudes (Burke 2012, 2014, 2017), which is strongly informed by Eduardo Bonilla-Silva's (1997, 2014) work on color-blind racism, which I will discuss further later in this chapter. Bonilla-Silva's earlier work critiques how racism was considered something a person "has," like a pathology, while racism's social basis was ignored. Rather, he argues, people exist within a racialized social system in which racialized categories and social meanings affect all social institutions. Burke maintains that our education and media systems fail to adequately dispel "structured ignorance" (McVeigh 2004) surrounding, for example, why racial groups experience poverty differently. Considered in this manner, the racialized social system cannot be avoided, and to suggest that only one population is "breathing the smog or doing so in ways distinct from the rest of us is wishful thinking" (Burke 2015, 6).

The Tea Party as a Version of Whiteness in the United States

The Tea Party's grievances rest on the idea that Americans—black and white—have turned their backs on the morality, responsibility, and patriotism of the founders. Their vision of America to a large degree relies on an idealized and white American past and a cultural identity espoused especially by Americans who happen to be white.

Burke (2015), however, does not utilize the concept of whiteness, which I maintain broadens our understanding of racial attitudes in the Tea Party. The concept of "whiteness" rests on a perspective that to understand the perpetuation and legitimization of racial inequality is to explore whites' understanding of themselves instead of a racial other (Hartmann, Gerteis, and Croll 2009). "The focus is on the identities, ideologies, and norms that privilege whites that are not always understood or even explicitly realized by those who benefit from them, and on the ways that these taken-for-granted assumptions can mystify, legitimate, and ultimately perpetuate systems of racial inequality" (Hartmann, Gerteis, and Croll 2009, 404). The Tea Party is an especially useful space to investigate the presence of an identity in American political culture that has not been explicitly recognized in hegemonic discourses as a raced identity. Even more importantly the "whiteness" of understandings and practices of the American Right are not generally recognized or remarked on in American political culture as "belonging" to whites. Frankenberg (1993) discusses three main characteristics of whiteness. First is the taken-for-granted or normative nature of being white, meaning whites have no acknowledgment of possessing any racial identity. Second, whites are unaware of the privileges that come with this race (e.g., McIntosh 1989), what Lipsitz calls the "value of whiteness" (Lipsitz 1998) or what Paul Street terms the "white fairness understanding gap" (Street 2001). Related to both is the third characteristic, "color blindness," in which whites are color-blind when it comes to racial inequality. They may see blacks as disadvantaged but attribute the lack of success to individual effort and the distinctive characteristics of black culture. Hence the lack of awareness regarding white privilege is related to an unawareness of structural, institutional, and interpersonal racism

I will focus on discourses of color blindness in the balance of this chapter, but before that I want to focus on how whiteness, "a sense of self and subjectivity unaware of its own social foundations" (Hartmann, Gerteis, and Croll 2009), is particularly manifested in the figured world and collective identity of my Tea Party consultants. Whiteness takes new forms under different conditions and in relation to specific places and identities (Hartigan 1997). Frankenberg (1993) terms these "social geographies," which may be racially marked physical environments, or conceptual frameworks (such as figured worlds), "which frame and limit what we see, what we remember and how we interpret the physical world" (Frankenberg 1993, 54). The TPM constitutes a unique social geography that illustrates a specific articulation and reproduction of whiteness.

Melanie Bush (2011) investigates mechanisms by which whiteness is reproduced on an everyday basis. As will be discussed in the section on color blindness, the structural aspects of American society that create racial and class inequality are rarely articulated. This mystification is exemplified by the first moments of the Tea Party movement, as Rick Santelli bellowed about "losers" who "bought more house than they could afford." This perspective and many descriptions of the subprime mortgage crisis ignore conditions such as the combination of predatory lending practices and the segregation and isolation of minority communities that led to people of color experiencing a higher rate of foreclosures in the housing crisis (Rugh and Massey 2010).

American whiteness, Bush writes, is also anchored in the concept of a common American experience. Balibar (1991) writes that racism is inherently implicated in nationalism owing to its creating of a unified "people" at the expense of diverse others. And as noted in chapter 1, nationalism and patriotism aim to resuscitate and celebrate the nation's founding myths and the heroes celebrated in the portrayals of school texts. There is, to Tea Partyists, an unquestioned greatness in the American founding story and in the character of the founders. Tea Partyists fear that the greatness of founding myths and heroes will be, or has been, forgotten or ignored. In such a sensibility, contesting the very foundation of that narrative does not make sense. Yet for many Americans, it is contested. It may be difficult to assign high moral rectitude to those founders espousing democracy and equality while holding slaves and restricting the franchise to white male property holders. Bush also mentions the different experiences regarding the meaning of and the ability to reach the "American dream," a level of comfort and security achieved through hard work and responsibility. The gender, racial, and class systems in America have handicapped the ability of many to reach such an ideal. Yet a critique of these structural features by those not achieving the dream is seen as un-American, ignorant of the myriad possibilities, and ungrateful.

Bush further maintains that whiteness is reproduced through what she terms "the regulation of discourse." There are boundaries for acceptable discussion of "poverty and wealth, justice and democracy, structure, agency, and the possibilities for the future" (Bush 2011, 207). This regulation of discourses is mediated through the education system, the justice system, and of particular importance in this case, the media. Generally, popular media polices the portrayal of racial inequality in America. "When diversity is shown, it often portrays blacks as assimilated or involved in interracial friendships that mask racial inequality" (Bush 2011, 131). This gives the indication that there must no longer be a racial problem in America. As discussed previously, conservative media is a key source of cultural resources for the figured world of the Tea Party. These media typically downplay racial inequalities or exacerbate tensions for ideological purposes (Jamieson and Cappella 2008; Street and DiMaggio 2011). We are reminded also of the concerted effort by conservative media from the outset of his presidency to show Barack Obama, not as incompetent, but as foreign and un-American, with paternity, citizenship, and values outside American society.

In a passage that appropriately captures the dilemma of the Tea Party with regard to racial inequality, Bush writes, "If as a nation, all people cannot count on freedom, justice, equality and opportunity, then the ideologies that say that these are the reasons the United States is special are undermined" (2010, 113). Blindness to these contradictions of the narrative of American exceptionalism is significant for the very foundation of the Tea Partyists' cultural world and evaluation of American society. Not only are contradictions invisible, but they *must* be invisible for the Tea Party to be possible.

Color-Blind Racism

Though white privilege may be invisible to them, Tea Partyists must nonetheless confront representations of themselves as racists. The concepts of white identity and the invisibility of white privilege rest on an ideology that is "putatively fair, meritocratic and universal" (Hartmann, Gerteis, and Croll 2009). Eduardo Bonilla-Silva (2014) argues that a new race ideology has emerged in the United States since the 1970s, and he attributes this ideology to the post–Jim Crow historical conditions in the United States. The claims that blacks and other minorities are subordinate categories of persons, both biologically and socially, has been replaced by a "color-blind racism" that claims contemporary racial inequality is the outcome of *nonracial* dynamics. "Whereas Jim Crow racism explained blacks' social standing as the result of their biological and moral inferiority, color-blind racism avoids such arguments of intrinsic inequality. Whites rationalize minorities' contemporary status as the result of market dynamics, the 'natural' desire of minorities to live with people similar to themselves and blacks imputed cultural limitations" (Bonilla-Silva 2014, 2).[7]

Omi and Winant (2015) argue that color-blind ideology and neoliberal governance each require the other for their success. Color blindness had its start with the "reverse racism" discourses that emerged in the 1970s. These helped to promote a perspective of "race neutrality" based on the assumption that blacks and whites *both* could be racists and in some cases were victims of discrimination. This further obscured for many any ideas of structural racism. Neoliberalism emerged in the 1970s as an anti-statist reaction to both the 1960s minority-based new social movements and the expanded government programs of the Great Society. Color-blind ideology was seen as a way to cleave the white working class from the New Deal coalition that included among others, minorities. Simply, color blindness undermined the salience of structures of inequality that marked protests of the 1960s and protesters' demand for state policies of redress. Together with neoliberal ideologies, color-blind discourses softened any opposition to the dismantlement of state efforts to redress race- and class-based forms of inequality.

Bonilla-Silva describes color-blind racism as characterized by the use of several interpretive frames. As I will show, these frames are useful in explaining Tea Party members' outlook toward race. However, my data point to some specific variations and elaborations of Bonilla-Silva's theory that help to explain color-blind racism in the context of current conservative populism.

ABSTRACT LIBERALISM FRAME

"Abstract liberalism" ignores structural racism, instead focusing on the ideas of choice and individualism as determinants of success. This perspective relies on the classic liberal tradition of equal opportunity, in which success is understood as a function of effort on an equal playing field.

While the abstract liberal perspective is often described as misguided in the context of supposedly overly generous public assistance, I also witnessed it being deployed in regard to criminal justice. During one meeting of the Greene County Tea Party, North Carolina Associate Supreme Court Justice Paul Newby, in the midst of his reelection campaign, was the invited guest. During a question-and-answer period, one audience member asked when the state was going to "start executing people again." Though capital punishment had not been exercised in North Carolina since 2006, the North Carolina legislature in 2009 passed the Racial Justice Act, which prohibited capital punishment for cases in which race was determined to be a contributing factor in the conviction or imposition of capital punishment.[8] Justice Newby's response, which elicited applause and verbal affirmations from the audience, illustrates the abstract liberal perspective:

Now the problem is that you have this Racial Justice Act that was passed by not this legislature, but the prior legislature. It was very controversial then. It's as if race were relevant to any of this. I have discussions with people who say that there are too many black people in prison. I don't disagree with that, there are. But they are not there because they are black. They are there because they committed a crime. [Audience loudly agrees.] I have not yet seen a situation where the dead person cared what color the person was that killed them. I mean, they are dead. That is the fallacy with this whole idea of hate crimes and all this kind of stuff. I mean, it's either a crime or it's not a crime. If you killed somebody, it's wrong. It doesn't matter what about them you didn't like.

Justice Newby articulates the Tea Party and conservative belief in personal responsibility and ignores the basis of the Racial Justice Act, specifically that blacks are disproportionately wrongly convicted and disproportionately sentenced to die. Speaking in a small, rural Tea Party group, Newby used his authority and cultural capital to draw on the premises of abstract liberalism and powerfully overwhelm any ideas of structural racism that some audience members may hold, instead making a link between color-blind racism and the Tea Party figured world.

My consultants more often articulated abstract liberalism in the context of public assistance. Paul, the evangelical Christian who traced his political awakening to Ronald Reagan and the Moral Majority, connects his Christian conservative beliefs to race: "We believe that the progressives are hurting people, not helping. Though conservatives may be more tough love, the point is that there is a better life out there. But if I talk about people taking care of themselves, I am termed a racist. It would be hard to find conservatives that wouldn't care about giving people a better life. My vision is that people should be empowered." Paul's statement illustrates the abstract liberal perspective of individual responsibility and the free will individualism related to white evangelicals (Emerson and Smith 2000). However, Paul's quote also shows resentment and defensiveness regarding how his beliefs are viewed as racist by many opponents of the TPM.

These two forces—color blindness and resentment—are clearly illustrated with Darrell. Darrell is a white, working-class, sixty-seven-year-old former civilian employee of the U.S. Army who spent his working years in New York before he retired to North Carolina. Darrell was raised in an Eisenhower era, conservative New Jersey family and enlisted in the army in 1960. He completed active-duty military service in 1963 and spent fifteen years as a mechanic. He returned to the army in the 1980s as a civilian transportation instructor. In my interview with Darrell, he constantly and easily shifted between different aspects of the Tea Party figured world and his conviction that many of the nation's present problems are derived from the rejection of the Constitution. When I asked about "American decline," he connected government spending to the Constitution: "And the Constitution . . . said the government . . . should not dictate what the people do or shouldn't. The people should be self-sufficient, and the government should be off the backs of the people. Basically, the federal government should protect our borders and keep us a sovereign country, but not interfere with people's private lives. Let the states take care of themselves as far as what they want to teach the kids in schools."

Darrell then articulates a linkage between government spending and individual "responsibility": "The government is giving money to people that don't need it or deserve it. No responsibility. People are going out and buying drugs and alcohol and big screen TVs. [They are] taking it from people that are working out there—working forty or fifty hours a week or just barely making it." This statement does not necessarily articulate racial grievance. In fact, at another point in the interview, he applied the corrosive nature of government assistance to his own family. This quote also gets at Darrell's thinking regarding the connection between patriotism and personal responsibility. I asked Darrell a definition of "patriotism." "If you are a patriot, you would honor the Constitution and what it stands for: The freedoms and not wanting to have a dictatorship where people get everything for free. Nothing is free. My granddaughter gets a little assistance from the state because her husband left. She once said something like, 'If I do this I will get free transportation.' I said 'Liz, it's not free. Some taxpayer is paying for that. Nothing's free.' These people get this idea that it's free. It's not free!"

Later, Darrell does, however, articulate a common stereotype circulating in conservative media of a black underclass of questionable responsibility, built on dependency and government largess. Throughout my interview with Darrell, he often articulated the theme of work and its inherent honor and righteousness. He saw himself as an example of his values on work, lifting himself into the middle class. For fifteen years after he had left the army, he worked as a mechanic at Lakehurst Naval Air Station and Fort Dix.

> I think that was in the eighties. When computers first came out, I didn't know nothing about computers and I certainly couldn't type. A light bulb went off in my head that said if I ever wanted to get out of this crappy mechanic trade, these computers are it. So I bought one, and I bought a typing program and taught myself how to type. Several years later a position came up for an instructor and one of the requirements was that you had to type your own lesson plans on a computer. 'Ah! I can do that.' So I got the job as a maintenance assistant on an instruction team, and we traveled all around New Jersey, Pennsylvania, and New York to Camp Drum . . . So that was good. I did that for twenty-eight years until I retired.

I ask a standard question in my interviews regarding the keys to success. Darrell replied, "Having ambitions and not being lazy . . . self-reliant and proud to make your own way."

Yet his next sentence injects a racially charged counterpoint to pride and ambition: "In the inner city, they have lost the concept of pride to make your own way. 'Why should I work when I can sit here and get public assistance?' . . . They have been born into it." Notice in this quote, the use of the term "lost" instead of saying "never had," implying a change that has occurred, instead of laziness being inherent. Some process has changed the *culture* of the inner-city poor. And to Darrell, it is government.

CULTURAL RACISM FRAME

The Tea Partyists' racial perspective is not simply that institutional and structural racism do not exist but that continued racial inequality is partially due to unfortunate, inherent qualities of black culture. Bonilla-Silva introduces the frame of "cultural racism," which uses culturally based arguments to make broad essentialist characterizations of blacks and other minorities (see also Ryan 1971). Bonilla-Silva describes this as "blaming the victim" and as related to the "culture of poverty" theory, which he traces back to the work of anthropologist Charles Lewis (1960). The contemporary legacy of the "culture of poverty" is that "minorities' standing is the product of a lack of effort, loose family organization and inappropriate values" (Bonilla-Silva 2014, 88).

Emerson and Smith (2000) recorded a variation of this, what they term "relationalism," in their research with white evangelicals. Humans have a propensity to sin, but proper social relationships, such as family and church, will prevent poor choices. Evangelicals, not blind to institutions such as government, have a similar outlook as my Tea Party consultants: the maladaptive cultural practices by poor people of color are not assumed to be inherent or primordial but rather the effects of "big government" progressives.

This perspective also reflects the continued influence of the argument made decades ago by Charles Murray in *Losing Ground* (1984) to the effect that government social programs create a culture of entitlement and dependency that does more harm than good. Returning to Darrell: "Blacks are the same as us but their culture and environment made them dependent. It's the liberals who are racists because they don't think blacks are smart because they just continue to bribe them into voting Democrat." In other words, they would be like us in terms of values and success if they hadn't become ensnared in a Faustian bargain by the Democratic Party.

Darrell's argument also includes an important corollary within the Tea Party: the Republican Party is falsely demonized as the enemy of African Americans. I noticed that some of the people I interviewed were puzzled as to why blacks supported the Democratic Party when it was typically Southern Democrats who stood in the way of the civil rights movement.[9] Chris makes both of these points:

> I feel that liberal ideology is detrimental to the economy, but they also say, "Those evil Republicans are going to repress you and go back to the sixties with fire hoses."
>
> Republicans have been more supportive of the black community than Democrats! Democrats prolonged Jim Crow and segregation. They were the ones responsible. Welfare has made the black community realize [think] that Democrats support them more. It is plantation politics, a politics of dependency.

Explicit in this perspective is that the Democrats not only demonize the Republicans but have succeeded in bribing the poor and specifically blacks into voting Democratic because of generous public assistance benefits. This perspective was articulated in the 2012 presidential campaign when Republican nominee Mitt Romney declared that 47 percent of Americans don't pay taxes, feel entitled to government largess, and consequently, will never vote for a GOP presidential candidate. As Darrell explains,

The way the Democrats do it is they say that if you vote for us, we will give you stuff. If you vote for Republicans, they will take your free stuff away. That's basically it. That's why we have ghettos in all the cities. All these people are on welfare, and they have all this free money, and it's just ingrained in them as they grow up that if you want to keep getting the free stuff, you vote Democrat. If you vote for Republicans, they're gonna take that money away from you. It's a plan. They got the black vote and the minority vote. These people were suckered into this. It is hard to take things away from people once you have given it to them.

This quote comes full circle back to Darrell's initial quotes regarding the decline of personal responsibility and government's role in it. Though it's apparent, such as in his reference to his granddaughter, that this decline in responsibility is not restricted to African Americans, he nonetheless does connect racial stereotypes to anti-statist frames of the Tea Party figured world.

More than just "bribery," however, Tea Partyists see a strong degree of group censorship perpetrated by liberal blacks on blacks who support conservative causes. Conservative commentator Ann Coulter put it memorably when defending black Republican presidential candidate Herman Cain: "Our blacks are so much better than their blacks because [they] have fought against probably [their] family, probably [their] neighbors . . . That's why we have very impressive blacks" (Fox News 2011). Darrell, also referencing Herman Cain, connects this censorship directly to why the Tea Party has trouble attracting black members:

Because they will be called Uncle Tom if they side with it [the Tea Party]. I just heard this guy talking about it the other night. The guy that bought the pizza place (Herman Cain, who formerly was CEO of Godfather's Pizza)—brilliant guy. He says he goes to black churches, and people whisper to him that they really like what he's saying. He asked them why they are whispering. They said that they don't want other people to know—people that agree with Obama. I feel sorry for this guy, I feel bad for him and Alan West.[10]

In a similar manner, Chris continues:

If you ask a number of small business owners who are Black, they get it. They know we don't have an environment in which you can succeed. But we have a government saying we have to go and get those conservatives, because it's your right to live in dependency. It's a cultural thing. The decline of the black families since welfare and the sixties; [the decline of] coherent two-parent families and a father figure in that community. That's not white people's fault that black fathers are leaving. I think there's some recognition to that in their community. They are part of what is responsible for the deterioration of their culture.

These utterances, which typically exclude any reference to institutional or structural racism (or class-based disadvantages either), portray my Tea Party consultants as blaming the liberal welfare state and the Democratic Party for maintaining a virtual "plantation" that keeps blacks tied to dependency. This also reaffirms the Tea Party figured world, especially the affect and fundamentalism that stresses the wickedness of their progressive opponents. Progressives are not simply espousing a different ideology in the marketplace of ideas; they are actively destroying the moral foundation of American cultural identity. Those blacks who "get it" are the business owners and those who are closest to the practices of classic liberalism and who have rejected the plantation politics of progressives.

NATURALIZATION OF DIFFERENCE

Many of my consultants saw blacks as purposefully segregating themselves from whites, reinforcing the naturalization of racial difference. Bonilla-Silva writes that whites may explain away racial difference as natural and nonracial "because they [blacks] do it too" (2014, 76). Darrell had close working relationships with blacks and whites, yet he was troubled by what he saw as self-segregation of blacks after decades of struggling for desegregation:

> When we had picnics (held by his employer), the blacks would all go and sit at their own table. Weird. All day long you work with these people, but when they got in the group, they would all sit at their own table. They didn't have to do that . . . Anyway, they perpetuate this racism themselves; they didn't have to sit by themselves. I don't know, it's weird. They want integration, integration. Okay, you're integrated. But then when you go have a party you go and sit at your own table. Now what are you doing that for? We work with you all day long, and you say that you're my buddy. But when there's a group of you, you also get your own table.

Darrell is noticeably frustrated by that memory. He had spent decades working side by side with black coworkers and did not understand the self-segregation. At the same time, he proudly sees the TPM as a movement for all Americans *qua* individuals—blacks included.

The earlier-mentioned idea of social pressure and fear of the "Uncle Tom" label have a deeper meaning when considering Tea Partyists' strong emphasis on individualism and loathing of concepts of "collectivism." One Tea Party group organized a reading group to discuss conservative-oriented books. One book was Austrian-school economist Frederick Hayek's *Road to Serfdom*, which critiques the idea of collectivism—what Hayek equates with the idea of "community."

> If the "community" or the state are prior to the individual, if they have ends of their own independent of and superior to those of the individuals, only those individuals who work for the same ends can be regarded as members of the community. It is a necessary consequence of this view that a person is respected only as a member of the group, that is, only if and in so far as he works for the recognized common ends, and that he derives his whole dignity only from this membership and not merely from being man (Hayek 2007, 162).

In conversations with me, Tea Party members often implied that blacks were focusing on their group membership or their black collective identity instead of individualism. Robert is a forty-year-old co-founder of the Hamilton County Tea Party. Hamilton County, containing one of North Carolina's largest cities, also has a very active black middle class and black Democratic Party establishment, which Robert called a machine. He co-founded that local Tea Party group as a direct challenge to the Democratic Party establishment centered on the county board of commissioners. He hoped that through careful organizing, his LTPG could help wrest control of the county commission from the Democrats and install "constitutional conservatives." Part of this was tapping into the county's black conservatives. Robert applied Hayek to the black community in his county:

> There are two thousand black registered Republicans in this county. I think that's an amazing number. Who would have thought? Then there are a whole lot of unaffiliated. There is so much social pressure for conformity to the black community. The use of that word, "community." In the book club, we read Hayek's *Road to Serfdom*. What he is saying is the conformity of a group into a certain ideal. Not a geographic community or a cultural community but a community. When we think of community, we think of the neighborhood or the town where we live. Liberals use that community to identify an ideology. And there is a lot of pressure for blacks to conform to the black community.

The relationship of group rights to individual rights has been an important component of conservative discourses about race in the United States since the emergence of the neoconservative movement in the 1960s.[11] Neoconservatives rejected white supremacy ideologies and Jim Crow practices because they contradicted the egalitarian values of American culture. However, they were equally opposed to the growing demands for cross-race equality that was emerging from the civil rights movement in the late 1960s (Omi and Winant 2015). To demand group equality as an *outcome* of policies conflicted with the neoconservatives' *opportunity-based* vision of American culture. As Omi and Winant write, the neoconservatives were opposed to individual or "negative" discrimination, such as denial of service at restaurants. Yet to go beyond that into, say, affirmative action would be committing "positive" discrimination. Being opposed to racial code words and Jim Crow while ignoring the structural racism that continues, the neoconservatives of the late 1960s and the Tea Partyists of today could argue that they are opposed to discrimination but also opposed to antidiscrimination policies based on ideas of group rights to equality.

Many Tea Partyists were resigned to the fact that blacks' collective identity prevented blacks who shared Tea Party values from participating in the movement. Sharon, co-founder of the Franklin County Tea Party, believed she had truly done her best to reach out to blacks in the community. Sharon was friends with Dr. Ada Fisher, the black Republican committeewoman representing North Carolina on the Republican National Committee who happened to reside nearby. "I've discussed it with Ada. Black candidates did come to our meetings [as speakers]. I got with Ada, and she gave us some names. I got the names of conservative black folks, and I've made calls and wanted to go to their churches and ask if we could get involved when they're doing cooking or reunions, and we just never got any response. We have reached out. I guess they don't trust us. I don't know."

Dr. Fisher offered a rather prejudiced explanation of blacks' aversion to conservatism when I heard her speak at a later Franklin County Tea Party meeting:

> The Tea Party and the Republican Party says that we are a party of limited and smaller government. Minorities hear that and say they're going to take away my benefits. The Tea Party and the Republican Party say we believe in less taxes. Poor and minority people don't pay taxes anyway. They don't care whether you cut them or not because they're not paying them. The Tea Party and the Republican Party say that we believe in free enterprise. They don't understand what free enterprise means because you have reality TV, football players, and all those people making big bucks.

In a sense Dr. Fisher is giving a crude and essentializing comparison of whiteness to blackness, arguing that social pressure is not excluding blacks from the TPM, but that the two groups are hailing from different cultural worlds.

Interestingly, the understanding that social pressure prevented blacks from joining the movement was strengthened when black supporters did participate and especially when they stressed their "Americanness" or whiteness instead of their black social identity. One supportive group was the Frederick Douglass Foundation (FDF), a black conservative organization that describes itself as "a national Christ-centered education and public policy organization with local chapters across the United States which brings the sanctity of free market and limited government ideas to bear on the hardest problems facing our nation" (Frederick Douglass Foundation). I was able to observe a speech given by the FDF's co-founder Timothy Johnson, who at the time was also the vice chair of the North Carolina Republican Party. The most interesting aspect of Johnson's address to the Burgoyne Tea Party was the way he attempted to divest himself of one of the primary aspects of contemporary black identity—historic links to Africa:

> The other thing that I want to make sure people know is that I am not an African American. I am from Cleveland, Ohio, and I'm an American. [Applause] I've never been to Africa, I didn't lose anything in Africa, and I have no intention of going to Africa. So when you see me and point me out, you can say there's a black guy over there. That's okay. Just don't say there's an African American because I am not African American. This is my country. [Applause] I'm a Christian and I'm an American, and last I checked, that is a majority in this country.

Johnson's confident approach and ramrod bodily *hexis* of a former military officer affirm an idealized American—Christian, disciplined, and successful. Johnson also doubles down on his claims of Americanness. As related to me by one of my consultants, at one presentation by Johnson, he asked a member of the audience when and from where his family had emigrated. After the audience member explained that his family emigrated from Germany during the wave of immigration at the turn of the twentieth century, Johnson responded that his family came over in the 1600s, and in addition he had spent several years defending his country in uniform, concluding with a direct and pointed observation that he was more American than many of them.

The figure of the Black Tea Partyist is the black person who disregards his racial identity and embraces an Americanism that is Christian and champions independence and success. It is more than coincidental that the most favorite black icons of the Tea Party are Herman Cain (corporate CEO) and Alan West (highly decorated veteran). Retired pediatric neurosurgeon Dr. Benjamin Carson's status among Tea Partyists skyrocketed when he publicly rebuked President Obama in his presence. In effect he was rejecting his racial affinity with the president and criticizing the Affordable Care Act using themes of moral decline.

This presence of highly successful black people who "get it" justifies interpretations that resonate with the color-blind frame of the Tea Party figured world. They cannot see themselves as racists. On the contrary, they are the ones that see the oppression. The government and liberals have created racial difference and, more significant, moral pathology.

During the period of my field research, Tea Party detractors commonly derided the movement as motivated by racism. Yet Joseph Lowndes asks an astute question: How do we "understand a movement that expresses the anti-statist discourse born of the racial logic of the modern right and which demonizes a black president but which emphatically disavows racial motivations, appropriates icons and narratives of the civil rights movement and successfully backs prominent candidates of color?" (2012, 161). This question becomes less puzzling through the engagement made possible by ethnographic research. Interacting with and observing Tea Partyists and the networks in which they participate discloses the identities on which conflicting positions make sense in the figured world in which Tea Partyists exist.

Bonilla-Silva's book on color-blind racism is titled *Racism without Racists*. This title is an accurate description of race and the Tea Party movement. The Tea Partyists I spent time with were not racist in the sense that they were motivated by hatred toward blacks. Instead, many of the cultural resources of the Tea Party figured world are based on pieces of the hegemonic understanding of America that is most ignorant of America's unequal racial society. Yet it is a movement that implicitly supports policies that perpetuate structural violence on the poor and people of color; it supports racist policies of libertarian economics stressing limited government and the shredding of specific components of the social safety net.[12] At the same time, most of my consultants truly wanted to share their social movement with people of color.[13]

I maintain that this can be explained by the "foundational" principles circulated within the Tea Party figured world to which Tea Partyists had already attached so much personal meaning. These values are idealized by the TPM and are considered to have been exemplified by the nation's founders and be gravely lacking in America today. These principles are based in a morality indicated by success in the market as tied to the qualities of individualism, achievement, and responsibility inherent in classical liberalism. This perspective privileges the individual and naturalizes a misguided impression that there is equality of opportunity. The classical liberal perspective ignores the invisible forms of power, such as structural violence, institutional racism, and implicit bias, which have no meaning in such a world. To them American greatness was achieved by people who overcame barriers and were successful, George Washington as well as Frederick Douglass.

Tea Partyists see, at the root of this decay, a powerful cultural hegemony of the liberal welfare state that negates individual agency and strengthens what they see as an artificial and destructive sense of black collective identity. This supposed cultural hegemony is driven by progressives, who are guided by the desire to maintain power and continue a failed ideology of collectivism. In the figured world of my Tea Party consultants, the state and the progressives maintain the plantation, driving the destruction of American cultural identity for blacks as well as whites.

4   Fellowship

LOCAL TEA PARTY GROUPS AS

COMMUNITIES OF POLITICAL PRACTICE

I have discussed how my consultants found or established a coherence between their own lives and the narratives, symbols, values, and emotions of the emerging Tea Party movement. Moreover, the cultural world of the Tea Party provided a lens for assigning meaning and blame for what they thought were the existential dangers facing America and for what a "true" patriot should believe and do. Yet how did the Tea Party evolve from affinity to identity? How were the Tea Partyists transformed from supporter to activist? To this point I have primarily portrayed Tea Partyists as individuals stating their beliefs, personal outlooks, and experiences, often in the context of the Tea Party figured world. However, the true vibrance of the TPM is shown when these individuals interact in spaces where the cultural world is practiced. The LTPGS were key to the movement's success because Tea Partyists in these social spaces performed, supplemented, and lived the cultural world of a Tea Party activist and patriot. Moreover, the local groups were spaces of learning where people gained political skills and taught others to be agentive political actors. Within these spaces Tea Partyists acquired strong feelings of political efficacy backed up by concrete skills of advocacy and organizing.

When the Tea Party emerged in 2009, many of my consultants sought out the early protest rallies and were energized by their participation. As is often the case, participation in rallies and protests temporarily relieves feelings of hopelessness partially through the sense of being part of a large, widespread collectivity. For many of my consultants, a sense of true belonging to a large, action-oriented community became palpable on September 12, 2009, during the Taxpayer March on Washington DC. Organized by Glenn Beck and several national Tea Party organizations, including FreedomWorks, Tea Party Patriots, and Resist-Net (Brown, Hohmann, and Bacon 2009), approximately seventy-five thousand participants (Markman 2009) marched from Freedom Plaza to the west front of the U.S. Capitol, where a rally was held with speakers and music.[1] As I learned, a large number of my consultants had attended and considered the experience a watershed moment. One consultant when asked about the experience said,

> I was overwhelmed. As we walked toward the Capitol, people were converging from everywhere. It was like 9/11 when people knew something dramatic was going on and so they hugged and got close with people. It must've been like this when World War II ended. We met people we didn't know but we right away knew them well because we were there for the same reason. We had surmised in our guts [that] we had to do something with other people of like minds to say to Washington, to all of our leaders, "You've gone too far with this. We're at a precipice. We're walking too close to a precipice like lemmings." We turned around and looked back and couldn't imagine all the people down the mall on side streets, surrounding the tidal pool . . . next to having a baby, it was the most exhilarating time in my life—crying, singing, [and] saluting the flag.

Janine, an Army veteran, was also moved: "And I'm walking, physically walking on the street [on Constitution Avenue toward the Capitol in Washington DC], surrounded—just surrounded by . . . I couldn't even venture a guess [as to the numbers of people]. Chills up my arms." I asked her why.

> Why? You ask me why? Because I was part of something that loved their country that I consider with even more pride than when I was in the military. The pride that I told you about when putting the uniform on. This was something that I thought when my children look back they're gonna say, "Mom was there, right there, she was a part of that movement." It was just, like I said, pride in my country that I

felt before, but not to that extent. It was just overwhelming. It made me want to cry on three or four different occasions.

Roberta, a retiree, felt overwhelmed by the numbers.

It was from watching Beck and Hannity and a lot of the guys on Fox. I told Susan [a friend]—we were very concerned where America is going—[that] we need to go to DC. We need to take a stand with these folks and let Washington know that there are people watching them. We put them there and we can take them out. The two of us girls got on the two o'clock train and rode up to DC. I tell you, Bill, that was the most exciting time. I swear everybody on that train was going. There were five or six cars on the Amtrak train; I wish you could've seen all the people piling off the train.

    We had taken our walkers and we were right on the front row . . . You don't know how inspiring it was. We had over 1 million people. 1 million people.

Few of my consultants who attended could remember—or in many cases even hear—what the speakers said because the impact they felt was, as related to me, being part of a large group. All indicated an emotion of relief and validation that there were thousands of other people like them, with the same concerns, fears, and values. A crucial aspect of movement building is when people from different backgrounds are able to recognize their feelings in the expressions of others (Morgen 2002). For them the TPM had transformed from isolated, small, tentative marches in local settings or scenes on television into a sense of a real tangible public of like-minded citizens across the country.

    This event suggests that the political identities emerging in the context of face-to-face contact were more substantial than simple political affinity as explained by framing theory (Flesher-Forminaya 2010) or than identification with the TPM as part of a media audience. At the rally, people built relationships, performed the figured world with others, and were left transformed by the experience. This materially grounded type of activist identity is not self-fashioned simply by watching Fox News or listening to Rush Limbaugh. As McAdam (1988) points out in his interviews with "Freedom Summer" activists, anyone who has been moved by participating in collective political activism is likely to understand the feelings of belonging and ownership imparted by the experience and the strong desire to relive it. By enacting and sharing an identity with others, the potential for activist mobilization increases (McAdam and Paulson 1993; Polletta and Jasper 2001).

Rallies and protests are empowering and, if significant, can serve as transformative experiences. However, they are discrete and often isolated episodes. The energy or what Durkheim termed "collective effervescence" dissipates as people return to their everyday lives as individuals. Regular contact between movement members reduces this entropy, maintains solidarity, and allows for the forging of movement identities (Flesher-Forminaya 2010; Juris 2012). After the Taxpayer March on Washington and other smaller rallies nationwide, individuals returned to their communities looking for local groups in their own areas or, if not finding one, forming their own. These newly energized activists wanted to put the ideals from the march into ongoing practice through educating others, advocating for their positions, and engaging in what many called "fellowship," or the sharing of concerns, experiences, and goals.

Unlike the large rallies, locally situated Tea Party groups and other successful movements provided submerged and discrete spaces where political identities could be fashioned and performed (Hetherington 1998; Juris 2012; Melucci, Keane, and Mier 1989). In the terms of social practice theory, these groups created "local spaces of practice" (Holland and Lave 2001) where others sharing their concerns could meet, talk, and discuss experiences, issues, and meanings. In these spaces of practice, participants grow into the figured worlds performed in such spaces (Holland et al. 1998, 83; see also Virchow 2007). Importantly, those who became part of Tea Party groups further developed sensitivities and sensibilities, as well as senses of self, attuned to the figured world that they were performing. More than simply assuming an affinity toward a specific ideology or applying an interpretive frame, these emerging Tea Party identities, like other movement identities, developed as embodied dispositions focused on political action (Melucci 1996; Polletta and Jasper 2001; Taylor and Whittier 1999). In the aftermath of the initial boost of enthusiasm, these groups were crucial in consolidating the movement, keeping people connected in face-to-face encounters with other activists, and putting into local practice the circulating messages of the wider movement. The local groups became primary sites or spaces where the figured worlds of the TPM were being performed and acquiring localized geographic and historical particularity.

In the balance of this chapter, I highlight the importance of the submerged spaces of the LTPGs using the concept of communities of practice (Lave and Wenger 1991) to build on earlier theorization of spaces of identity formation in social movement studies. I then describe the workings of some typical LTPGs and the circulation of the cultural resources that are used to fashion local Tea Party identities. The next section discusses how the figured world is generated, contested, and animated by new resources. Finally, the forging of these identities occurs as a process that also includes internal tensions, disagreements, and the setting of boundaries regarding what may be said and done.

Authoring Selves

After its first year of existence, the Hawthorne County Tea Party held an election for new members to their "executive committee," a group designed to guide and promulgate policy and activities for the group. Members' names were put into nomination at a prior meeting, giving other members time to consider them. At the next meeting the candidates were asked to stand up and say a few words about themselves. Their utterances were more than just expressions of interest and qualifications but were small performances of the symbolic and discursive components of the Tea Party. These individuals were claiming their membership in the movement through evoking several different components of the Tea Party figured world, such as historical narratives, indignation, and fundamentalist sensibilities.

The first candidate stated, "I saw some names of people I respect, so it must be a good outfit. I came to the protest. I believe in four cornerstones: limited government, fiscal conservatism, free markets, and national defense. I want to make sure the so-called Republicans do what they say."

Another evoked American history and the responsibilities of citizenship through a historical anecdote familiar to most Tea Party members:

"I love my country, and I love what this movement stands for. We need to keep those guys [politicians] accountable, and if I'm in, I will give it 110 percent. There is a story from the Constitutional Convention. After the Constitution had been drafted and signed, Benjamin Franklin was asked by a woman, 'What have you given us?' He replied, 'A republic, madam, if you can keep it.'"

The next to speak highlighted how the Tea Party discourse is continually informed and built on through media such as talk radio. "I have never been politically active, but with the current regime in office, I had to get active." His use of "regime" is most likely appropriated from Rush Limbaugh, who throughout the Obama presidency, used that term whenever referencing the administration. Though the term means a ruling government, it is commonly used to refer to a government that is foreign, illegitimate, or despotic. One typically does not hear references to the "British regime"; one does hear references to the "Iranian regime."

And finally, two evoked the image of flinty, idealized citizenship by articulating the cultural politics of the TPM through values and beliefs that in their views had made America exceptional. "I'm not a poet; I believe in God, family, and country. We need to turn this country around. I am a realtor. I believe in free enterprise. I work on commission, which means no work, no pay." And the other: "Freedom is granted by God. I'm a strong believer in the Second Amendment. I believe in extreme limited government. I was raised in a conservative family, and my grandparents grew up in the Depression so they had the right values."

This small episode illustrates how collective identities are "action systems" (Melucci 1995) in which participants collectively construct meanings and negotiate a collective "we." Individually, each appropriated discourses, symbols, texts, and values of others, both media and other members, and "authored" themselves within the space of the Tea Party movement (Bakhtin 1981; Holland et al. 1998; Holquist 1990; Lachicotte 2002). Given the premise that selfhood is socially constructed (e.g., Mead 1934; Voloshinov 1986), individuals did not enter the groups as fully formed Tea Party members, rather movement actors "pinned down" (Lachicotte 2002) a sense of self through dialogue and in practice with others. As we saw with Darrell in chapter 1—not exactly sure what to do at his first protest—Tea Partyists are orchestrating multiple and manifold voices identifying what a Tea Partyist is and does. This dialogue occurs, of course, with others in the LTPG. But it also occurs with imagined others, such as relatives from the Depression era with the "right values," and even opponents, such as "so-called Republicans" and those who the real estate agent believed get paid for *no* work. Last, these voices include the other components of the TPM, such as the conservative media, as in Limbaugh's use of "regime" and the Ben Franklin quote.[2]

LTPGs as Communities of Political Practice

Local Tea Party groups provided spaces where self-authoring occurred and where small groups collectively explored and fashioned what it meant to be a Tea Party member (see Braunstein 2017). These processes forged a political style that created durable identities within boundaries and relationships of power. The local groups I participated with were all organized by a core of two to four individuals who were already acquainted as neighbors, through churches, or through prior political activity. Though LTPGs were independent of each other, their meetings, at least at the start, followed a similar pattern. Local group meetings were typically held once a month in a large public space. In some cases these spaces were rented meeting halls, such as an American Legion post, but most commonly, meetings were held in large restaurants—often in their private dining rooms. In several counties the meetings were regularly held in the cavernous 1970s era family-style seafood restaurants that dot the North Carolina landscape. These restaurants were typically very large with high ceilings and able to seat a hundred people easily in open spaces where a speaker could be heard throughout the room. Meals were typically inexpensive, featuring deep-fried seafood and hush puppies. Often the meeting would begin with an hour of mealtime before the actual program started.

Meetings of local Tea Party groups varied in size. At some locations the meetings were regularly attended by at least a hundred people. Other LTPGs, primarily in rural counties, would have meetings of twenty to thirty individuals regularly. Occupations, age, and class positions also varied across different LTPGs. The Burgoyne County Tea Party, with regular attendance of over a hundred was typically made up of middle-class retirees. While the Adams County Tea Party, in a more rural location, tended to be younger, with the average age below sixty, and made up primarily of working-class individuals.

All the LTPG meetings I attended began with the Pledge of Allegiance and some form of prayer. The more urban Revere County group, not wanting to appear sectarian, did not use the word "prayer," substituting the term "invocation" or "meditation." In that group the invocation was often grounded in historical terms and themes and had a less sectarian tone resembling more the "civil religion" Robert Bellah (1967) describes. For example, one week the invocation was the prayer that Franklin Delano Roosevelt read over the radio on the occasion of the Normandy invasion on June 6, 1944. More commonly, however, groups reflected the points of contact between the Tea Party and Christian evangelical figured worlds I mentioned earlier. The prayers were a blending of political, historical, and religious themes, typically ending with "in Jesus's name." The following were voiced in three different groups:

> I will pray for the president because the king's heart is in the Lord's hand. Obama may have his agenda, but there is a sovereign God that rules this universe.

> We come to you as a needy nation and a needy people. We put our trust in parties and politicians and governments, and we are poorer for it. We need a revival that takes us beyond political parties, that demonstrates your power and glory. We pray that they will look to you, that it will speak to them.

> Your creation is perfect. Our stewardship has not been so. We pray for guidance. We pray for an awakening and the stirring in our leaders, national, state, and local. We are not necessarily asking for it to be our way, but we are asking them to open their hearts and have it be your way.

One prayer delivered by a member at a Hawthorne County meeting included a nostalgic reference that was probably before his own memory, yet nonetheless related back to earlier idealized times that participants often drew on for their ideas of change.

We need to put feet on our prayers; we need to talk to these elected representatives, we need to write the letters, we need to make them understand what we're here about and what we want to see done. But I pray most of all that we put you first in everything that we do and say and not put ourselves out there to get the praise and the honor for the work that we do. But that we all move in the same direction to turn this country around and set it back how it was back in the forties. I realize that there were some things that were missing in the forties, but there were a lot of good things too. I pray that you will guide us and direct us and help us in every way that we can and we will acknowledge you. In Jesus Christ's name, I pray. Amen.

From those commonalities Tea Party local group meetings typically then engaged in the primary activity of the meeting. The activity might have entailed planning political actions or reporting from specific committees formed to do certain tasks, such as monitoring county commissioners or following legislation or communicating with other Tea Party groups. Sometimes a group engaged in open-ended conversations on social and political topics. Often Tea Party groups had a scheduled speaker who could be a local officeholder, an organizer from a national political organization, a candidate running for office, or sometimes members of other Tea Party groups discussing strategies that they had successfully employed. After the opening rituals of the LTPG meeting, which were consistent across the groups I observed, the interactions and practices of the group illustrated the dynamic, practical, and symbolic processes of identity formation.

The idea of separate spaces for social movement activity is well pursued in social science (e.g., Hirsch 1990; Melucci, Keane, and Mier 1989; Morris 1984; Scott 1990; Taylor 1989; Taylor and Whittier 1999). Such spaces provide social centrality for the groups, but also serve as sites of identity production through the performances of symbolic acts (Hetherington 1998, 103). These spaces can also be "pre-figurative," whereby participants model or "figure" the practices and values that their movement envisions. However, little has been written of the negotiated and emergent quality of movement identities formed in social practice in such spaces.

Anthropologists studying cultural processes in schools, workplaces, and the performance of skilled cultural practices, such as midwifery, have developed the concept of communities of practice (Lave and Wenger 1991; Eckert and McConnell-Ginet 1992) to account for the dynamic process of learning and producing in collectives. The concept elucidates the relationship between knowledge, action and identity. Communities of practice are aggregates of people coming together around common endeavors and producing new activities and meanings in the course of the mutual endeavor (Eckert and McConnell-Ginet 1992; Westermeyer 2016).

The Burgoyne County Tea Party (BCTP) clarifies the importance of local Tea Party groups in providing spaces for the realization and production of individual and collective identities. The BCTP also illustrates the mix of local and trans-local components that constitute the movement. Through strong leadership and organization and by attracting others with similar moral certitude and unique talents, the BCTP was the most vibrant Tea Party group of the eight I studied.

One of the first Tea Party groups in North Carolina, the Burgoyne County group's initial rise and subsequent success were due to the work of three retirees, all women, motivated by the Tea Party's initial message and their dissatisfaction with the local Republican Party organization. Sue, the chairperson, and her two friends organized a taxpayer protest to coincide with the initial national protests on April 15, 2009. Hearing through Fox News of protests being organized nationwide, they connected with organizing resources on internet sites provided by the TV channel and by the NTPO FreedomWorks. After the initial protest at their community post office surprised them by drawing an attendance of nearly a thousand, they initiated regular meetings and organized multiple activities.

The group's monthly dinner meeting was held at an aging seafood restaurant. Close to a hundred people regularly attended the meetings, during which the group reported on and planned activities, listened to speakers, and circulated information picked up, for the most part, from conservative media and local politics. Through the everyday happenings of BCTP, we see activities that marked performances of the figured world of the Tea Party: emotional displays of indignation and solidarity, deployment of assumed historical legacies of patriotism as an interpretive frame and as defining qualities for everyday practice; and insistence on political and economic fundamentalism most vividly displayed in steadfast adherence to what participants considered the literal meaning of the U.S. Constitution.

The BCTP meetings I observed, from beginning to end, were places where the figured world came alive and where people realized and performed the identity of a supporter of Tea Party politics. I was first struck by the history and patriotism embedded in the language of the Tea Party group. As with most groups I observed, meetings began with the Pledge of Allegiance and a Christian prayer interwoven with political themes.

Part of being a BCTP member was memorizing the preamble of the U.S. Constitution. This was a core ritual of the group, which became apparent from my first meeting with Sue. Early in my research, I had learned from other Tea Party activists that the Burgoyne County group was one of the best organized in the state. I then went to a protest that I knew Sue would attend in order to meet her. Approaching her, I identified myself as an anthropologist and mentioned I had heard of her Tea Party group and was very interested in having the group as one of my research sites. She eyed me suspiciously and then asked, "Do you know the preamble to the U.S. Constitution?" Having learned the preamble as a youngster, I surprised myself by reciting it almost perfectly. Sue said the words with me, and I was slightly uncomfortable at her slow, deliberate delivery, which indicated that the words had much deeper meaning for her than for me. At the BCTP meetings the recitation, which occurred during every meeting and many events, assumed a similar ritualistic tone, said in a manner similar to what I was used to in intonements of the Apostles' Creed, a Catholic liturgical statement listing articles of belief and faith.

This re-signification according to the horizon of meaning supplied by the figured world is also indicated in practices surrounding the U.S. Constitution as a whole. As already mentioned, the Burgoyne group put great stock in the Constitution. At the event where I demonstrated my bone fides and intention of good faith to Sue, she was participating in a protest outside a public high school where that Saturday the Mexican consulate from Raleigh was issuing matrícula consular identifications to Mexican nationals—some of whom the Tea Partyists believed lacked proper immigration documentation. Just as our conversation concluded, a second carload of BCTP members arrived at the protest. Sue gathered her group together and, as I learned was customary on their many road trips, said a prayer. The nine people gathered around Sue and bowed their heads. Sue began a simple prayer thanking the Lord for their safe passage on the sixty-mile drive. As Sue led the group, she raised her right arm above her bowed head clutching her pocket-size copy of the U.S. Constitution. "Our group is small," she said, "but we represent thousands who say *no* to this infringement of these rights guaranteed to us by these United States and that we pledge to you, dear God, that we will do what it takes to uphold this Constitution and restore our beloved America. God bless America. Amen." In a brief conversation with Sue later, she told me how tragic it was that people were using fraudulent documents in order to gain the ability to illegally vote and that it was going on right there in front of her a few dozen feet away.

At this early point in the research, I was a bit perplexed. The prayer seemed odd and didn't make much sense to me, and Sue seemed to me to be obviously misinformed about what was going on in the high school gym. After spending hours in BCTP meetings and interviewing Sue, I understood that she was framing her opposition to undocumented immigrants through the belief that allowing them to vote defiled the Constitution; they could not enjoy the rights guaranteed by the document without upholding their responsibilities to obey the law. For Sue and others in her group, the Constitution epitomized American values and democratic citizenship. They used the Constitution as a lens to evaluate government programs and to judge people (like me).

Additionally, the Burgoyne group had developed a core political activity around the distribution of pocket-size versions of the U.S. Constitution to the general public. While such distribution was a common practice in the other LTPGs that I observed, the BCTP outpaced all the others by distributing in their first year and a half over thirty thousand pocket Constitutions at polling places, at holiday parades, at their own rallies, and even in everyday interaction outside Tea Party events.[3] To BCTP members, the foundation for restoring core American values was having its citizens read, understand, and embrace the words of the U.S. Constitution.

Embedded in all these practices and dispositions was a shared affect, or an "emotional collective," which Virchow (2007) defines as activity-spawned emotions that integrate supporters, shape a worldview and attitude, and encourage followers to get more fully engaged. As mentioned in chapter 1, social movements, including the Tea Party, are successful partially because of their effect in channeling inchoate fears toward specific threats and targets (Gamson 1992) and finding spaces where the emotions made possible by the movement can be expressed and shared. This emotional tenor was generated within the group at times by its members' utterances drawing attention to an especially noteworthy news item and also through media emanating from outside sources, such as YouTube videos.

One song proved to be especially evocative in the Burgoyne group. The song, by a relatively unknown country singer named Bruce Bellott, was titled "We Ain't Going Away" (2010) and included these lyrics:

> You can talk all day till you're blue in the face.
> We don't buy your lies.
> Sit on the scene till you come clean, and
> Buddy, you better get it right.
> We Ain't Goin' Away!

The song, by way of an easily sung tune and lyrics, relates to mistrust of politicians, the frustration caused by political powerlessness, and the theme of movement perseverance. Groups' singing the song together created powerful moments of solidarity. Playing the song and an accompanying video showing individuals at Tea Party rallies mouthing the words became a regular feature of BCTP meetings for several months. The video also became an unofficial Tea Party anthem among many groups across the nation, making Bellott a minor celebrity in Tea Party circles.

On occasion other groups would create a similar mood through the 1984 song by Lee Greenwood "God Bless the USA." The chorus gives an example of the song's emotional tempo:

> And I'm proud to be an American
> Where at least I know I'm free

These songs, played and sung within the group, illustrate the interplay of emotion and aesthetics within the Tea Party figured world and their function in building solidarity and solidifying identities. I use aesthetics to mean the sense one feels from experiencing an object, text, work of art, or for our purposes, a cultural resource. The aesthetics of a political movement often say a great deal about the relationships, goals, and members of the movement (Sartwell 2010). Songs act as especially potent cultural resources because they tell participants about themselves, provide familiarity to new participants, and provide emotional comfort (Payne 1995). Both songs helped constitute a collective "we" through statements of belief and the affect triggered by the songs' images. Additionally, as mentioned earlier, Tea Partyists related a sense of stigma regarding public expressions of their patriotism. Both songs are what non–Tea Partyists might term "corny," or more aptly, maudlin, mawkish, or saccharine. Yet they are appropriate for the sentimental patriotism that the Tea Partyists felt and that they believed was not shared by most Americans. Moreover, singing is a kind of teaching tool, or as T. V. Reed writes, "the halfway house to commitment" (2005, 28). Unlike all but the most rousing of political speeches, songs are remembered and more successfully imprint the messages of the movement on the memory.

The LTPGs, as described in this case of the Burgoyne group, create spaces where the figured world comes alive for Tea Party supporters. The U.S. Constitution is not simply referenced; it is used as an artifact that mediates one's political identity by being used, quoted, and shared. In addition, members are free to talk sing and share emotions of patriotism and indignation.

Invigorating the Figured World

The participants in LTPGs, as part of a wider network, often introduced fresh stories and issues picked up from media and their own personal networks. These included videos, news items, letters to the editor, and even their own personal opinions introduced through announcements or everyday interaction. And as mentioned, LTPGs also hosted speakers at their regular meetings. Though sometimes the speakers were from NTPOs, such as Americans for Prosperity or Heritage Action, more often they represented local groups and individuals. These small organizations that exist outside the TPM saw the LTPGs as ways to access high-propensity voters, further their goals, and in some cases procure funds.

For instance, I watched a presentation by the North Carolina organizer for a flat tax organization several times during my research as he visited each group. There were also presentations by local officeholders, religious figures, and former members of the military, such as former Navy SEAL and Obama critic Ben Smith and former Marine and Fox News analyst Col. Bill Cowan (who later married one of the members of the Adams Tea Party). In the most basic sense, the speakers were introducing or framing new information on political issues and dispositions within the meaning system of the figured world.

One of the most interesting events I observed was designed to enhance an anti-liberal emotional disposition by framing the liberal perspective in a pathological and conspiratorial manner. One of the reoccurring practices of American right-wing populism, beginning with the early nineteenth-century Anti-Freemasons, is the demonization of opponents (Berlet and Lyons 2000, 7; Hofstadter 2008). The goal is to figuratively define an enemy and place that enemy outside the circle of wholesome mainstream society. A common tactic is to paint enemies as a foreign conspiracy perpetrated by individuals with psychological and moral defects. I referenced this early in chapter 1 regarding the media-generated fears of Barack Obama. This particularly effective presentation was carried out at a meeting of the Revere County Tea Party by Greensboro political consultant Tim Daughtry, who at the time was one half of a team of psychologists who had formed a political consulting firm named Concord Bridge.[4] The purpose of his firm was to advise candidates on political communication. He gave a similar presentation in a breakout session at the 2010 North Carolina GOP convention, gave talks at numerous Tea Party group meetings, and appeared on Glenn Beck's news website, *The Blaze*. The Concord Bridge website reads: "Our workshops are designed to help mainstream activists and candidates understand the strategy and tactics of the far left, to understand why our normal responses to those tactics are ineffective, and to learn and practice more effective skills. As a foundation, we use methods from sports psychology to help participants stay calm, focused, and confident under the stress of political exchanges. Only from this calm and focused stance can mainstream activists recognize common leftist tactics, avoid getting trapped in a defensive position, and seize the political offensive."

The talk was titled "Liberal Minds, Liberal Methods: How to Break Their Grip on Power." Daughtry as a psychologist presented his ideas using scientific discourse and framed his argument to display conservatism as normative yet repressed by a liberal elite. He presented conservatives, though a plurality of Americans (Saad 2015), as a minority that is oppressed by the hegemony of the liberal welfare state. Relying on Gramscian terminology, Daughtry claims liberals dominate the cultural institutions and the only way to win is through "a long march through the institutions."

Daughtry began by painting conservative views as the mainstream ideological position in American society. Conservatives' lives are devoted to the traditional occupations of the ideal citizen. "We want to raise a family, go to work, mind our own business. We will cooperate with each other when it is in our mutual interest." Mainstream conservatives play by the rules, but their problem is that conservatives "confuse civics with politics," meaning that conservatives don't fight, they defend and debate. As Daughtry sees it, "If you are debating, you are defending 'normal.' If you are defending normal, then you have already lost."

To Daughtry and many conservatives, America is a population of good people adhering to traditional values. However, a small minority of liberals has seized control of the country through altering the culture, the institutions, and the ways of thinking and knowing. "What is culture?" he asks.

Well, if you want to understand water, don't ask a fish. It's just what there is; the way things are. By changing these assumptions, liberal thought gets infused into everyday thinking. If you grow up in a school that teaches us that Franklin Roosevelt got us out of the Depression by spending money, then that just looks normal, doesn't it? There was another Depression a few years earlier where the government didn't do anything, and we were out of that within a year. And they don't realize it that we could've been out of the one right now two years ago without the stimulus plan. But the idea of immersing people in Marxist thinking was brilliant if you think about it. You don't consciously decide. Do you remember the moment you decided to stand for the Pledge of Allegiance? You don't decide. It's just what we do.

He continues by employing the Gramscian concept "war of position" (Gramsci, Hoare, and Nowell-Smith 1972), in which, as opposed to direct confrontation with the state (war of maneuver), revolutionary forces seize power through the culture, civil society, and intellectual traditions: "Culture is just what we do . . . Marxists realize that you take over a country through immersion not conversion. That's a critical point. You don't have to convert anyone to radical left-wing thinking. You actually come in under the radar. If you subvert the culture, you subvert the government that rests on that culture." This subversion is possible because conservatives are disengaged from politics: "This is accomplished because the real Americans are not constantly political. Conservatives are engaged in living, not politics; we do not stay to protect our institutions after the election. We are the summer tourists; liberals are the locals. When we win an election, the next day our students are taught by the ones that lost the election."

The conspiracy of cultural Marxism is a common trope in some corners of conservatism and a contemporary manifestation of the conspiratorial anticommunism that animated the grassroots conservatives of the 1950s and 1960s (McGirr 2001; Nickerson 2012). Conservative authors such as David Horwitz and Michael Lind have circulated the account, and it is also vividly portrayed in the documentary *Agenda: Grinding America Down* (Bowers 2010), which was shown at meetings of several of the Tea Party groups I observed during my fieldwork.

The account claims that "cultural Marxists" have made a concerted effort throughout the second half of the twentieth century to undermine the culture of the United States. Daughtry explained to his audience that Gramsci and other Marxists "realized that middle-class countries didn't fall to revolutions—only agrarian ones did." Their solution then was to seize the institutions. Yet Daughtry stresses that this is not conspiratorial thinking. "It was in the open in the early 1900s, and if you didn't read Marcuse when you were in college in my day, you were not sophisticated."

Daughtry's talk continues on this theme by attributing the dramatic changes in society and culture to the concerted effort of a sinister group from foreign shores working to undermine the nation: "Many of those of the Frankfurt School came to America and taught at the New School at Columbia University [*sic*]. Their first target was the School of Education. If you want to infect an entire community with a virus, infect a teacher. I'm not saying that your child's teacher is a Marxist. I'm saying that your child's teacher and textbooks were taught by somebody who was taught by somebody who was taught by a Marxist. The ideas have been embedded in the curriculum."

Daughtry then shifts from the Marxists' long march through the institutions to a representation of the Left as psychologically abnormal compared to mainstream America. Groups construct an enemy through "mythmaking" (Aho 1994, 29), relying on historical or biological accounts that legitimize the "evil" of an enemy. Through a disease, developmental maladaptation, or evolution, an enemy is in possession of some flaw that explains the evil. Daughtry lays out the liberal worldview as a pathology—a result of poor parenting and incomplete childhood development. He argues that a child will grow up with a healthy personality through "average" parenting. However, if a child is the object of "fawning or spoiling," he will develop a narcissistic personality. With good parenting a child will grow up as a responsible and cooperative member of society. With poor parenting,

> the world is a dangerous place. It's like the training wheels came off too soon or they never came off at all. They never learn to make it on their own. Either way the world is a threatening place. And here's the punch line: they are totally dependent on others for survival and approval . . . What do they do with that fear and insecurity? It comes out as anger and resentment . . . The hole they are trying to fill is a spiritual hole. No earthly power can fill it. You cannot make them happy. They are striving for power, blaming, accusing, and criticizing; their inability to handle disagreement is all because of a hole inside of them that we cannot solve for them. That leads to the insatiable desire for power over others. If you can't make it on your own, the only path is to manipulate and control others.

By framing the stances of liberals in this way, Daughtry depoliticizes them, making the merits of the liberal perspective illegitimate. The liberal perspective is based on an illness or defect of character as opposed to the conservative perspective, which is common sense and normative. Moreover, the liberal, as a maladjusted child, is to be managed, ignored, or marginalized.

Daughtry is an example of how the spaces created by local Tea Party groups are settings where the circulating discourses of conservative politics meet, fill in, and further animate the figured world of the Tea Party. The power of perceived expertise coupled with scientific discourse provides material useful for the fashioning of subjectivities (Dumit 1997). Furthermore, Daughtry adds new urgency to the Tea Party's goals. The extra-constitutional expansion of government, the increases in dependency, and the rejection of tradition and morality are not simply the result of actions of people holding a few differing views. Nor are they simply un-American and akin to foreigners. They are emotionally, spiritually, and dangerously abnormal. They present an existential threat to America. Daughtry's presentation fills in the figures of those whom the Tea Party is up against. More broadly, it helps to better understand the processes of demonization that have become instrumental in the greater polarization of American politics—a polarization that contributed to making the TPM possible (Dionne 2016).

Differences, Boundaries, and Contentiousness

Thus far, I have portrayed the LTPGs as operating with relatively few differences and disagreements. But Tea Party groups were not free of tensions. The introduction of new information and dispositions, as well as the different trajectories people take into social movements, can lead to groups being sites of contestation over meanings and practices (Wolford 2010). For instance, by the end of my fieldwork, many of the groups had organized "conceal and carry" classes, which is the instruction required in order to acquire a permit to carry a concealed firearm. Seeing the permits as a display of support for the Second Amendment, several of the Tea Party groups I observed organized these workshops. Possessing a permit became a popular goal for many members. This desire was not shared by all. In one conversation with Sue of BCTP, she seemed troubled that though many members were pursuing the permits, because of a traumatic experience that involved a firearm, she did not want one. The experience struck me because she looked at the permit as having become a near obligation of BCTP membership and she was noticeably torn.

In chapter 1, I mentioned the desire to "shut it down" during the congressional budget stalemate in 2011. Several members of the Burgoyne and Greene County Tea Party thought that shutting down the government was a needed remedy and a true means to shrink the government. Everyone did not share these sentiments as several members made it clear to me and to other group members in meetings. They argued that a government shutdown would have unforeseen effects, would most likely hurt people, damage the economy, and lessen American standing in the world.

In her comparison between a local Tea Party group and a faith-based progressive community organization, Ruth Braunstein describes how the two groups were shaped by different "democratic imaginaries" that produced contrasting forms of activism and contrasting ideas regarding the proper roles as activists. She found that there was negotiation over the meaning of each respective group in which members worked out "appropriateness" of different practices and actions based on how they envisioned "groups like them" (Braunstein 2017, 154). And while my analysis shows similar negotiation, my multi-sited observations point to a fairly wide assortment of perspectives negotiated and wide variation among Tea Party groups.

Practice theory emerged in order to build a better understanding of the dynamic relationship between structure and agency (Ortner 1984). As noted, individuals find meaning in the Tea Party through reflecting on their own lives and on the way those lives make sense in relation to the Tea Party figured world. And as shown, their lives vary greatly. Human interaction creates the performances of the figured world in the LTPGs. Yet those performances always have an unfinished quality as individuals continually respond to new and emerging actors and circumstances. Taylor and Whittier (1992) and Melucci (1995) write how social movement participants continually negotiate the meanings of their political identities—new ways to think and act in their collectivity.

This happens as people collectively work out the symbolic meanings of the social movement with one another (Allen, Daro, and Holland 2007; Strauss and Friedman 2018; Taylor and Whittier 1999) and, often, through dialogue with opponents (Satterfield 2002). Holland, Fox, and Daro (2008, 97) write that movements should not be seen as unified actors but as multiple sources of discourses competing to inform everyday actions of participants. This negotiation can take several forms, most commonly through the informal talk that occurs between Tea Party group members. These negotiations are undertaken within fields formed by diverse geographical, cultural, and social landscapes among people of different social positions and personal histories. Yet negotiations are also characterized by relations of power based on unequal relationships of structural power as well as symbolic and cultural capital.

One of the most interesting negotiations I witnessed over meaning occurred in a meeting of the Adams County Tea Party. The leaders of that group placed a high value on informal discussions and deliberations over issues and meanings. At one meeting they decided to break the attendees up into small groups at each of the large white folding tables in the aging American Legion hall where the meeting was held. The table at which I was sitting was made up of eight people, three women and five men, who came from noticeably different perspectives. The facilitators asked people to discuss what they believed were the main challenges facing America. The ensuing conversation illustrated the different conservative identities that typically come into play within the Tea Party groups I observed. It also showed the tension between how senses of political dislocation animated activism for some and reinforced crippling cynicism in others.

The first to talk was a man in his late seventies who began by saying that the Republicans and Democrats are both complicit and the biggest problem was "sending jobs overseas and bringing foreign people in to do the jobs in America so that the lower man has no money and as a result the government has no tax revenue."

Next to speak was Randy, a fixture at the Adams County Tea Party who was known for his strongly expressed views of various insidious intentions of government formed from his membership in the John Birch Society. Randy claimed that America had become a nation defined by corporate fascism and guided by the Bilderberg group, a secretive meeting of European and American government and economic elites held yearly to discuss transatlantic cooperation. He believed that regular people could do little to change the country as long as it was being controlled by a transnational conspiracy of global corporations and secretive government elites.

A female member of the group then spoke up, saying that she heard the Bilderberg group mentioned on the *Sean Hannity Show* and that he had claimed the conspiracies surrounding the group were "nonsense."

Randy responded that that explanation is what should be expected from the mainstream media because they are "controlled opposition." Randy continued with information gleaned from the website Infowars .com, produced by the right-wing conspiracist Alex Jones, and argued that very little could be done in America as long as powerful, multinational corporations and their political servants were running the country from an invisible and unapproachable perch.

The older man who initially spoke mentioned the problem with imported workers and how "illegal immigrants" were receiving "food stamps." In these first few minutes of the table's discussion, the conversation was dominated by the more negative perspectives articulated by Randy and the older gentleman.

However, Steve and David, leaders of a Tea Party group in neighboring Greene County, stepped in to redirect the conversation back to more hopeful topics. Steve was a leader in his county's Republican organizations years before. He chimed in quickly trying to direct the conversation in a more positive direction: "We have to look at realistic choices." David added, "It's easy to get discouraged and feel that there is nothing that can be done. But we forget it is 'we the people.' When we unite together, we can get things done." Steve then responded directly to Randy, saying that both parties do not reflect the feelings of most Americans, only the Democrats are becoming "communist." "We need to get good people into [Republican] primaries and get them elected."

Another gentleman then joined the conversation. Diverting the topic toward Christian fundamentalism and millennialism, he predicted end times in which the emerging "beast" mentioned in the biblical Book of Revelation will be "electronics."

At that moment a younger man in his late thirties asked whether the group had a Facebook page. In what seemed a direct reaction to the prior statement, he argued that the group and the movement needed to attract young people: "I am putting that on my agenda: I want to get some young people involved and get them some knowledge. The reason there are no young people here is because they don't have any knowledge of what's going on." He then punctuated his statement with his own biblical reference from Proverbs 29:18: "'Because where there is no vision, the people perish.' Just one or two [young people] will do. They text and post things." A common concern among many Tea Party groups was their inability to attract younger people and so several members at this point chime in with agreement.

The man stressing millennialism replied, "The colleges are controlled by liberals. You drive down the road here and you will see some little Toyota with an Obama sticker on it and some little girl with her painted toenails up on the dash. She's smoking a cigarette and drinking a Mountain Dew. Kids are not smart enough to believe."

Undeterred, the younger man replied, "There is a young person's group that I know about. Time to try to get some information to them."

Steve, relieved that the conversation had moved to more practical solutions, agreed, "We need to get young people involved. That's one of the problems isn't it? How do we educate them?"

David then said that we needed to find out what it was about their culture that attracted them and go there. "You are going to have to go to where they are if you can reach them."

This brief portion of a discussion illustrates the contentiousness within the spaces formed by local Tea Party groups, where different visions of America and political empowerment meet. Randy's position, informed by the John Birch Society, represents a segment of conservatism—a fringe segment nonetheless—that still claims adherents, including listeners to conspiracist Alex Jones and Infowars. At the same table is an economic populist perspective in which people see that power is put in the hands of corporate and government elites. The first man who spoke attempted to place blame for people's declining income at the feet of a government that has enabled jobs to be sent overseas and cheap labor to be imported. I heard this perspective several times during fieldwork and was initially struck that it seemed to borrow more from left-wing populism than free-market Tea Party conservatism.

This perspective, in which blame for white working-class dislocation is placed on a corrupt relationship between capitalism *and* government—what many on the right term "crony capitalism"—has caught the attention of social scientists and was successfully tapped by Donald Trump (J. Williams 2016; MacGillis 2016). Trump's rejection of multilateral trade agreements and the imposing of tariffs has often frustrated traditional free-market conservatives yet has proved to be very popular among many working-class conservatives. Moreover, it is oddly coincidental that at this table a more conspiratorial conservative was sitting alongside the white working-class populist. Though I know of no reference by Trump to the John Birch Society, he has relied on conspiratorial narratives such as those of Alex Jones several times in his public life. The table was a brief foreshadowing of Tea Party support for Trump.

Another man placed blame on the rejection of God by citizens and government. The importance he puts on the much-anticipated Second Coming articulated a hope for change that rests on the intervention of God. Yet he also believed that humans have enabled the bad state of the country through their reliance on and fetishizing of technology. On the other side, in opposition to those who paint pictures of hopelessness, we see those energized by their Tea Party experiences. Steve and David were trying to capture the discourse of taking power back in spite of the political class's corruption. Their desire was for the slow incremental change that will eventually restore the country through careful organizing and the cultivation of conservative candidates.

The scene also discloses another source of conflict. To some degree the conflict within this meeting was generational. The younger man, enthusiastic about finding young people and knowing that with knowledge young people would realize the TPMs importance, directly confronted a fear of technology. In his account, young people have embraced and taken advantage of social media, and so it is an actual means by which the Tea Party can be successful with younger generations. He highlighted the generational divide through his own elaboration of the importance of technology. For the younger man, "electronics" will bring new people in through social media. For the older man, electronics are going to be the platform for an Antichrist.

And finally, the discussion in the small breakout group discloses unique subject positions that vary across LTPGs, which are further discussed in the following chapter. This exchange was likely gendered. Since the social fields that affect local spaces of practice are characterized by disparities in power and symbolic capital (Bourdieu 1991), these sites are charged by the assignment of position and struggles over social identification (Wortham 2006; McDermott 2001). LTPGs become spaces where the meanings of inequalities are reproduced and viewpoints silenced or self-censored. The men at the table did all the talking. Of the three women present, one made a single statement while the other two remained silent throughout. As is discussed in the next chapter, this was quite different from other LTPGs in which women were the drivers and leaders (see also Burke 2015; Deckman 2016). In fact, women were the primary or co-founders of five of the eight LTPGs with which I participated.

Other local Tea Party groups were more clearly negotiating the boundaries between what the group would and would not do. The Franklin County Tea Party's meetings were typically attended by fifty to seventy-five people in a large seafood restaurant. The group was involved in few activities outside the monthly meetings during the time of my fieldwork. During the 2010 election, many of the members became involved in supporting a local Republican candidate to the state House of Representatives. That candidate won narrowly, upsetting the Democrat who held the seat. After that, however, the group was rarely involved in any activities aside from their monthly meeting or setting up a table at their county fair or float at their Christmas parade. This low level of activity did not sit well with Jack, a newer member of the Franklin County group.

Jack was a transplant from New Jersey who had been involved in an extremely large and active Tea Party group there. He often related to other members of the Franklin group the level of energy, emotion, and activity that was present in his former group. Jack saw the Franklin group as too timid and too unwilling to press for change. "You folks need to play politics and throw a few bombs. We need to try to put things on the agenda, and when we are refused, we need to draw attention to it."

Jack's idea was to suggest that the local school district sponsor an essay contest for students based on their impressions of the U.S. Constitution. Believing that the school district would reject their proposal, Jack argued that it would then be time for them to protest and create a controversy around what should be considered an uncontroversial act—having students write about the nation's founding document.

Jack's proposal was met with a lack of enthusiasm with many arguing that downtown protests of more than one person were "banned."[5] In later interviews it became apparent that many were more comfortable volunteering for candidates or being involved in less confrontational political activities. Part of this was because being based in a small town, some members were acquainted with many of those they would be confronting. Though Tea Party groups often contained political neophytes, they often also, at least in small southern towns, included local citizens with long-standing ties in the community—some reaching back generations. Such citizens, as opposed to newcomers, were sometimes more hesitant to adopt a confrontational style.

Sometimes the boundaries on group discourses and activities were more implied and enforced through silence or redirection. The Hawthorne Tea Party included an elderly man who attended each meeting and never missed an opportunity to warn of the dangers of teaching evolution and the way it corrupts unknowing youth. The man would get very emotional, seeing Darwinism as a rejection of Christianity and a "dag dastardly deed." He often brought up this concern in a group forum where his statement did not necessarily require a response. His declaration was often simply met with silence, though at one meeting, people tried to redirect the man to bring up these concerns with family members. The chair of the group related to me his frustration and his anxiety about these clearly religious concerns. He thought that such commentary would harm the group's ability to recruit new members, who could be deterred by the overtly Christian themes in a movement that supposedly focused on strictly fiscal matters.

The previous example also illustrates how LTPGs police the points of contact between the Christian conservative figured world and the Tea Party figured world. Along the same lines, one member, an early participant in the Hawthorne group, would as part of the program give a short history "lesson" that was often based on interpretations of history that linked events to divine intervention or signs that God favored the American nation. For example, one history lesson described the Dunkirk-like retreat of George Washington's army from Brooklyn Heights across the East River in 1776, arguing that the persistent fog that hid the evacuation from the British was proof of God's intervention. Eventually the chair of the group asked the member to discontinue these stories.

As compared to boundary setting, the proffering of support for discourses voiced in the Tea Party meetings was even more complex. Sometimes there was a noticeable silence in instances when I expected people to challenge some statements. On one occasion at a Franklin Tea Party meeting, an "expert" on Islam gave a presentation that was dangerously inaccurate in its description of Muslims, for instance, claiming that the Koran directs all Muslims to kill those of other faiths who do not convert to Islam. The noticeable silence gave credibility to the outlandish and intolerant claims, even though the group's cochair later apologized for his talk and regretted inviting him. In any social field the perceived value and possession of symbolic capital may lead some individuals to ignore what a speaker has to say (Bourdieu 1977, 1991). Simply, "does this person have the credibility to say these things?" Or it may lead some individuals, as in this case, to self-censor and not voice their reservations about what another is saying. These effects of symbolic capital may lead to the propagation of incorrect or even harmful information.

Many issues are introduced to a group, and as seen in the Franklin County episode, the fringe is given a voice equal to the mainstream. People may be polite or not feel able to adequately argue a point. Or at other times a closed network of Tea Partyists may circulate and build support for falsehoods in a kind of collective process that Julian Sanchez (2010) called "epistemic closure." The introduction of unchallenged falsehoods may lead Tea Party groups (and of course, other exclusive groups in general) to appear "out of touch" and extreme. This often occurred with discourses originating on the internet but also with misinformation from more mainstream conservative media, such as Fox News. For example, while Texas was evaluating its public school history curriculum in 2010, Gretchen Carlson on the Fox News morning show mistakenly claimed that Texas was considering not teaching any U.S.

history before 1877 (Stutz 2010). I heard the point mentioned in several Tea Party groups, and though Fox later corrected the mistake, it persisted and few questioned the obvious absurdity of the claim. The claim made sense, however, in relation to the wider Tea Party narrative of American society turning its back on America's founders.

During the period of my fieldwork, the LTPGs were crucial for forging, mobilizing, and retaining everyday Tea Party activists. The groups provided the spaces where the figured world of the Tea Party was performed and where meanings were broadened and strengthened on a continual basis through the introduction of new information supplied by the media, through participants' own stories, and through visiting "circuit riders," such as Tim Daughtry. However, just as LTPGs were not the unwitting extensions of elite conservative groups like Americans for Prosperity, neither did the groups uphold a unified set of discourses, positions, and practices. As shown previously, the Tea Party movement addressed many different types of concerns held by participants.

Less discussed here is the variation across LTPGs as to what qualified as appropriate Tea Party practices. The LTPGs I observed, across different landscapes and represented by people from different social positions, had varying definitions of what a Tea Party group should do or what was realistic in their case. For example, the essay contest that was met with such a lukewarm response among the Franklin County group was successfully implemented in the Hamilton group. Moreover, as shown in the next chapter, the Hamilton members would have willingly pushed the conflict that the Franklin group sought to avoid.

The next chapter discusses how those unique personal histories and social positions led to differences in what the Tea Party means and how to practice membership. Tea Partyists holding different meanings regarding the movement led to LTPGs with widely varying characteristics, including the forms of political activism, if any, that the groups engage in.

5 Trickle-Up Politics

LOCAL TEA PARTY GROUPS AS

MOVEMENT ACTORS IN LOCAL POLITICS

Local Tea Party groups as communities of political practice were vibrant sites where the figured world and associated identities were created, learned, and performed; where new material invigorated the communities of practice; and where boundaries, support, silence, and dismissals were negotiated. The prior chapter, however, spoke little to the externally oriented political actions of local Tea Party groups. This is crucial: the LTPGs enlivened and localized the TPM, but were they effective political actors? All the LTPGs that I researched to some degree or at some point in their history were involved in some form of outward political activity.[1] Some groups stopped being active after the success of the 2010 elections. Yet three of the groups with which I participated remained politically active and actually increased the intensity of their political activities after 2010. In all three of these cases, the political activity was undertaken primarily in local political arenas that were fairly invisible to national media coverage. Although the TPM is portrayed as focused on national- and societal-level concerns, Tea Party frustrations surrounding taxes and spending are experienced more intimately close to home through, for example, local taxes and local school districts. Local-level politics is also the site where some of my Tea Party consultants experienced early frustrations that led to their political activism. Local political party organizations were resistant to change and often run by entrenched elites. Processes like budgeting and legislation were mysterious "black boxes" with arcane rules and bureaucratic gatekeepers. Moreover, the close relationships of town elites, elected officials, and bureaucrats sometimes gave off the hint of corruption or cronyism.

Of course, grassroots conservatives' working at the local level is not new. Some local Tea Party actions are strikingly similar to the New Right suburbanites of the 1950s and 1960s (McGirr 2001). Numerous clubs and organizations sprang up in the postwar years to provide opportunities for everyday citizens to protect schools from progressivism, fight communism, and resist desegregation and the civil rights movement.

Furthermore, some of the activities undertaken by some of the LTPGs I observed were remarkably similar to some of the tactics of Ralph Reed and the Christian Coalition in the early 1990s. Organizing the Christian Coalition in the early 1990s, Ralph Reed sought a permanent, precinct-level organization, made up of autonomous chapters and staffed by volunteers who would support issues instead of candidates. As in the Tea Party activism described later in the chapter, Christian Coalition activists waged campaigns in city councils and school boards; they captained precincts in county GOP organizations and distributed candidate information to voters before Election Day. Moreover, like Americans for Prosperity and FreedomWorks, Reed also provided workshops to train neophyte activists for political advocacy and to teach how to peer into and decipher the machinations of government (W. Martin 1996; R. Reed 1993).[2]

The spaces of practice created by the LTPGs could be thought of as multiple and very loosely connected centers of leadership, high energy, and enthusiastic cooperative activity. Beyond providing such gathering places, however, these sites, as alluded to in the previous chapter, constituted a space in which many individuals developed and realized an activist political identity. Newcomers to political activity acquired political skills such as speaking, organizing, and lobbying and learned the intricacies, interrelationships, and decision-making practices of their local governments and of local Republican Party organizations. Since the LTPGs collectively approached the public environments, newly forming activists were supported in the acts of protesting, questioning officials, and organizing.

Little research describes the workings of the Christian Coalition chapters, but given the level of autonomy Reed describes, it should be assumed that they varied in practices and styles as local Tea Party groups did. Social practice theory, with its focus on local spaces of practice as potentially independent sites of cultural production, encourages attention to spatial variation. Thus, the sites of action, the actions undertaken, and the longevity of each group's activism varied. The chapter will begin with a discussion of the primary descriptive distinction between different LTPGs, namely, whether they engaged in outside activism or not. I will trace part of this distinction to the relationship between leaders and members in the different groups. To a substantial degree, the character of each related back to the organizers' motivations and political biographies. And the final section discusses how LTPGs did not simply appropriate issues from elite organizations and media but at times generated their own issues, which then gained significance within the wider conservative movement.

Audiences and Activists

Members in seven of the eight groups I worked with were involved in electioneering before the 2010 election (Pierce being the only relatively inactive group). This included making phone calls to voters or leafleting at polling places. Three groups did not organize their own activities but rather invited candidates to speak and recruit members for their campaign activities. Four of the groups organized campaign activities within the LTPG. After resounding victories in 2010, the groups with members who volunteered on political campaigns were unable to maintain their commitment and energy and settled into simply meeting, interacting among themselves, and doing very little outside political activism. Three of the four groups that organized their own activities, maintained a high level of activity—Hamilton, Burgoyne, and Adams. Those three groups, primarily because of a strong core of active members, continued to grow and develop new forms and targets for political activism.

Each group seemed to settle into one of two types: what I term "audiences" and "activists." An audience group had two main characteristics. First, the group meetings were predominantly educational; info was presented to the group, and there was a low degree of interaction. Second, there was an absence of a second tier of leadership. In other words, the leaders—the two or three primary organizers—were carrying out most of the activities of the organization. In some of these groups, the leaders, either owing to their own time commitments or personal styles, could not seem to move their groups onto more activist footings.[3]

It is nonetheless important to note that an audience group is still important in the broader Tea Party movement. Even without involving themselves in externally oriented, contentious local politics, these groups circulated and repurposed the cultural resources that served to invigorate the figured world. These were large groups of high propensity voters who were going to use the interpretive frame of the Tea Party during elections in evaluating issues and candidates. Through visits by elected officials and other organizers who often sought out these groups, these members were educating themselves regarding politics and political activity in their local community and nationwide. Many would also be drawn on as foot soldiers in later campaigns. Conversely, they were educating candidates on the issues most important to the most ardent conservatives in their constituency. Finally, the groups were still nodes in the Tea Party network, where information was continually circulated to other Tea Party groups and individuals.

The activist groups were all vibrant, local, political organizations. In the last year of my fieldwork, with no general election on the horizon, three of the eight groups—one third of the groups that I worked with— were engaged in ongoing activism (refer to the chart in the introduction that categorizes the different LTPGs). The meetings were interactive, and though presentations occurred, they were not the only activity. Often a microphone would go around the room so that people could give updates on multiple activities, as in the first vignette in the introduction in which members spoke of event planning, budget advocacy, essay contests, and the recording of Van Jones. The leaders did work, of course, but other members did many of the necessary tasks and were empowered to initiate committees and activities on their own.

For the groups in Burgoyne County, Hamilton County, and Adams County, activism became a primary component of the Tea Party figured world. Lave and Wenger (1991) theorized communities of practice in the context of "situated learning"; in this case, political knowledge was gained through the co-participation of novice and experienced activists in local political settings. These activist groups were ongoing workshops of political socialization in which members learned practical political skills, including setting up phone trees, organizing rallies, speaking at legislative bodies, and electioneering. Those LTPGs had small yet significant effects on their local political culture and elections and transformed their members into experienced dedicated advocates, protesters, and campaigners.

For example, soon after the 2010 election, I spoke with Patricia, a woman of seventy, who said she had handed out leaflets at early voting sites. I asked if she had ever done anything like that before. With a chuckle and a smile, she said, "No! I can't believe I did that." She continued, telling me that because of the candidate forums held during the group's meetings, she learned more about how "government budgets" worked. For instance, she mentioned that because of the group-sponsored debate between school board candidates, she better understood the budgeting and financial priorities for the county school district.

Patricia's experience is central to understanding a key aspect of the importance of these local Tea Party groups. Patricia was motivated early on to become involved with the Tea Party and sought out the local group. Through that participation she had the opportunity to do something that was outside her comfort zone, have a small influence on a historic election, and become more versed in the workings of her government. This sense of efficacy, reinforced through the LTPGs' regular face-to-face meetings, made these groups of regular citizens potent political actors in their local political cultures. The Hamilton and Burgoyne groups illustrate the creation of such activists in dissimilar ways.

HAMILTON COUNTY TEA PARTY

The Hamilton County Tea Party, the first of the three "activist" groups, assumed a form that was strongly influenced by the class position of the members and the political landscape of their county. Their unique skills, backgrounds, and sense of their own cultural capital provided the context for a more instrumental approach to activism and a bitter conflict with their local county government.

The Hamilton County Tea Party was formed in late 2009 by four people who attended the same Sunday church service. Between the regular service and the later Bible study group, they would meet over coffee and donuts to discuss the issues of the day. They were becoming more and more troubled by the direction of the country as President Obama's health care reform was nearing passage.

The drive behind the formation of the group was led by Sandy, an energetic, upper-middle-class stay-at-home mother of two in her late thirties, and Robert, a small business owner in his mid-forties. Sandy was motivated by Tea Party inspiration, former Alaska governor, and vice presidential candidate Sarah Palin.

In December of 2009 I went on a business trip with my husband and took Sarah Palin's book [*Going Rogue*] with me. What I got out of the book is that if Americans would just take care of their little piece of America, their own backyard. If they got involved locally and cleaned up the corruption, the good old boy network and found out where their tax money is going . . . If everybody took care of their little city or county, oh my gosh, we would see such a difference. It's called trickle-up politics as Dan [Sandy's husband] calls it. I was so inspired by that because I think a lot of times people feel very helpless watching the news. They see all these huge national issues in Washington DC and these politicians; these things that you will never be able to get your hands on to do anything about. And every couple of years you get to vote. But local was all of a sudden, "Gosh, I think there are politicians who do stuff locally." But I didn't really know. I had never been to a city council meeting or a county commission meeting, never. I had never been in the building; I didn't know where they were downtown, the whole nine yards. So I thought that we needed to do something. We have to do something on this local level. The one friend I have had these political conversations with at church was Robert.

She began attending the local Republican women's club meetings but became disillusioned quickly. It became apparent to her that a relatively young, energetic newcomer was going to have limited influence on reinvigorating an entity that had for years been more of a social arrangement for older members of the local conservative establishment, whose biggest activities were fund-raising dinners for the local GOP. "So Robert and I decided that we needed to sit down and have coffee and decide what we were going to do." Robert agreed about the importance of the local political field, and together Robert and Sandy gathered some friends, some people Robert knew from the local GOP, and a few who Sandy met at the women's club.

Later on, maybe a month, we had a meeting at night; there were six of us there. We talked about what we could do, and we decided that nationally we couldn't do anything, and we didn't think we could do anything statewide. But locally, let's look at it. Who controls the government locally? Six people on the Board of Education—there are eleven board members, and you need six. Six county commissioners and five on the city council . . . So in our conversations we figured that all we needed were seventeen people that could change the dynamic of the county. So let's start there. So we agreed that that's what we could do. Seventeen. So all of a sudden it was smaller. Instead of it being just too big for one little me, it didn't seem very big.

Their first target was their county government. Their reasoning went as follows: Hamilton County is one of the larger counties in North Carolina, and its county seat is one of North Carolina's ten largest cities. Democrats make up a majority of voters and include a very prominent black middle class and a black political elite. The county-level legislative body, the County Board of Commissioners, had the most direct impact on people's lives through their control over property tax rates and the way those funds are spent.

The Hamilton group was made up of mostly middle-class and upper-middle-class professionals, as well as some retirees and their spouses. The membership was overly represented by people in finance, consulting, and marketing, many of whom would form a dedicated second level of leadership that coordinated different activities. There was, for example, a city council committee, an outreach and membership committee, a school board committee, and a committee to liaison with other Tea Party groups.

Hamilton members' first activities were preparing and making comments to the commissioners during the public comment period at the beginning of the twice monthly county commissioner meetings. The purpose of these short, three-minute presentations was to draw attention to different aspects of spending that the group deemed wasteful or unnecessary. The comments read by participants often held a modest degree of conceit and disrespect toward the Democrats on the commission and especially the chair, a politically powerful African American real estate broker. The commission meetings were always broadcast live on local television and often reported on in the local daily newspaper and a free weekly newspaper that gave the group sympathetic coverage. Members of the group recorded the comments themselves and began circulating video clips of each other's presentations through social media, such as Facebook and a YouTube channel.

The production and circulation of these videos was the focal point of a unique space of practice created by the group. Though the group did have meetings occasionally, such as the scene portrayed in the introduction, much of their interaction was done either in small groups at the county commissioners' meetings or through the exchange of videos and comments over Facebook, e-mail, and the organization's YouTube channel. The county commissioner meetings were events at which the members would meet and talk, and the three-minute comment periods were the primary activity. I would hear members ask each other, "Are you speaking tonight?" Some would and some would not. Some had no difficulty writing and presenting a three-minute public comment. For others the process was new and challenging. More accomplished speakers worked with new members, helping them craft concise and compelling comments. Sandy, herself a political neophyte when she launched the group, became a very effective speaker with comments that were hard-hitting and aggressive with an underlying tone of contempt toward the commissioners. The group had no illusions that their comments were actually going to change the commissioners' minds on policy. As Sandy put it, "But my audience is not really the commissioners but the group that is going to view these videos. These videos are designed to get people to the tipping point a little bit quicker. The commissioners already know how many people are on the disability rolls. They already know what's going on with the federal mandates and who gets help and who doesn't. So my mission is for the people. It's for the people that are on the Facebook page. We have 700 people on our e-mail distribution list."

Owing to the class positions of the members, the group developed a style that reflected their own sense of privilege, entitlement, and symbolic capital. It's customary for Tea Partyists to protest, address complaints to elected officials, and often work for or against candidates. Many Hamilton members, being quite privileged, believed that they could do the job better than those in office. This disposition came out through utterances about the group's outlook on governing, which they equated with running a business. In a comment before the county commissioners about school district funding, one of the group's members, a retired executive, justified his argument for budget cuts in this way: "I ran multibillion-dollar enterprises for forty years. My last ten years I spent turning around financially troubled companies. Really tough stuff. On the school board there is a lot of money that's being wasted . . . The administrative staff of Hamilton schools needs to be cut by 50 percent. This is a strategic imperative . . . They need to cut $20 million out of their budget to maintain their fiduciary responsibility to the taxpayers."

The Democrat chair of the commission, over time, built up greater and greater contempt for the organization owing to their constant complaints and accusations. On more than one occasion, he lashed out at the group for their sense of privilege: "You're not the only smart people here. We have brains too. And we have concerns too. Just because we're not doing it the way you want it to be done, doesn't mean were not doing it. People are elected on the school board by people who trust them to do the right thing. Just because you don't like it, doesn't mean they're wrong."

At one point in late 2010, after months of repeated challenges to the commission, one Democratic member suggested sarcastically that since the group was so well versed in taxes and spending, maybe they should come up with their own budget to back up their words. The group accepted the challenge with enthusiasm. They organized themselves into several working groups to analyze different areas of the budget, including human resources, transportation, general services, and health care (but not law enforcement). Members researched budget items and visited different county agencies to discuss their budgets and responsibilities. The group claimed to have found over $70 million in savings, more than enough to offset the planned increase in property taxes.

Seeking a means to present their findings, the group learned that the ornate room where the commissioners met was open to the public and groups when not in use. They reserved the room and invited the county commissioners to attend. Four of the eleven county commissioners attended (not including the chairman) and in a brilliantly executed act of spatial power politics, the commissioners were placed at tables below the dais where those giving testimony usually sit. Members of the Hamilton County Tea Party placed themselves just in front of the dais, higher than the commissioners. Owing to those spatial arrangements, for a few hours that spring night, it looked as though the Tea Party was driving the agenda of Hamilton County.

After the event, unsurprisingly, the commissioners ignored the group's budget suggestions and passed their own budget, which was finalized behind closed doors at the home of one of the commissioners. Regardless of the defeat, which most members expected, the group recruited new members and began monitoring and speaking at meetings of the school board and the city council for the Hawthorne County seat.

Though they didn't change the Hamilton County budget, the Hamilton LTPG achieved several important goals. First, the group earned a degree of "standing," or in Bourdieu's (1991) terminology, the symbolic and cultural capital necessary to participate in that political field. Because of their constant presence, people saw them as representing an ideological position and an aggressive style that had been absent—even from the county Republican Party. Second, though many members were quite privileged, many translated their personal skills—for better or worse—to public policy and policymaking. They taught this expertise to new, less experienced members. Finally, the members, to a degree, opened the "black box" of governing, realizing their own sense of possibility in the political arena. As one member related to me, "I had a feeling that I may be just as smart and capable as the people on the dais, but now I am positive of it. We are as smart as they are and could do their jobs if we had to. I didn't really feel that way before." And as with Patricia earlier and many other consultants, he felt empowered and confident that he knew about civic issues and could tell people about them. He thought the people could come to him and that he was a resource. "It makes me feel good to be able to help them with issues."

By 2012 Robert and Sandy had achieved one of their primary goals with the help of the massive election gains by the GOP in the 2010 "Tea

Party Wave" election. In addition to Republicans' winning control of the U.S. Congress in 2010, they also gained control of several state legislatures, including North Carolina's for the first time since Reconstruction. In 2011 the new legislative majority then intervened in the makeup of the Hawthorne County Board of Commissioners, eliminating one at-large seat and one district entirely and reapportioning the districts to favor Republicans (Killian 2012). In 2012 Republicans gained three seats and a one seat majority on the board. One of those victors was a Hamilton Tea Party member I interviewed for this research.

As shown with Robert and Sandy, the initial organizers of each group had a substantial influence on the early direction of the groups. I will not argue that the leaders necessarily dictated the subsequent form of the group, but their backgrounds and motivations to some degree influenced the style that the group developed and displayed at least initially. The process of movement formation, as detailed in the introduction, was triggered by the resonance of the Tea Party movement frames with people's sense of unease regarding the direction of the nation. And as noted in chapter 1, these concerns were not uniform, but rather the product of different biographies. The primary organizers, guided by their own biographies, often set the initial tone as they brought people together in their first meetings and provided direction for their group's initial activities. Moreover, their direction was often related to their own experiences with politics. Two examples will show the influence of initial organizers and the personal histories they brought to the movement. Burgoyne is the second activist group, which will show striking contrast to the Pierce County Tea Party, a less active audience group.

SUE AND THE BURGOYNE COUNTY TEA PARTY

In the prior chapter I described the Burgoyne County Tea Party and the way they performed the Tea Party figured world in their monthly meetings and activities. As mentioned, Sue and several of her friends founded the group, though at least during my time with them, Sue was the hands-on center of the group. Youthful in her mid-seventies, a New Hampshire transplant, former elementary school teacher, and mother of grown children, Sue remembers sewing for the Red Cross as a young child during the Second World War and saw her generation as enduring sacrifice in order to give the next generation newfound opportunities. Though generally conservative her entire life, she had become strongly aware of her conservatism a decade earlier as she rejected the increasingly liberal principles emerging in her church. She tells me, "I had been an unconscious conservative and [then] became a conscious conservative." Upon moving to North Carolina and becoming involved in the local Republican women's club, she was, like Sandy, disappointed that the group and the local GOP were not sufficiently conservative, nor were they facilitated in a democratic manner.

I asked Sue to describe her vision should the Tea Party be successful. Articulating common Tea Party themes, she replied:

> Conservative, constitutional principles are taught . . . There is a president who is running a transparent government and understands what its responsibilities and limits are. The judiciary gets it, and that they don't get to change the Constitution whenever they want to. There is also a sense of patriotism that you can feel in communities all across the country. People are not afraid to put up a flag. People are proudly saluting the flag. People want to learn about our heritage. Parents wake up to how much importance there is in birthing a child and giving the child principles.

In this quote we hear familiar Tea Party themes of limited government, constitutional literalism, patriotism, and the removal of the stigma associated with expressing love for the country. Sue's statement also illustrates how gender identity relates to Tea Party activism. In conversations Sue would often reference motherhood. The "motherhood frame" (Deckman 2016) describes how the social position of women in the family grants them a moral position that men often lack and that motivates social action. For generations women's gender roles have driven involvement in conservative (and progressive) activism, for example, the temperance movement, military preparedness before U.S. entry into the First World War, and protests against the growth of the New Deal (Nickerson 2012). Historically, women saw themselves as fulfilling key roles, rearing children and instilling values of citizenship. Many Tea Party women have expressed these moral claims in the context of fiscal concerns, such as how government programs that lack the social relationships and values of family replace the family as a source of social support and moral guidance. Sue often framed motherhood as a sacred national duty, reflecting the moral claims of the Tea Party figured world. As her quote indicates, motherhood fulfills a crucial role in building democratic values. In other cases women were motivated by the idea of generational theft, that the debt and excessive spending concerns of the Tea Party would saddle their children and often grandchildren with crippling debt.

Women played an oversized role organizing the LTPGs I participated with and in the Tea Party movement in general (Deckman 2016). This is partially due to the unpleasant experience women had with their local Republican Party organizations. Sue and Sandy both experienced this. Republican committees were often hierarchical or overly bureaucratic. Moreover, the Republican women's clubs were less interested in advocacy and organizing, unlike those clubs in the 1950s and 1960s, when they were widespread, well attended and quite activists in their orientation (Nickerson 2012; Rymph 2006). The more "open source" nature of the local Tea Party groups was an ideal fit for activist-oriented, conservative women who felt unwelcome or unmotivated in traditional GOP organizations.[4]

Those influences shaped Sue's identity as a Tea Partyist and influenced how she steered the group in its early days. I already mentioned some of the common internal practices of the Burgoyne County Tea Party, such as saluting the flag and reciting the preamble of the U.S. Constitution. They were also one of the most politically active groups of the eight I followed. Sue's vision of conservatism was strongly influenced by her transition to conscious conservative and her disappointing experience with the local GOP. As a result of her rejection of the local Republican Party practices, the group's members all but seized and transformed the local GOP. The Burgoyne County Tea Party's active, committed members became Republican captains of a majority of the voting precincts in Burgoyne County, influencing the direction of the county party organization.[5] Burgoyne Tea Party members outorganized the local GOP establishment by developing a political organization that was not simply more ideologically explicit, but that more successfully involved citizens in political activities, such as protests, grassroots lobbying, and electioneering. As part of the state structure of the Republican Party, their influence in the county party eventually had broader effects, leading to Tea Party–inspired, state-level convention fights over platform language and senior statewide party officeholders. Skocpol and Williamson (2012) write that the TPM contributed to the ideological hardening of the Republican Party. The sources of this hardening, they argue, came from each of the different components of the movement. Considering the work of the Burgoyne LTPG, we also see how this hardening may start almost imperceptibly at the precinct level and work its way through the party hierarchy.

Beyond those activities the group organized its own electioneering campaigns. Burgoyne Tea Party members actively worked the polls, including early voting sites and Election Day polling places (Hamilton Tea Party did electioneering too). In 2010 and 2012 the group sent out questionnaires to all the local candidates seeking their positions on several issues relevant to the Tea Party. They made an easy-to-read table that displayed candidates' responses (and lack of response) and published them in a space bought in the local paper. They also compiled the answers onto a simple leaflet that would then be distributed to voters (along with a pocket-size U.S. Constitution, of course) as they entered the polling places. The group maintained a schedule and map to ensure that as many of the polling places and early voting sites were covered as possible.

Additionally, many BCTP members wrote and read political commentaries on airtime provided to citizens by the local AM talk radio station. The group seized on this opportunity as a cost-free way to express their political views and recruit new members. Often members practiced their commentaries at BCTP meetings and encouraged others to write and broadcast their own. The few presentations I heard included themes from conservative media but given local voice and color by county citizens. The BCTP also fund-raised thousands of dollars to place several self-designed, Tea Party–themed billboards along North Carolina highways before the 2010 and 2012 general elections.

The Burgoyne Tea Party was a beehive of political activity. During my research one could feel Sue's imprint on the group, yet there were many different leaders and coordinators working on many different activities.

From the start, members began to take responsibility for a host of activities. Sometimes these activities, such as choosing who would become a precinct captain, were collectively decided on. Other times they were independently launched by members; for example, one man took it upon himself to videotape meetings and events and create a Vimeo channel. A year after I had completed my fieldwork, Sue stepped down as chair and a member of the second-level leadership took her place.

DALE AND THE PIERCE COUNTY TEA PARTY

Fifty miles away in Pierce County, the LTPG assumed a very different form. Dale was the founder of the Tea Party in Pierce County, a primarily rural, agriculturally based county with two primary small towns that before the 1990s had substantial textile and furniture manufacturing sectors. Its largest city and county seat is a town of twenty thousand. I was initially struck by Dale's vision of his Tea Party group as one that wasn't "hollering and carrying signs." At the time his claim struck me as a rejection of a defining Tea Party characteristic. It was after speaking with Dale and observing the development of his group that I started to realize his and the other members' devout fundamentalist faith was influencing the style and practices of the Tea Party group. Dale became an evangelical Christian in the late 1970s and embraced his faith with missionary zeal. At one point he and his wife ran an unlicensed home for runaway girls, scouring the streets of Greensboro for homeless teens to feed, clothe, and minister to.

Unlike Sue's, Dale's vision of the Tea Party seemed to be informed by different motivations and emotions. When I initially asked him what the Tea Party was to him, he responded, "The Tea Party is the same—all it is is 'Taxed enough already!' That's all it stands for. We are living today where one party is either 'tax and spend' or 'borrow and spend.' The 'borrow and spend' is where we're at today."

To Dale, the primary threat to America was much greater and deeper than "tax and spend" or the immediate threat to the Constitution by President Obama and progressives. "Every movement revolves around the sitting president. Obama just happens to be the sitting president that is making bad decisions and getting bad advice." To Dale, American decline is manifested in the secularization of society and the breakdown of the postwar nuclear family. Further, whereas many Tea Party members, including Sue, would champion the restorative powers of the Constitution as the key to American revival, Dale's hope was placed firmly in Jesus Christ. At one group meeting, Dale complained, "I don't know what's going on in our country. But I do know that we need to start inviting people into our churches and letting them get the gospel of Jesus Christ. The Constitution is not gonna fix what we got. There is nothing that any man has written that's going to fix our country. We are morally bankrupt." For Dale, American decline emerges from the removal of God from people's lives, government, and public schools. Often the rejection of God was undertaken by government, which after inserting itself into more and more areas of public life, removed faith in the name of multiculturalism and "political correctness." In some cases the government was more hostile to religion. I often heard Pierce County members express fear that the government will remove tax exempt status or even shut down Christian churches that were too politically oriented.

Unlike Sue's group, which focused on patriotic and political concerns, the Pierce County group traced American decline loosely through the Tea Party frames of morality and individual responsibility. Moreover, the Pierce County Tea Party also differed from many Tea Party groups in the activities that its members undertook. The Pierce group was an audience group. In the year that I attended PCTP meetings, I never once saw the group engaged in externally oriented contentious politics. The events and activities were based largely in faith and charity with distinct working-class concerns. As Dale told me early in my fieldwork, "We want our group to be a community organization. We want to help people. We collected supplies for the schools. On October 2 we had a big fund-raiser with Children's Miracle Network. And I want to see some kind of a support system for seniors that have to make a choice between food and prescriptions. We can only do that if we have the numbers and people that put others before themselves. If you put yourself before others you will never get anything done except fight with your ego." During my fieldwork I never saw any work done on behalf of seniors. However, Dale and some members did organize a school supply drive, a Children's Miracle Network fund-raiser, and a "buy American" fair, at which a dozen vendors sold their made-in-America products from stands in a vacant lot.

Since Dale formed his group in the summer of 2010, over a year after Sue and her friends started theirs, it seemed that to Dale, the Tea Party was a vehicle through which he could impress and organize around his religious interpretations of the Tea Party. In this case, harking back to my earlier discussion of the Christian Right and the TPM, the figured world of the evangelical and the Tea Party had thoroughly overlapped. At times I wasn't sure whether the Pierce County Tea Partyists were a politically focused church group or a religiously oriented political group. This resulted in a unique style practiced in the PCTP group. At one meeting Dale had so combined the spiritual and the political that he conducted a type of "altar call"; having participants close their eyes, he invited them to raise their hands if they wished to make a new spiritual commitment to Jesus Christ after the meeting. This group style, I believe, alienated some people and prevented the group from growing quickly. However, it also attracted a consistent core that shared this understanding of American decline and appreciated the style by which the group operated. Diane, for example, the strongly devout person that we met in chapter 2, was an early and regular attendee at PCTP meetings. By the end of my fieldwork, the group meetings were well attended, and while the religious tone seemed diminished, the group became a forum that candidates would visit seeking support. At that point, nonetheless, the group still didn't engage in any contentious politics, and it didn't seem as though Dale was really interested in doing so.

These two examples show how different motivations coupled with strong and charismatic personalities could have a strong effect on the type of action that an LTPG took. The groups often attracted a group of people who were able to relate to the primary organizers, creating a strong relationship between the members and leaders. Dale and Sue attracted people like themselves—social conservatives in Dale's group and middle-class, retired conservative Republicans in Sue's. Conversely, these styles can repel many would-be Tea Partyists. The unique style of the Pierce County group focusing on Christian fundamentalist themes repelled some would-be members. At the meeting that Dale did his altar call, one first-time visitor pointedly asked about the outward political activity that he expected from a Tea Party. Dale's response was noncommittal saying, "We could do that if people want." But he quickly moved on to another topic without asking the group as a whole if they'd like to engage in external political activity and what that activity might be.

Although it is easy to say that the leaders were the ones that made all the difference in the local groups, my research among several groups showed the dynamics to be more complex. In many cases the leaders were a means of building solidarity and focusing energies facilitating effective activism. However, in the most active groups, there was a second level of leadership below the primary organizers. The groups that were most active and energetic were characterized by multiple centers of activity. In the Burgoyne group a few people coordinated the precinct work; another who proofed members' radio commentaries before they were read on the radio; and another, a woman, handled the collection of petitions that were to be delivered to policymakers. In the Pierce group there was no such second tier. Dale and his wife organized the limited activities the group undertook. In the monthly meetings people mostly listened and agreed and were given few opportunities to do more.

The Cultural Production of New Grievances

Local Tea Party groups that I observed varied by tactics, priorities, organizational structure, and their chosen targets. The Hamilton County group engaged in innovative types of activism, such as the alternative county budget. Burgoyne seized their local GOP organization, whereas the Hamilton group was unsuccessful when they attempted it. The Pierce group forged an interpretation of the Tea Party that though probably unrecognizable to some, successfully attracted dozens of concerned citizens to regular meetings.

These examples show the ability of these LTPGs to develop new repertoires of action. However, groups also developed new sets of grievances, often not included in the original Tea Party concerns of taxes and spending. Figured worlds, as mentioned, include interpretive frames, allowing people to evaluate and act on many different issues and situations. They "distribute people by relating them to landscapes of action" (Holland et al. 1998, 41). The associated collective identities, while acting as interpretive frames, are also characterized by the dynamic rearticulation of variegated meaning and relationships across different political and social fields (Gregory 1998, 11). "Freedom" and "liberty";

key documents, such as the Constitution; and allusions to ever-creeping government interference in everyday life evoke these worlds as the relevant horizon of meaning against which to read recurring as well as *newly encountered* political situations.

Tea Partyists continually encountered new issues that might resonate with the Tea Party figured world. The most obvious example was the importance of the Second Amendment to Tea Partyists at least in my area of North Carolina. Though the Second Amendment was not one of the initial Tea Party issues in 2009, the underlying theme of constitutional protections and the arbitrary actions of government easily adhered to Tea Partyists' existing concerns. A second issue was Common Core, a set of national education standards developed by forty-eight state governors that set a minimum curriculum for primary and secondary education. The reform, passed with bipartisan support and signed by President George W. Bush, was seen by conservatives as another betrayal of conservative principles (Dionne 2016) but was generally not a prominent issue. However, during its early implementation, it became identified with the Obama administration by conservative politicians, media, and NTPOs as another example of heavy-handed government actions interfering in local community issues. The concerns were often voiced by local Tea Partyists, and several previously supportive Republican officeholders becoming strong opponents of Common Core owing to the pressure exerted by Tea Party groups, large conservative organizations, and talk radio personalities (Wallsten and Layton 2013).

Sometimes, however, LTPGs themselves bring entirely new issues into the Tea Party network. One of the most unique I've encountered was the "Green Tea Coalition" in Georgia in 2013. The founder of the Atlanta Tea Party Patriots, a local Tea Party group, joined with the state chapter of the Sierra Club to promote the home ownership of solar panels (Martin 2013). The Sierra Club wanted to make it easier for consumers to install solar panels; the Tea Partyists saw Georgia Power's monopoly and their refusal to purchase electricity produced by home solar panels as anticompetitive. Interestingly, their successful effort to open up the market ran into a roadblock. The Green Tea effort did not catch on with other local groups maybe partially because of opposition from Americans for Prosperity, a project of Charles and David Koch, whose holdings include many energy and fossil fuel concerns. Nonetheless, the Atlanta Green Tea Coalition joined forces once again to protest the Atlanta Braves' plans to build a new stadium in the suburbs of Atlanta (Terbush 2013).

The crucial point is the network structure of the TPM. In all these cases activism circulated through the network of local Tea Party groups, national Tea Party groups, and conservative media. Sue learned some of her tactics through workshops that were organized by Americans for Prosperity. She was sought after for her experience to speak at larger Tea Party events and often gave advice to the organizers of other groups. The Hamilton group continued to circulate videos and improve the quality of their production (Sandy's preteen son became an accomplished video editor). Sandy once shared her experiences during one of the Hawthorne group's meetings. As mentioned in the beginning of the introduction, one of the group's videos of Van Jones discussing social justice went viral, appearing on Glenn Beck's and Bill O'Reilly's shows on the Fox News Channel. And in all these cases new individuals were brought into the Tea Party movement, developed senses of themselves as Tea Party activists, and burnished the perception of their own agency.

THE ADAMS COUNTY TEA PARTY:
THE INSTIGATION AND ENACTMENT OF NEW ISSUES

In one instance local Tea Party groups developed new issues and conflicts that not only circulated to other LTPGs but became major issues in the wider national conservative political universe. The issue, which I watched evolve locally, regarded Agenda 21, the United Nations–sponsored nonbinding, voluntary plan for sustainable development originally drafted at the Rio Earth Summit in 1992. The purpose of Agenda 21 was to create guidelines for sustainable development for national and local governments (International Council for Local Environmental Initiatives [ICLEI] 2008). Against the horizon of meaning of the Tea Party figured worlds, the narrative of Agenda 21 was read, beginning at the local level, as an international conspiracy to deprive America of its sovereignty. That reading emerged and circulated within Tea Party circles quickly in 2010. My research found little mention of Agenda 21 before that year, and those references were in small, obscure libertarian and conspiratorial online sources (e.g., Strzelczyk and Rothschild 2009).

The Agenda 21 narrative began to gain attention in early 2011 with the election of a firebrand county commissioner in Carroll County, Maryland. He had campaigned on the Agenda 21 threat and led a successful effort to withdraw the county's membership in ICLEI, which he viewed as the localized incarnation of Agenda 21. Word spread through social media, and in the coming months LTPGs in municipalities nationwide flooded meetings of local government boards and commissions loudly opposing ICLEI, land use ordinances, and transportation projects (Whittemore 2013). Yet outside the profession of city and regional planning, these disruptive actions were fairly unnoticed by NTPOs or major broadcast media.

I was able to observe the Agenda 21 narrative develop within the third activist group, the Adams County Tea Party, located in a small rural county in the foothills of the Appalachian Mountains. The county is anchored by Dixon, a picturesque community popular with tourists for its preserved early twentieth-century downtown. The Adams County Tea Party (ACTP) included a small yet highly committed group of people. Regular meetings rarely included more than thirty individuals but were typically, as mentioned in the previous chapter, characterized by free-flowing and guided discussions on local and national issues among the members. The group had been very active since its launch in early 2010. It held candidate forums during the 2010 campaign season, and many of the members volunteered for GOP candidates for the county commission, helping contribute to the victory of three candidates who formed a new conservative majority on the board. The group continued pressuring the county commission after the election, successfully organizing for property tax reductions.

I first heard of Agenda 21 at an ACTP meeting in November 2010, when Paul, who had been researching sustainable development, warned the group of Agenda 21 as "a danger that Glenn Beck isn't even talking about." Some members voiced skepticism to me regarding the conspiratorial nature Paul claimed for Agenda 21, yet he continued to speak of it at meetings, supplying more and more information he gleaned from the internet, including the emerging protests by local Tea Party groups in other states. The issue was finally discussed on *The Glenn Beck Pro-*

gram in the early summer of 2011. Later that summer, the fight against Agenda 21 came to Adams County, and ACTP mobilized to oppose it.

As rural economies transition away from local manufacturing and agriculture, more and more rural North Carolinians commute to cities, precipitating the need for regional transportation planning. When a representative of the nascent regional transportation planning authority came to Dixon for an information session before the city council, ACTP members saw what they considered to be an Agenda 21–inspired effort as a real and present danger to the picturesque southern town. During the question-and-answer period after the presentation, the mild-mannered representative was asked point blank how the regional authority would infringe on local sovereignty and impose onerous regulations that would consolidate housing and force the city to fund and build transportation hubs and greenways. Tea Party concerns regarding "social equity" resulted in this exchange:

COUNCIL MEMBER AND TEA PARTY ALLY: Can you explain the social equity component?
CONSORTIUM REPRESENTATIVE: Right now, we have 1.6 million people in the region. We will grow to about 2 million, so says the state demographer. We have a diverse population already. We have new immigrants and people who've been here for a long time. We have disparities within the region. The region is fractious, but that is one of our strengths and diversity, people working together on common problems will be a better place to be.
COUNCIL MEMBER: So it really is social engineering.
REPRESENTATIVE: I wouldn't call it that.
TEA PARTY MEMBER: But that is what you just said.
REPRESENTATIVE: I wouldn't call it that.

Unfamiliar with the questions, the soft-spoken representative was left to answer limply, "I'm not aware of that restriction" or "There is no plan for that by the consortium." Discussing the experience with him later, he complained to me that many of the concerns were not germane to the scope or goals of the consortium. I suggested to him that they in fact were because of the unique meanings of sustainable development and Agenda 21 held by Tea Party members.

As a result, two members of the city council were noticeably more confused than when they arrived at the meeting and less certain about joining the regional authority. One council member, a conservative who was already skeptical, became a stronger opponent of sustainable development, offering enthusiastic support and credibility to the Tea Party members' interpretation of the issue. The group then circulated information about the meeting through social media to other Tea Party groups in the state, including a link to a local newspaper article, written under the headline "Citizens Blast Sustainable-Communities Plan at Meeting." The ACTP not only had a pronounced effect on the city's hesitation to participate in regional governance, but it also contributed to propelling the narrative of the dangers of Agenda 21.

The discourse of the Agenda 21 scheme circulated among North Carolina Tea Party groups, emboldened members, and helped push the issue in more and more counties. Later in my research, the Burgoyne County group protested land-use ordinances in their county, framing the policies as the creeping influence of Agenda 21. More broadly, Tea Party protests and organizing also led planning professionals to reexamine the usual practices of citizen participation (Trapenberg-Frick 2013; Whittemore 2013). The circulation of and credibility given to the Agenda 21 fear by Tea Party members in local groups helped push the issue into the national conservative political consciousness. Glenn Beck released a dystopian novel on the topic of Agenda 21 in 2012. By the summer of 2012, in addition to resolutions passed at the North Carolina Republican Convention, the Republican National Committee at their convention passed a platform plank opposing Agenda 21.

From the perspective of anthropology, conspiracy narratives, regardless of their validity or "truth value," should be considered for their "use value," tracking their sociopolitical locations and trajectories within relations of power and investigating them as commentaries on how informants view the world (Pelkmans and McHold 2011). How are what might be considered unsubstantiated conspiracy theories appropriated, and how do they gain traction? In a small county such as Adams and in the closed information networks of today, these fears can gain an audience and influence local policymaking.

The Agenda 21 controversy however also resembles some of the early grassroots actions by the emerging New Right in the 1950s and 1960s against the United Nations and its agencies, the United Nations Educational Scientific and Cultural Organization (UNESCO) and the United Nations International Children's Emergency Fund (UNICEF). To many postwar conservatives, the United Nations was a centralized distant government by people from foreign and often socialist or communist nations (McGirr 2001). Education guidelines from UNESCO were seen as usurping local control over school curriculum (Nickerson 2012).

The perpetuation of the Tea Party conspiratorial narrative of Agenda 21 also fulfills the wider pro-business goals of conservative interests. Elite conservative think tanks have been the primary drivers behind skepticism about environmental problems such as human-caused climate change (McCright and Dunlap 2003). This skepticism, a common theme in Tea Party groups, resonates with their core distrust of government, the perceived biases of the "mainstream media," and the suspect intentions of the Obama administration. As these conspiratorial readings are fed back into the wider conservative network, they, regardless of their veracity, nonetheless accomplish the conservative goal of complicating the promotion of environmental regulation. Although it is common for people to seek out and process data to conform to preexisting biases (Kunda 1990; Taber and Lodge 2006), elite conservative actors have a disincentive to present scientific views that dispel the Tea Party–Agenda 21 narrative.

Though opposing Agenda 21 furthers the Republican goal of less environmental regulation and gives the impression of heeding the grassroots, the rise of the Agenda 21 narrative is still remarkable. In the course of a year, the Agenda 21 threat had grown through social media from a fairly negligible concern inhabiting a small corner of conservatism to an issue that was embraced by the national-level GOP.

This and the prior chapter illustrate several dimensions of the importance of the local Tea Party groups in relation to the other two components of the TPM. The different components of the Tea Party have produced a multilayered figured world evoked by symbols, narratives, and emotional displays. Nonetheless, the LTPGs did not simply reiterate the cultural resources produced by the more elite segments of the movement, such as Americans for Prosperity, FreedomWorks, or Fox News. While these sources are important in generating the materials by which local Tea Party activists invigorate the figured world, the local groups appropriated, repurposed, altered, and combined these wider discourses and images into unique styles. And though many of their practices were consistent, there were many differences. Most dramatically, the Pierce group under the strong tutelage of Dale, envisioned an entirely different meaning of the Tea Party and its use a tool to further political change. Nonetheless, for participants, the LTPGs provided an easy avenue for people to *be* a Tea Partyist and share that experience with others. Moreover, participants were often transformed by the experience. They not only were able to forge a collective identity, which helped to assign meaning and alternatives to the political landscape, but many developed identities as political activists with the support of the solidarity and instruction provided by other group members.

Political activism became a defining characteristic of the Tea Party figured world for many, making the groups workshops for democratic citizenship. Experienced political activists found a new venue for engagement, while those with no experience in politics were able to learn skills, whether public speaking or learning the intricacies of the county budget. Although these groups were small, they often successfully inserted themselves into political decision-making forums. North Carolina counties are small, and in such municipalities, several loud protesters at the county commission meeting can have an effect and be noticed, as indicated by the Adams County group.[6] Furthermore, several dedicated precinct walkers can make the difference in local and state house elections, in which winners and losers are often separated by just a few hundred votes. Though the Tea Party declined in national influence after the 2010 election, many groups showed that at the municipal level LTPGs continued to build growing political organizations that were exerting a strong influence on their local governments, elections, and policymaking.

The networked architecture of the groups allowed tactics, discourse, and issues to circulate and stimulate all the groups. Although some of the groups were unable to maintain a similar level of energy and political activity, they did maintain a networked collection of conservative citizens. Moreover, the Adams group contributed to the development of new conflicts that fed the wider conservative universe. This movement of cultural resources "up" into the wider political culture may end up being one of the TPM's most enduring legacies. Watching the 2012 Republican presidential primaries, it was apparent that Newt Gingrich was tapping into Tea Party language better than any of the other candidates, possibly contributing to his win in the South Carolina primary (Gardner and Helderman 2012; Knickerbocker 2012).

However, Donald Trump is the full realization of the Tea Party discourses uploaded to national politics. From the anti-elitist "Drain the Swamp" to the danger of undocumented immigrants to the unwarranted accusations against Barack Obama, Trump brought Tea Party issues into the Republican mainstream. Additionally, his "says what he means" candor and conspiratorial narratives hark back to Sarah Palin and the styles that enchanted nascent Tea Partyists from the start.

Conclusion

POLITICAL ANTHROPOLOGY OF
U.S. RIGHT-WING POLITICS

In May 2014 a video circulated online showing U.S. House of Representatives majority leader Eric Cantor of Virginia being booed and shouted
down at a town hall–style meeting held to elect the seemingly inconse-
quential chair of the Virginia Seventh Congressional District Republican
Committee (Portnoy 2014). Reminiscent of resistance to Agenda 21 at
the Dixon City Council meeting and suggestive of the Burgoyne Tea
Party's seizure of their local GOP organization, this small-scale drama
in Virginia turned out to be a harbinger of the powerful congressman's
primary election defeat the following month at the hands of a "Tea
Party" candidate. Some media commentators on this nationally covered
political upset declared that national-level Tea Party organizations did
not contribute to Cantor's defeat (Goldmacher 2014), attributing it
instead to "local conservative activists," though not mentioning the
nearly eighty *local* Tea Party groups in the Commonwealth (Tea Party
Patriots 2014a).[1] Five years after the emergence of the movement, media
were still presenting the TPM as elite groups and media personalities.

In these pages I have presented an analysis of the significance of local
groups of Tea Party activists in the success of the wider movement. Presenting the complexities of LTPGs as a link between everyday citizens
and elite components hopefully problematizes oversimplified characterizations of the structure of the Tea Party movement. Is it the machinations of elites or a spontaneous eruption of conservative populism?
As illustrated by a close examination of the local groups that have
emerged, it is both. The Tea Party groups were organizationally auton-

omous; they had no formal ties to the NTPOs, such as Americans for Prosperity or Tea Party Patriots. Even so, the groups often repeated and localized elite and Fox News–generated discourses, incorporating them into their members' collective political identities. Nonetheless, the LTPGs can validly be portrayed as grassroots activism because of the energy, morale, and drive they generated in meetings and activities and because of the innovations they collectively generated and fueled. Finally, as links in a wider network, the LTPGs I observed were productive, contributing new themes and domains of action to the wider Tea Party movement and conservative universe.

However, beyond the mere presence and significance of grassroots Tea Partyists, this analysis also demonstrates the complexity and agency of the Tea Partyists and the groups that they form and the deep and complex personal and interpersonal relationships and processes that make the Tea Party movement so effective. First, at the personal level, there was widespread and active "identity work" undertaken by everyday political actors. Possibly owing to the depth of their concerns regarding the future of America, a wide assortment of individuals was able to link their complex life histories and experiences to the meaning of the Tea Party movement. Many were transformed by the experience and will never look at public life the same again. Others have become more directly active in the institutional political sphere by running for office and managing conservative political campaigns.

Second, there were powerful dialogic and collaborative processes within the local Tea Party groups. As shown in chapter 4, meanings were negotiated (not without tension), leading to a decentralized social movement with unique, localized particularities. These groups were characterized by movement and action, and new information and cultural resources were continually being introduced, accepted, and rejected. These groups of individuals exploring new meanings and possibilities injected dynamism and improvisation into the social movement.

Accordingly, small interpersonal groups continue to be important components of social movements even as computer and information technology (CIT) become the standard equipment of contemporary social movements. The nearly contemporaneous emergence, yet dissimilar outcomes of the Tea Party movement and the Occupy movement invite further research and comparison on the relationship between the digital social networks and actual co-presence of individuals in the two movements. The Tea Party, like Occupy, organized large gatherings and took advantage of CIT such as social media. Yet the TPM more successfully utilized widespread, locally situated, ongoing, face-to-face meetings and activities important for maintaining group cohesion and enabling the ongoing formation of political subjectivities fitted to local areas and to individual biographies. Whereas subjectivity may be fashioned within movement networks (Juris 2008), Occupy needed and lacked the "free" or "marginal" spaces where the process of collective identity and movement building occur. Granted, the general assemblies and the encampments were such spaces; however, when those spaces were shattered by authorities, few of the small organizations re-formed under new and safer conditions.

Of course, the seemingly greater longevity of the TPM cannot be solely attributed to its greater success at generating enduring local groups. Although the media to a degree effectively circulated the powerful Occupy slogan "We Are the 99%," the conservative broadcast media remains unprecedented in its ability to circulate consistent conservative discourses and images across a range of media sources (Jamieson and Cappella 2008). While there is quantitative research on conservative media affecting mobilization through reporting and framing, there is less on media as active social movement organizations (e.g., Walgrave and Manssens 2000).[2] It is clear that conservative media played a very different and much more significant role for the Tea Party than for Occupy.[3]

These observations add an important corollary to the literature on networked movements, showing the continued importance of direct, recurring personal interaction *alongside* CIT in movement success. The rise of Twitter and Facebook—and even listservs twenty-five years ago for that matter—has revolutionized protest and social movements. Some organizations, like MoveOn.org, successfully operate exclusively online and have enduring activist memberships. However, research suggests that face-to-face organizations offer an enduring and powerful space for the sharing and development of the repertoires and activist subjectivities. An example is demonstrated on the American left by the continued effectiveness of the organization formed around the 2004 presidential campaign of Howard Dean, which had a centralized campaign organization supplemented by local face-to-face chapters around the nation. The successor organization of Dean's campaign apparatus, Democracy for America (DFA), effectively uses computer-networked activism and is a loud, prominent voice in the liberal netroots. Yet despite its primarily online presence, today, more than a decade later, there are forty local groups that meet regularly and act as effective local community advocacy groups (Charles Chamberlain, DFA Executive Director, personal communication).

The rise of the Indivisible movement since the election of Donald Trump as president of the United States provides a more contemporary example of this style of political organization and activism. Indivisible was initially an online pamphlet written by former congressional staffers containing effective organizing strategies for those resisting the new administration (Indivisible n.d.). According to the authors, the model for the strategies was taken from the TPM, most significantly, the focus on local political arenas. And though the pamphlet omits some important points about what made the Tea Party successful, the document is nonetheless a testament to the importance of this type of political activism.[4] According to the Indivisible website there are as of 2018 "thousands" of local Indivisible groups across the United States. Although I doubt that there are thousands of Indivisible groups engaged in actual contentious political activity, even a fraction of that is a substantial grassroots movement. However, Indivisible, though successful, does not have a widespread liberal mass media circulating its messages and symbols and recruiting new members because such a mass media infrastructure does not exist.

Social Movements, Electoral Politics, and Political Anthropology

Indivisible and the Tea Party movement are unlike many social movements because they are firmly engaged in electoral and party politics. Writing in the political science journal *Perspectives on Politics*, social movement theorists Doug McAdam and Sidney Tarrow (2010) challenge scholars to look more closely at the relationship between electoral politics and social movements. Many social movements studied by social scientists are considered outside electoral politics. In fact, one of the definitions of social movements is that they are "extra-institutional," working outside institutional politics because those avenues are blocked or the institutions are unable to adequately address grievances. However, the authors argue that social movements and electoral politics are often linked indirectly. For example, innovations introduced by social movements are often taken up by institutional political actors. McAdam and Tarrow maintain that the internet tactics of the alter-globalization movement were drawn on by the online organizing of Howard Dean's 2004 presidential campaign. These tactics were then subsequently taken up by the successful Obama presidential campaign in 2008 and perfected even further by the Bernie Sanders's presidential campaign. Or in my experience, GOP platform committees appropriated the Agenda 21 narrative that had circulated among LTPGs.

Social movements are also reactions to elections, for example, the "green revolution" in Iran in 2009 and, of course, the Tea Party movement vis-à-vis the election of Barack Obama. The authors also speculate that the broad trends in party control of the White House (Democrats, 1932 to 1968; Republicans, 1969 to 2008) were greatly determined by social movement organizing (i.e., the labor movement in the former and the Christian Right in the latter).[5] Finally, they see social movements often as actors in rifts within major political parties, for example, the collapse of the New Deal coalition as southern whites fled the Democratic Party after the civil rights movement. And of course, in the case of the TPM and Occupy, social movements disrupt the terms of debate within parties and expand ideological differences and possibilities (Schlozman 2015).

The present research works toward the aim of the two authors to bridge the "casual indifference" between scholars of discrete disciplines of political contention. It is easy to miss the most important effects of social movements on electoral politics that became apparent in the TPM. First, dramatic proliferation of ideologically oriented broadcast media, such as Fox News and talk radio, is reducing the relevancy of political parties and their ability to control the electoral process and the direction of policy.[6] Second, the rise of new media technologies is further eroding the formal structure of political parties through the easy connection and mobilization of activists and the multiple and dizzying variety of sources for political information. In other words, social movements like the Tea Party, in addition to media and other online sources, are changing the structural characteristics of American institutional politics resulting in a political culture in which political parties no longer have the power to conceptualize, focus, or even respond to the broad ideological terrain of American political culture. This was further illustrated in 2016 by Donald Trump, who against the best efforts by the party establishment, essentially seized the GOP through a coup d'état enabled by the news media.

Anthropological study of the Tea Party movement offers a vivid example of how the discipline can contribute to the study of American politics. Anthropology, especially political anthropology, offers an important perspective that is typically lacking from traditional perspectives offered by political science and sociology. In a decades-old article on political anthropology, Abner Cohen (1969) argued that the main contribution of anthropology to the study of politics is the exploration of the relationship between symbolism and relations of power.[7] Cohen wrote, "Symbols are systematized together within the framework of dynamic ideologies, or worldviews, in which the symbols of the political order are integrated with those dealing with the perennial problems of human existence: the meaning of life and death, illness and health, misery and happiness, fortune and misfortune, good and evil" (1969, 217). In 2009 conservative Americans, fearful and concerned, were unsatisfied by the direction the nation and by the way conservative political leaders were framing and addressing their concerns. According to Cohen, in times of change, new symbolic forms, which can provide better solutions to the current problems of the group, are sometimes adopted. As we've seen, the Tea Party figured world, a new practical and symbolic formation, allowed people to link the movement's new configuration of symbolic meanings to their own problems of human existence, concerns, and biographies. This new symbolic configuration, however, was not simply deployed through media and at the grassroots level. Components of the figured world were appropriated by institutional political leaders on the right, intensifying and giving new life to the half-century schism between conservative and establishment Republicans. Often these Tea Party–aligned lawmakers advocate more for the symbols created by the Tea Party movement than for actual public policy.

Tea Party symbols—the Constitution, emotional displays, uses of historical figures, the lack of compromise, and the outlook about American decline—have become organizing certitudes by a significant faction of the Republican Party. Some of those same themes, with notable omissions, animate the Trump administration and its allies today. The Tea Party didn't create the schism in the GOP but gave it form and reconfigured the relations of power that characterize it. These cultural resources became integrated into the wider political system as most vividly displayed by the willingness of GOP lawmakers to shut down the government in 2011 and 2012 or by the open revolt of many "Tea Party conservatives" against the leadership of Senate majority leader Mitch McConnell, Speaker of the House John Boehner, and more recently, House Speaker Paul Ryan. That political style, characterized by a lack of compromise or any desire to work with the President Obama, had a dramatic effect on governing, as illustrated by the near absence of any substantial legislation emerging from Congress in Obama's last term.

Unfortunately, anthropology is contributing little to the study of this historic change to American political culture. Anthropological study of the sociopolitical Right in the United States, with some excellent exceptions, is limited. In researching for this book I found the primary works about the American Right have been published by sociologists and political scientists. Moreover, these works are not simply quantitative; they effectively utilize ethnographic methods more associated with anthropology (Braunstein 2017; Burke 2015; Meyer and Pullum 2014; Deckman 2016). Yet although these works are ethnographically rich, they often don't utilize the theoretic grounding from anthropology that draws attention to the dynamic, diverse, and symbolic aspects of culture and power relations that undergird them. Interestingly, owing to the Tea Party–induced controversy over Agenda 21, there are more published works on the TPM from the discipline of city and regional planning than there are from the discipline of anthropology (e.g., Filion 2011; Trapenberg-Frick 2013, 2018; Trapenberg-Frick, Weinzimmer, and Waddell 2015; Whittemore 2012).

This omission by anthropologists is often attributed to a belief that anthropologists are more likely to study people "we like" (Tretjak 2013; Bangstad 2017; Gusterson 2017) or, as one has suggested, that anthropology in recent decades has become focused on "the suffering subject," those living in pain, poverty, or oppression (Robbins 2013). Yet if anthropology is to confront the critique that it doesn't speak to the concerns of the day and, as the American Anthropological Association motto reads, "solve human problems," we should heed Hugh Gusterson's (2017) call following the election of Donald Trump: "If we are to contribute to the analysis of current menacing trends, and to help find a way to reverse them, we need rich, deep, nuanced encounters with the conservative Other, encounters that will require all the skills of reflexivity, relativism, and humane critique that our discipline can summon." Anthropological study of the Right also may, as in the Green Tea Movement, uncover alliances and points of contact between right-wing and marginalized groups and suffering subjects. Moreover, "such studies can simultaneously offer tools for thorough yet vigorous critique and intervention—a counter to the plethora of well-intentioned but overly generalized, ill-informed, and unpersuasive criticisms pouring forth particularly from left-oriented spaces within and outside the academy alike" (Tretjak 2013, 61).

Edelman (2001) has observed the politico-cultural right wing occupies a "parallel universe in collective action research with inconsistent connections to social movement theory." And though the anthropologists may not share the values of the right-wing populists, the evangelicals, or the anti-immigrant activists, one finds groups from opposite ends of the political spectrum share and differ on ideals, narratives, and practices of democratic citizenship (Braunstein 2017). The people-centered, engaged approach of ethnographic methods uncovers the importance of these differences and similarities and tells us something about the world we live in today. The Tea Partyist is seeking change, is being changed by the experience, and is experiencing the same inspiration and despair as activists chasing different horizons.

Epilogue

While I was completing this book manuscript in late 2018, the political landscape in America was changing rapidly. I cannot complete a book on the TPM at this point without recognizing the elephant in the room. Apt metaphor or not, Donald Trump and his supporters present another form of conservative populism that exists separate from, yet in tension with, Tea Party populism. The foregoing analysis does help us better understand the attraction of Trump. Moreover, my Tea Party consultants' eventual support of Trump helps us understand the state of the Tea Party figured world today.

I attended a Trump rally in October 2015 and was struck by the atmosphere. It was not like a Tea Party event, which though often addressing strongly conservative topics, always had a degree of "structure," meaning topics and symbols were fairly consistent and emotions were focused in specific ways. Someone carrying a Confederate flag or an outrageous or racist sign was the exception not the norm. At the Trump rally the atmosphere was reversed; people were angry—not Tea Party indignation, but rage. The group was noticeably working class and primarily older whites, but there also were many eighteen-to-thirty-year-old males, a group one would rarely if ever see at a Tea Party gathering. I got a sense that many of these people would not be interested in knowing how Benjamin Franklin would interpret current events or in sitting around for two hours on a Monday evening to talk about it. These people were hearing interpretations (whether realistic or not) of their feelings about material, cultural change, and loss and were being directed toward whom to blame. The atmosphere was generally chaotic. The difference between what motivates Trump supporters and what motivates Tea Partyists is Trump supporters are not drawing on the moral claims that Tea Partyists are. Tea Partyists will make America great again on a path that passes through the social and individual transformation of values. Trump supporters make no such detour. I concluded from that experience that the TPM cleared a path for Donald Trump by allowing certain submerged and objectionable political beliefs and actions to become sayable and doable. But these beliefs and actions took on new life in hyper-partisan spaces of practice forged at Trump rallies and circulated through the nation's broadcast media. Trump supporters, many newly politically active, were more connected to economic and cultural resentment, more strongly attuned to—owing to Trump—nativism, xenophobia, malice, and ferocity.

However, today most Tea Party people are firmly in support of Trump. At this point, only two of the local Tea Party groups I observed meet on a regular basis. Many of the group organizers are still involved in politics—some have run for office; some are part of their local Republican organizations. However, many have just gone back to their everyday lives. In his large and more resource-oriented longitudinal research on local Tea Party groups, Berry (2017) found that the number of local Tea Party groups declined by nearly 40 percent between 2010 and 2017; he primarily attributes this decline to lack of resources. He maintains that the very fact that LTPGs were not directly funded by national Tea Party organizations contributed to their decline because the local organizations needed significant resources to transition into more substantial political actors. I would also maintain that the very nature of the local Tea Party groups—energetic interactive groups of people—required that those groups maintain meaningful activities focused toward clear goals. It became clear in my research, as indicated, that outside the brief periods before national elections, purpose and energy proved to be difficult to maintain.

The LTPGs in my area were also weakened by the tension between Christian conservative and fiscal conservative Tea Party members. A dramatic rupture within and between several of the local groups occurred during the 2014 election. During the primary campaign for a U.S. Senate seat from North Carolina, deep divisions formed within and between several groups over support of two of the candidates. One candidate was a pastor representing a more social conservative perspective, while the other, a successful businessman, represented a more fiscal, constitutional conservative perspective. The differences became quite personal and divisive for several of the groups, to a point where some members left groups and some LTPGs would not attend joint events with others who supported an opposing candidate. North Carolina voters eventually chose neither of the two candidates, and the seat was eventually won by Republican Thom Tillis. But it seems the damage was done at a time when the national TPM was also in decline.

Many of the Tea Party consultants that I have spoken with recently or followed on social media now strongly support Donald Trump, which left me slightly perplexed. Initially support for Trump was lukewarm at best among my Tea Party consultants. In 2015 I attended a kind of Iowa-style "caucus" organized by Tea Party groups, and Trump received one vote out of approximately a hundred. All others favored either Ted Cruz or Ben Carson. Their early lack of support made sense, though, when considered in the context of how Tea Partyists interpret people and events. Trump is a pragmatist, often capricious, and not a political fundamentalist. He will not base his policies on constitutional literalism and most likely will not guide his actions on the basis of what George Washington or Benjamin Franklin would have done. After Trump won the nomination, most of my consultants grudgingly and expectedly supported Donald Trump with a wait-and-see attitude; not to mention that a vote for his opponent, Hillary Clinton, would have been intolerable.

However, their outlook changed dramatically after the election; apprehension morphed into unwavering support. Trump has filled his administration with Tea Party favorites, like Mike Pompeo as secretary of state, Mick Mulvaney as director of the Office of Management and Budget, Dr. Ben Carson at the Department of Housing and Urban Development, as well as with participants in the Tea Party network, like (temporarily) Steve Bannon from Breitbart News and Education Secretary Betsy DeVos, a billionaire donor to conservative causes (Mayer 2016). He also has nominated highly conservative judges to the Supreme Court and the lower federal courts. This final point must not be underestimated. The courts were a recurring theme throughout my research with Tea Partyists, who often decried "activists judges" who were seen as rewriting or reinterpreting the Constitution or "legislating from the bench." Evangelicals, Tea Partyists, and Trump supporters all understand the significance of installing relatively young, highly conservative jurists to the federal courts, including the Supreme Court. Trump's nomination of these jurists is a primary source of strong support from the Far Right and may well be Trump's most lasting legacy.

Yet I believe there are two other foundational factors that help explain the shift in Tea Party members' support. First, the figured world that so effectively circulated through the Tea Party network and maintained and cultivated the LTPGs broke down after 2013 as the LTPGs faded. However, as noted previously, much of the Tea Party style (lack of compromise, demonization of the Left, and self-righteousness) remained embedded in the conservative political culture. That Tea Party style is indicative of and contributes to a wider shift in American political culture.

Thomas Edsall (2018) writes of researchers who are publishing work on "negative partisanship," the development in American politics of voters aligning against one party instead of affiliating with the other (Abramowitz and Webster 2018; Iyengar and Krupenkin 2018). Though this process has been going on for two decades, it has intensified since 2010. The TPM, including its media allies, contributed to this through the demonization of Barack Obama and liberals in general, as in Tim Daughtry's talk on cultural Marxism. I believe that instead of my Tea Party consultants necessarily embracing Donald Trump for his policies, they may support him because of the level of hatred he generates from the Left and his systematic dismantling of Barack Obama's signature achievements.

This was vividly illustrated in a photographic "meme" on social media from a Facebook group called Deplorables United for Trump. Under a photograph of President Trump holding up two fingers, the caption reads, "I have two goals when I wake up in the morning: making America great again and pissing-off liberal crybabies."

An even stronger explanation lies in the reconfigured notion of class that I wrote of in chapter 2, whereby people feel dislocated from a political class. I wrote that we need a different conception of class that stresses the relationships of nonmaterial forms of capital, namely, cultural and symbolic power. Social theorist Pierre Bourdieu (Bourdieu and Johnson 2007) wrote extensively about the idea of symbolic capital: "the degree of accumulated prestige, celebrity and honor which is founded on the dialectic of *knowledge and recognition*" (emphasis added). Bourdieu wrote that when people recognize their lack of symbolic capital, they often self-censor—what Bourdieu terms "symbolic violence." For example, a person may recognize his or her southern accent has lower status or even stigma among a group of non-southerners and thus be reticent to participate in a conversation. White working-class Americans and Tea Partyists recognize a lack of symbolic capital in contrast to urban, political, and coastal elites. However, instead of self-censoring, Trump supporters without symbolic capital lashed out with resentment and fashioned a collective identity around that stigma. Hillary Clinton termed Trump supporters as a "basket of deplorables." Rightfully insulted by such a description, the rural and Rust Belt working class and Tea Partyists (who have been struggling with the racism label since 2009) were not silenced; rather the embraced the label by, for example, wearing T-shirts that read, "Proud member of the basket of deplorables."

Simply, we see two Americas divided by their interpretations and uneven possessions of symbolic capital: the unrefined, rural, Rust Belt, southern, and typically white working class and the refined, multicultural, urban, and coastal "cultural" elites. Considering this and the Marxian conception of class, one can see how Trump bridges them. Trump is wealthy and operates comfortably among the wealthy. One sees this vividly in many of his cabinet picks. However, Trump also lacks or embellishes his lack of some refinements, and this leaves him outside the circles of those possessing high levels of political and symbolic capital—what many call the "cultural elite." Trump lacks measured language, has never been a benefactor of the arts, is proud of his lack of political correctness, and makes no apologies for his aversion to healthy eating habits. He is the bourgeois yet anti-cultural elite.

This resonates with conservatives today. As mentioned, Trump lacks the capital of the cultural elite who are viewed as looking down on conservatives. But he also lacks the symbolic capital of a political elite—the ease of movement through the halls of political power—one of his strongest assets was the GOP establishment's disdain for him. He speaks of draining the swamp with more credibility than any politician. As one of my consultants told me, "Trump has never been at the table with the elites," not meaning the wealthy elite, but the political and cultural elite. In contrast, Trump's opponents Jeb Bush and Hillary Clinton are firmly in that group.

But is the Trump phenomenon grounded in an organized public that may coalesce into a collective identity like the Tea Party? Is there a horizon of meaning that through networking and symbols may form a figured world? Yes, to some degree. But I believe it's too early to tell. The sustained activism in submerged spaces and the ideological consistency of the Tea Party is not, to my knowledge, present to such a degree among Trump supporters. However, there is a similar if not more powerful media architecture. Media personalities like Sean Hannity and Rush Limbaugh have been as important to forging Trump's support as they were with the TPM. Yet, even more significant, the mainstream media circulates the discursive and symbolic components of Trump through the unprecedented, continual live coverage of Trump rallies and the circulation of most of his Twitter messages—a degree of coverage that was rarely afforded his predecessors. Broadcast networks' pursuit of ratings through the coverage of ever more outrageous utterances and outbursts by Trump facilitates the circulation of a Trump figured world to a greater degree than it did a TPM figured world.

The primary components of this emerging figured world are nationalism, nostalgia, white social identity, and the belief that Trump and his supporters are the antithesis of those on the left, who are viewed as elite, un-American, nefarious, and effete. The question is whether in the coming months and years President Trump proves able to maintain and transform a coalition of support into a unified, effective movement and whether that will persevere when he is no longer in the bully pulpit. Nonetheless, many Tea Partyists seem to easily slip into these new garments. The material is a bit coarser and of a different shade, but at present it seems to be a good fit.

Notes

Introduction

1. When first developing the concept of three components, I considered including Tea Party–aligned politicians in the structure. South Carolina senator Jim DeMint and Minnesota representative Michele Bachmann were the most prominent. I decided to not include them because I did not think that my consultants would have considered them part of the movement, I did not see nearly the same activity by them as compared to NTPOs, and because the anti-politician sentiment was so strong among members of the movement. There was a Tea Party Caucus in the U.S. House of Representatives at that point, yet it seemed short on action and results. Furthermore, when the Tea Party Caucus was formed, some Tea Partyists believed it was an attempt by the Republican Party to co-opt the emerging movement (Vogel 2010).

2. I use pseudonyms for research consultants and the locations of local Tea Party groups. All but one of the eight groups I participated with used their respective county in their name. The counties in North Carolina are typically small. The median population of North Carolina's one hundred counties in 2014 was fifty-six thousand. Since counties often contained a few small towns as well as rural areas, referring to the groups by county indicated a realistic geographic orientation.

3. Because of the equal time principle of the fairness doctrine, the twenty-four-hour programing of conservative talk radio programs (e.g., Glenn Beck followed by Rush Limbaugh followed by Sean Hannity, etc.) would not be legal without the programing of competing liberal views. Ronald Reagan's Federal Communications Commission rescinded the doctrine in 1987 on the grounds it restricts a free press.

4. The cultural turn was a movement that transcended several academic disciplines beginning in the late 1970s. It sought to shift the focus of inquiry away from positivist epistemologies to questions of meaning, emotion, and symbolism.

5. Melucci writes that contemporary social movements are characterized by both visible action, such as political confrontation, and latent action conducted in less visible or "submerged" spaces. These submerged spaces, which are "dispersed and fragmented . . . act as cultural laboratories," in which participants produce new meanings, relationships, and perceptions (Melucci, Keane, and Mier 1989, 60).

6. Politics, as defined by Stephen Gregory (1998), "refers to a diverse range of social practices through which people negotiate power relations. The practices of politics involve both the production and exercise of social relationships and the cultural construction of social meanings that support or undermine those relationships."

7. It's important to note that collective, social, and personal (intimate) identities draw on many sources and are always in process (Escobar 2008; S. Hall 1985, 1996; Laclau and Mouffe 1985; Holland et al. 1998).

8. I use the less common term "consultant" (e.g., Basso 1979; Hinson 1999) as opposed to "informant" to refer to my Tea Party interlocutors. Though still not an ideal term owing to its business-like tone, I believe that it better captures the dialogic and shared nature of anthropological research.

9. Others have raised epistemological concerns with the research as well. See, for example, Shapira (2017).

1. Patriots

1. Alvarez, Dagnino, and Escobar (1998) define cultural politics as "the processes enacted when sets of social actors shaped by, and embodying, different cultural meanings and practices come into conflict with each other."

2. I had a similar experience while attending a union-organized rally on the North Carolina capitol grounds in Raleigh during my research in 2011 at which Tea Party groups counterdemonstrated. Toward the end of the rally, as each body of protesters eyed the other across the street, the union protesters began singing "God Bless America." Tea Partyists, seeing themselves as the true patriots of the two groups, began singing the same song. Each group attempted to sing louder in order to successfully possess this mantle of true patriotism.

3. Attendees of AA programs are not always there by choice. Often those convicted of an offense involving illicit drugs or alcohol must attend several AA meetings.

4. The opposite side of the sign read, "I am AFP," an attempt to show that the organization, largely founded and funded by the billionaire industrialists Charles and David Koch, had a grassroots component.

5. I have also decided to use the term "patriot" because not only is it the language of my consultants, but also the language of their models, the founders

of the country. According to the *Oxford English Dictionary*, Revolutionary Americans considered themselves "patriots," as opposed to, say, nationalists. Finally, when discussing the American Right, nationalism is easily associated with Far Right nationalism or what is called "white nationalism," a nebulous term that is characterized by white supremacy, neo-Nazi ideology, anti-Semitism, etc. In fact, an early study on the Tea Party attempted to make this connection (I critique their approach in chapter 4), titling their document "Tea Party Nationalism" in order to make that link.

6. Janine lived in a town in Pierce County, and an LTPG had already been organized in a different town ten miles away. However, I don't believe that was the primary reason she failed in organizing a chapter. I speculate that Janine, a newcomer in the town, did not have the personal network necessary to attract an initial core of people. It is possible also that her timing, in the late summer of 2011, was past the critical time in 2009 and 2010 when enthusiasm for the movement was high and people were seeking out the emerging movement.

7. Again, the inconsistent methodological definition of Tea Party supporter among researchers, which I discuss in the introduction, plagues the analyses of the TPM.

8. Braunstein (2014) makes a similar argument, though drawing on a different body of theory. Though not mentioning a religious identity specifically, she describes Tea Partyists "mapping" themselves in multidimensional and contradictory identity "fields."

9. In the following chapter we meet a woman from the religion-based LTPG I referenced earlier who has successfully forged a strikingly consistent web of Christian Right discourse, Tea Party patriotism, and white working-class angst. This was made possible partially through the specific figured world created in an uncharacteristically religious local Tea Party group I will discuss in chapter 5.

10. In 2015 Tea Party Patriots publicly supported the Christian-owned retail chain Hobby Lobby's lawsuit to not be compelled to offer contraception under the Affordable Care Act. However, Tea Party Patriots framed the argument as a First Amendment issue, based on its "free exercise clause" (Tea Party Patriots 2014b).

11. I should also stress that displays of emotion are culturally specific and gendered. The impact of the emotional displays by Beck and my consultants had more significance because all three were males. American society circumscribes and strictly polices the boundaries of masculinity. In other cultures these displays of emotion may be far from out of the ordinary.

2. Troubles

1. During the same period, the North American Free Trade Agreement (NAFTA) was implemented and China joined the World Trade Organization (WTO), precipitating the irreversible decline of textile and furniture manufacturing, the other mainstays of the western and central North Carolina economy.

2. Many of my consultants had minimalist definitions of "political," often claiming the Tea Party wasn't political. I was puzzled by this early on but later realized that political was more than often a pejorative term representing the struggle between individuals for power, status, and financial gain.

3. This is not meant to say that such beliefs are not anathema to some conservative perspectives. One goal of the New Right characterized by William F. Buckley and *National Review* was to find common ground or "fusion" between the traditionalists, libertarian, and anticommunist wings of conservatism (Dionne 2016).

4. It should also be noted that though David considers himself conservative, those occupations David saw as most important, the schoolteacher and sheriff, as well as his father, were agents of the state.

5. North Carolina was the second to last state to secede and was deeply divided by the decision. More than twenty-five thousand white North Carolinians fought for the Union. Support for the Union was strongest in the Piedmont and western mountains, where there was little slaveholding.

6. Given that most of the LTPGs I observed were in the western third of North Carolina, many of my consultants' families were antislavery Republicans during and after the Civil War. Such family histories were sometimes used as an indication that not all southerners are white supremacists and as a subtle counter to the charge that Tea Partyists were often racists.

7. Jesse Helms was an oversized figure in North Carolina and national politics from the 1970s into the 2000s. He was known as a staunch anticommunist, foreign policy hawk and opponent of abortion and gay rights. He was accused of using white racial resentment as a campaign strategy on several campaigns.

8. It should also be noted that Jesse Helms was known for making constituent services a priority of his office. Before Helms, U.S. representatives, not senators, focused on constituent services. According to Link (2008, 133), Helms's constituent services were "legendary."

9. One could also make a strong argument that Jesse Helms exacerbated racial resentment to win elections.

10. At the same time, as will be discussed later, personal and local meanings shape the Tea Party.

3. Plantation Politics

1. The racial landscape in America is, at the time of this writing, a quickly shifting terrain. The disposition of whiteness and color-blind ideology are more in the spotlight than when the research was conducted. Owing to the Blacks Lives Matter movement, the Alt-Right, and the election of Donald Trump, most Americans, Tea Partyists included, are being led down a new path of racial awareness.

2. My consultants used the term "black" as opposed to "African American" in nearly all my encounters.

3. The theme of racial unity is fairly clear given the timing and place of the event, including the inclusion of Martin Luther King Jr.'s niece Alveda. However, the rally was more focused toward the unity of faith and a celebration of the honor demonstrated by those in the military.

4. It should also be pointed out that negative attitudes toward blacks' personal and moral qualities are not restricted to conservatives. As recently as 2012, the General Social Survey found 41 percent of white Democrats thought blacks "lack the motivation to pull themselves out of poverty" (Silver and McCann 2014).

5. Also critiquing the impression that racism is the primary driver of the movement, Lowndes (2012) does not dispute that individuals with racist leanings most likely populate different aspects of the TPM. In fact, he writes that he would be more incredulous if a modern, conservative, populist movement emerged without attracting a number of racists. But the presence of isolated racist signs and utterances in a wide-ranging decentralized movement only goes so far in explaining the presence of racial animus in the TPM.

6. His speech included the following lines: "I believe in states' rights. I believe we have distorted the balance of our government today by giving powers that were never intended to be given in the Constitution to that federal establishment." He continued by pledging to "restore to states and local governments the power that properly belongs to them." Reagan was advised against delivering that speech in Philadelphia because the discourse was similar to that used by segregationists in the 1950s and 1960s and because Philadelphia was the site where three civil rights workers, James Chaney, Michael Schwerner, and Andrew Goodman, were murdered by the Ku Klux Klan in 1964.

7. It is important to note that the shift in racial attitudes from the belief in biological inferiority to color-blind racism did not eliminate racialized thinking or belief in racial stereotypes. Bobo and Smith (1998) describe a concept like color-blind racism that they call "Laissez-faire racism." They argue that

the end of Jim Crow and the progressive change in attitudes by whites toward blacks did not "[bring] an end to negative stereotyping of blacks. Instead the character or extremity of stereotyping has changed" (Bobo and Smith 1998, 200).

8. A repeal of the Racial Justice Act was passed by the Republican-controlled North Carolina legislature in 2013 and signed by Governor McCrory.

9. Many seemed unaware of the defection by many Southern Democrats to the Republican Party after the signing of civil rights legislation in the 1960s. They would probably be surprised that both Jesse Helms and South Carolina senator and segregationist Strom Thurmond began their political careers as Democrats.

10. Alan West was a former Florida congressman and Tea Party favorite.

11. Though often thought of as a movement focused on foreign policy, the original neoconservatives were former moderate leftists who were equally motivated by a rejection of the domestic New Left and Black Power movements (Horwitz 2013).

12. Lisa Disch (2012) argues that Tea Partyists have supported racialized cuts to the welfare state by supporting middle-class social insurance programs like Social Security and Medicare while calling for huge cuts in programs directed toward the poor and people of color, such as Supplemental Nutrition Assistance Program (SNAP) benefits and Temporary Assistance for Needy Families (TANF).

13. In fact, Parker and Barreto themselves show that 65 percent of Tea Party "supporters" "approve of Barack Obama as a person" (2013, 208).

4. Fellowship

1. As one would expect, there is some dispute as to the number of people in attendance at the rally. The Washington DC Fire Department unofficially estimated "in excess of 75,000." Some NTPOs claimed as many as 800,000 people. The Washington DC Metro reported that there was an increase in ridership that Saturday of approximately 87,000 compared to a typical Saturday.

2. Though that individual may have discovered that quote independently and on his own, the quote is nonetheless familiar to many Tea Party participants, especially those who watch Glenn Beck, who used the story both in his book *Glenn Beck's Common Sense: The Case against an Out-of-Control Government, Inspired by Thomas Paine* (2009) and on his TV program.

3. BCTP purchased pocket constitutions for approximately thirty-five cents each from the National Center for Constitutional Studies (NCCS), the same organization that published *The Five Thousand Year Leap*, which describes

the biblical foundations of the United States' founding documents. There were many sources from which Tea Party groups procured the many different versions of the pocket Constitutions I saw during my fieldwork. NCCS was not affiliated with any of the elite NTPOs. Its versions of the Constitution, which I believe reflected the religious views of BCTP members, contained additional pages with quotes from the founding fathers, some of which focused on religious themes, as well as information about purchasing some of the organization's other materials.

4. The name Concord Bridge itself is a reference to patriotic and historical themes. A bridge in Concord, Massachusetts, was the site of the first shots of the American War for Independence.

5. More than likely, large protests required a permit.

5. Trickle-Up Politics

1. I will, however, discuss one group for which the outward activity was more of what is considered social service or charitable work. I have argued that any outward activity aimed at improving the lives of the disadvantaged is inherently political (Westermeyer 2009).

2. Although there were numerous Christian Coalition chapters across the nation in the 1990s, none of my consultants mentioned participating. Like many social movements, participants often have unique "awakening" experiences that motivate them in specific times and places. Many of my consultants related their Tea Party activism to such an event. In other words, many Tea Partyists were not activists before 2009.

3. One exception was the Revere County Tea Party, which though not engaged in outward political activity, was nonetheless full of excitement. The group met weekly and typically had many activities, such as the talk by Tim Daughtry in the previous section, classes on understanding the U.S. Constitution, and films.

4. However, Tea Party women, as portrayed in the motherhood frame, are nonetheless faced with a difficult paradox. By framing involvement through the specific roles of motherhood, women are attempting to empower themselves as political actors, while at the same time, employing culturally constructed gender roles that are reified as natural and essentialized characteristics (Burke 2015, 71).

5. Today precinct organizing in many parts of the nation often takes place in the three to six months before general elections and then goes dormant again until the next election cycle. So unlike in earlier times, today many constituencies do not have long-term precinct captains. At the time of my research, the member in charge of tracking voter registration and precinct

organizing declared to me that 72 percent of the precincts in Burgoyne County were headed by BCTP members and 60 percent of the county Republican Party officers were members of BCTP. One of Sue's cofounders and friends would leave the group early on because she disagreed with Sue on strategy. The friend believed the group should be working closely with the local Republican Party rather than against it.

6. There are one hundred counties in North Carolina; California, which has three times the area and four times the population, has fifty-eight.

Conclusion

1. The third component of the TPM was also present. Talk radio host Laura Ingraham drew attention to the race on her show and made a speech at a meeting in the district.
2. Hervik (2011) is an excellent illustration of the possibilities of such research.
3. Any comparison with Occupy, of course, would also need to account for Occupiers' different goals, such as its prefigurative focus, not to mention its rejection of institutional and bureaucratic politics in place of demonstrating alternative democratic practices.
4. Unlike the TPM, Indivisible groups rarely confront their own side, namely, Democrats. Owing to Tea Party influence and the danger of being challenged in primaries by even more conservative candidates, incumbents often moved right with the TPM, sometimes grudgingly.
5. I will differ with them on this point. There was a very strong grassroots component of the New Right in the 1950s and 1960s that I would argue was more significant (Diamond 1995; Dionne 2016; McGirr 2001; Nickerson 2012).
6. In an interview about the 1994 Republican electoral sweep of Congress, conservative direct mail pioneer Richard Viguerie said Rush Limbaugh was a savior: "Every day, Limbaugh would give us our marching orders, if you would" (Jamieson and Cappella 2008).
7. Edmund Leach (1954) in a foundational work of political anthropology makes a similar point.

References

Abramowitz, Alan I., and Steven W. Webster. 2018. "Negative Partisanship: Why Americans Dislike Parties but Behave Like Rabid Partisans." *Political Psychology* 39 (S1): 119–35.

Abu-Lughod, Lila. 2002. "Egyptian Melodrama: Technology of the Modern Subject?" In *Media Worlds: Anthropology on New Terrain*, edited by Lila Abu-Lughod, 75–102. Berkeley: University of California Press.

Aho, James. 1994. *This Thing of Darkness: A Sociology of the Enemy*. Seattle: University of Washington Press.

Alinsky, Saul. 1971. *Rules for Radicals: A Practical Primer for Realistic Radicals*. New York: Random House.

Allen, Kim, Vinci Daro, and Dorothy Holland. 2007. "Becoming an Environmental Justice Activist." In *Environmental Justice and Environmentalism: The Social Justice Challenge to the Environmental Movement*, edited by Ronald D. Sandler and Phaedra C. Pezzullo. Cambridge MA: MIT Press.

Alvarez, Sonia, Evelina Dagnino, and Arturo Escobar, eds. 1998. *Cultures of Politics, Politics of Cultures: Re-Visioning Latin American Social Movements*. Boulder CO: Westview Press.

Alvarez, Sonia, and Arturo Escobar. 1992. *The Making of Social Movements in Latin America: Identity, Strategy, and Democracy*. Boulder CO: Westview Press.

Anderson, Benedict. 1984. *Imagined Communities: Reflections on the Origin and Spread of Nationalism*. New York: Verso.

Armey, Dick, and Matt Kibbe. 2011. *Give Us Liberty: A Tea Party Manifesto*. New York: HarperCollins.

Aronowitz, Stanley. 2003. *How Class Works: Power and Social Movement*. New Haven: Yale University Press.

Bakhtin, M. 1981. *The Dialogic Imagination: Four Essays*. Austin: University of Texas Press.

Balibar, Etienne. 1991. *Race, Nation, Class: Ambiguous Identities*. London: Verso.

Banerjee, Tarun. 2013. "Media, Movements and Mobilization: The Tea Party Protests in the United States 2009–2010." In *Research in Social Movements,*

Conflicts and Change, edited by Patrick G. Coy, 39–75. Bingley, UK: Emerald Group.

Bangstad, Sindre. 2017. "Doing Fieldwork among People We Don't (Necessarily) Like." *Anthropology News* 58 (4): e238–43.

Barker, David C., and Christopher Jan Carman. 2000. "The Spirit of Capitalism? Religious Doctrine, Values, and Economic Attitude Constructs." *Political Behavior* 22 (1): 1–27.

Barton, David. 1993. *The Bulletproof George Washington: An Account of God's Providential Care*. Aledo TX: WallBuilders.

———. 1995. *America's Godly Heritage*. Aledo TX: WallBuilders. DVD, 95 min.

———. 2001. *Setting the Record Straight: American History in Black and White*. Aledo TX: WallBuilders.

Basso, Keith H. 1979. *Portraits of "The Whiteman": Linguistic Play and Cultural Symbols among the Western Apache*. Cambridge: Cambridge University Press.

Bean, Lydia. 2014. "Compassionate Conservatives? Evangelicals, Economic Conservatism, and National Identity." *Journal for the Scientific Study of Religion* 53 (1): 164–86.

Beck, Glenn. 2009. *Glenn Beck's Common Sense: The Case against an Out-of-Control Government, Inspired by Thomas Paine*. With Joseph Kerry. New York: Mercury Radio Arts/Threshold Editions.

Bellah, Robert N. 1967. "Civil Religion in America." *Daedalus* 96 (1): 1–21.

Bellott, Bruce, vocalist. 2010. "We Ain't Goin' Away." By Bradley Ray Gudgeon, Pamela Gudgeon, and Bruce Bellott. Published September 15, 2010. YouTube video, 3:38. https://www.youtube.com/watch?v=G7xPMq45p6Q.

Benen, Steve. 2011. "Rick Perry and 'The 5,000 Year Leap.'" *Washington Monthly*, August 23, 2011.

Benford, Robert D., and David A. Snow. 2000. "Framing Processes and Social Movements: An Overview and Assessment." *Annual Review of Sociology* 26 (1): 611–39.

Bennett, W. Lance, and Alexandra Segerberg. 2012. "The Logic of Connective Action: Digital Media and the Personalization of Contentious Politics." *Information, Communication and Society* 15 (5): 739–68.

Berkowitz, Peter. 2009. "Conservatives Can Unite around the Constitution." *Wall Street Journal*, January 2, 2009.

Berlet, Chip. 2012a. "Collectivists, Communists, Labor Bosses, and Treason: The Tea Parties as Right-Wing Populist Counter-Subversion Panic." *Critical Sociology* 38 (4): 565–87.

———. 2012b. "Reframing Populist Resentments in the Tea Party Movement." In Rosenthal and Trost 2012, 47–66.

Berlet, Chip, and Matthew Nemiroff Lyons. 2000. *Right-Wing Populism in America: Too Close for Comfort*. New York: Guilford Press.

Berry, Jeffrey. 2017. "Tea Party Decline." Paper presented at the Annual Meeting of the American Political Science Association, San Francisco.

Black, Earl, and Merle Black. 2002. *The Rise of Southern Republicans*. Cambridge MA: Belknap Press of Harvard University Press.

Bobo, Lawrence D., and Ryan A. Smith. 1998. "From Jim Crow Racism to Laissez-Faire Racism: The Transformation of Racial Attitudes." *Beyond Pluralism: The Conception of Groups and Group Identities in America* 198: 182–220.

Bonilla-Silva, E. 1997. "Rethinking Racism: Toward a Structural Interpretation." *American Sociological Review* 62 (3): 465–80.

———. 2014. *Racism without Racists: Color-Blind Racism and the Persistence of Racial Inequality in America*. 4th ed. Lanham MD: Rowman & Littlefield.

Bourdieu, Pierre. 1977. *Outline of a Theory of Practice*. Cambridge: Cambridge University Press.

———. 1991. *Language and Symbolic Power*. Edited by John B. Thompson. Translated by Gino Raymond and Matthew Adamson. Cambridge MA: Harvard University Press.

Bourdieu, Pierre, and Randal Johnson. 2007. *The Field of Cultural Production*. Cambridge: Polity Press.

Bowers, Curtis. 2010. Agenda: Grinding America Down. N.p.: Black Hat Films.

Boykoff, Jules, and Eulalie Laschever. 2011. "The Tea Party Movement, Framing, and the US Media." *Social Movement Studies* 10 (4): 341–66.

Braunstein, Ruth. 2011. "Who Are 'We the People'?" *Contexts* 10 (2): 72–73.

———. 2014. "Who Are 'We the People'? Multidimensional Identity Work in the Tea Party." In Van Dyke and Meyer 2014, 163–88.

———. 2017. *Prophets and Patriots: Faith in Democracy across the Political Divide*. Berkeley: University of California Press.

Brody, David. 2012. *The Teavangelicals: The Inside Story of How the Evangelicals and the Tea Party Are Taking Back America*. Grand Rapids MI: Zondervan.

Brown, Emma, James Hohmann, and Perry Bacon Jr. 2009. "Tens of Thousands Protest Obama Initiatives at Capitol." *Washington Post*, September 13, 2009.

Burghart, Devin, and Leonard Zeskind. 2010. *Tea Party Nationalism Report*. Kansas City MO: Institute for Research and Education on Human Rights. http://www.irehr.org/2010/10/12/tea-party-nationalism-report-pdf/.

Burke, Meghan A. 2012. *Racial Ambivalence in Diverse Communities: Whiteness and the Power of Color-Blind Ideologies*. Lanham MD: Lexington Books.

———. 2014. "Colorblindness vs. Race Consciousness—American Ambivalence." In *Color Lines and Racial Angles*, edited by Douglas Hartmann and Christopher Uggen, 165–76. New York: Norton.

————. 2015. *Race, Gender, and Class in the Tea Party: What the Movement Reflects about Mainstream Ideologies.* Lanham MD: Rowman & Littlefield.

————. 2017. "Racing Left and Right: Color-Blind Racism's Dominance across the U.S. Political Spectrum." *Sociological Quarterly* 58 (2): 277–94.

Bush, Melanie E. L. 2011. *Everyday Forms of Whiteness: Understanding Race in a Post-Racial World.* 2nd ed. Lanham MD: Rowman & Littlefield.

Cain, Carole. 1991. "Personal Stories: Identity Acquisition and Self-Understanding in Alcoholics Anonymous." *Ethos* 19 (2): 210–53.

Carbone, Nick. 2011. "Would You Send Your Kid to a Tea Party Summer Camp?" *Time,* June 19, 2011. http://newsfeed.time.com/2011/06/19/would-you-send -your-kid-to-a-tea-party-summer-camp/.

Carbonella, August. 1996. "Reconstructing Histories and Geographies: Some Dissident Remarks on Historical Anthropology's Unwaged Debate." *Focaal: Tijdschrift Voor Antropologie* 26 (27): 159–65.

Castells, Manuel. 2000. *The Information Age: Economy, Society and Culture.* Vol. 1, *The Rise of the Network Society.* Oxford: Blackwell.

————. 2007. "Communication, Power and Counter-Power in the Network Society." *International Journal of Communication* 1 (1): 29.

————. 2012. *Networks of Outrage and Hope: Social Movements in the Internet Age.* Cambridge: Polity.

Chavez, Leo R. 2013. *The Latino Threat: Constructing Immigrants, Citizens, and the Nation.* 2nd ed. Stanford CA: Stanford University Press.

Christie, Les. 2010. "Foreclosures Hit Record High in 2009." CNN Money, January 14, 2010. http://money.cnn.com/2010/01/14/real_estate/record _foreclosure_year/.

Cohen, Abner. 1969. "Political Anthropology: The Analysis of the Symbolism of Power Relations." *Man* 4 (2): 215–35.

Cohen, Jean, and Andrew Arato. 1984. *Civil Society and Political Theory.* Cambridge MA: MIT Press.

Cohen, Stanley. 1972. *Folk Devils and Moral Panics: The Creation of the Mods and Rockers.* London: MacGibbon & Kee.

Converse, Philip. 1964. "The Nature of Belief Systems in Mass Publics." In *Ideology and Discontent,* edited by David Apter, 206–61. London: Free Press of Glencoe.

Cox, Daniel, and Robert P. Jones. 2010. "Religion and the Tea Party in the 2010 Elections." Public Religion Research Institute. https://www.prri.org/research /religion-tea-party-2010/.

Cramer, Katherine J. 2016. *The Politics of Resentment: Rural Consciousness in Wisconsin and the Rise of Scott Walker.* Chicago: University of Chicago Press.

Crapanzano, Vincent. 2000. *Serving the Word: Literalism in America from the Pulpit to the Bench*. New York: New Press.

Cross, William E., Jr. 1971. "The Negro-to-Black Conversion Experience." *Black World* 20 (9): 13–27.

Crowder-Meyer, Melody. 2010. "The Party's Still Going: County Party Strength, Activity, and Influence." In *The State of the Parties*, edited by J. Green and D. Coffey, 115–34. Lanham MD: Rowman & Littlefield.

Deckman, Melissa. 2016. *Tea Party Women: Mama Grizzlies, Grassroots Leaders, and the Changing Face of the American Right*. New York: New York University Press.

Deutsch, Kenneth L., and Ethan M. Fishman. 2010. *The Dilemmas of American Conservatism*. Lexington: University Press of Kentucky.

Diamond, Sara. 1995. *Roads to Dominion: Right-Wing Movements and Political Power in the United States*. New York: Guilford Press.

Diani, Mario. 1995. *Green Networks: A Structural Analysis of the Italian Environmental Movement*. Edinburgh: Edinburgh University Press.

DiMaggio, Anthony. 2010. "What 'Populist Uprising?' Part II: Further Reflections on an 'Astroturf Movement.'" *Znet* (blog), April 29, 2010. https://zcomm.org/znetarticle/what-populist-uprising-part-ii-further-reflections-on-an-astroturf-movement-by-anthony-dimaggio/.

———. 2011. *The Rise of the Tea Party: Political Discontent and Corporate Media in the Age of Obama*. New York: Monthly Review Press.

Dionne, E. J. 2016. *Why the Right Went Wrong: Conservatism—From Goldwater to Trump and Beyond*. New York: Simon & Schuster.

Disch, L. 2012. "The Tea Party: A 'White Citizenship' Movement?" In Rosenthal and Trost 2012, 133–51.

Doukas, Dimitra. 2003. *Worked Over: The Corporate Sabotage of an American Community*. Ithaca NY: Cornell University Press.

Dumit, Joseph. 1997. "A Digital Image of the Category of the Person." In *Cyborgs and Citadels: Anthropological Interventions in Emerging Sciences and Technologies*, edited by Gary Lee Downey and Joseph Dumit, 83–102. Santa Fe NM: School of American Research Press.

Eckert, Penelope, and Sally McConnell-Ginet. 1992. "Think Practically and Look Locally: Language and Gender as Community-Based Practice." *Annual Review of Anthropology* 21 (January): 461–88.

Edelman, Marc. 2001. "Social Movements: Changing Paradigms and Forms of Politics." *Annual Review of Anthropology*, 285–317.

Edsall, Thomas B. 2018. "What Motivates Voters More Than Loyalty? Loathing." *New York Times*, March 1, 2018.

Emerson, Michael O., and Christian Smith. 2000. *Divided by Faith: Evangelical Religion and the Problem of Race in America*. New York: Oxford University Press.

Escobar, Arturo. 2008. *Territories of Difference: Place, Movements, Life, Redes*. Durham NC: Duke University Press.

Fetner, Tina, and Brayden King. 2014. "Three-Layer Movements, Resources, and the Tea Party." In Van Dyke and Meyer 2014, 35–54.

Filion, Pierre. 2011. "Toronto's Tea Party: Right-Wing Populism and Planning Agendas." *Planning Theory and Practice* 12 (3): 464–69.

Fitch, William. 1989. *Some Neglected History of North Carolina: Being an Account of the Revolution of the Regulators and of the Battle of Alamance, the First Battle of the American Revolution*. Bowie MD: Heritage Books.

Flanagin, Andrew J., Cynthia Stohl, and Bruce Bimber. 2006. "Modeling the Structure of Collective Action." *Communication Monographs* 73 (1): 29–54.

Flesher-Fominaya, Cristina. 2010. "Creating Cohesion from Diversity: The Challenge of Collective Identity Formation in the Global Justice Movement." *Sociological Inquiry* 80 (3): 377–404.

Formisano, Ronald P. 2012. *The Tea Party: A Brief History*. Baltimore: Johns Hopkins University Press.

Fox News. 2011. "Herman Cain Blame Game." FoxNews.com, October 31, 2011. Video, 7:29. http://video.foxnews.com/v/1251781128001/herman-cain-blame-game/.

Frank, Thomas. 2004. *What's the Matter with Kansas?: How Conservatives Won the Heart of America*. New York: Metropolitan Books.

Frankenberg, Ruth. 1993. "Growing Up White: Feminism, Racism and the Social Geography of Childhood." *Feminist Review* (45): 51–84.

Frederick Douglass Foundation. N.d. "About Us." Accessed March 2, 2019. http://tfdf.org/about_us.html.

Gamson, William A. 1992. *Talking Politics*. New York: Cambridge University Press.

Gamson, William A., and Andre Modigliani. 1989. "Media Discourse and Public Opinion on Nuclear Power: A Constructionist Approach." *American Journal of Sociology* 95 (1): 1–37.

Gardner, Amy. 2010. "Gauging the Scope of the Tea Party Movement in America." *Washington Post*, October 24, 2010.

Gardner, Amy, and Rosalind S. Helderman. 2012. "Newt Gingrich Using Energy, Power of Tea Party Movement." *Washington Post*, January 24, 2012.

Gerlach, Luther, and Virginia H. Hine. 1970. *People, Power, Change: Movements of Social Transformation*. Indianapolis: Bobbs-Merrill.

Giddens, Anthony. 1991. *Modernity and Self-Identity: Self and Society in the Late Modern Age*. Stanford CA: Stanford University Press.

Ginsburg, Faye. 1998. *Contested Lives: The Abortion Debate in an American Community*. Berkeley: University of California Press.

Goldmacher, Shane. 2014. "Eric Cantor Lost Even as the National Tea-Party Groups Sat on Their Hands." *National Journal*, June 10, 2014. http://www.nationaljournal.com/politics/eric-cantor-lost-even-as-the-national-tea-party-groups-sat-on-their-hands-20140610.

Goodwin, Jeff, James M. Jasper, and Francesca Polletta. 2001. *Passionate Politics: Emotions and Social Movements*. Chicago: University of Chicago Press.

———. 2004. "Emotional Dimensions of Social Movements." *The Blackwell Companion to Social Movements*, ed. David A. Snow, Sarah A. Soule, and Hanspeter Kriesi, 413–32. Malden MA: Blackwell.

Graeber, David. 2002. "The New Anarchists." *New Left Review* 13 (6): 61–73.

———. 2009. *Direct Action: An Ethnography*. Edinburgh: AK Press.

Gramsci, Antonio, Quintin Hoare, and Geoffrey Nowell-Smith. 1972. *Selections from the Prison Notebooks of Antonio Gramsci*. New York: International Publishers.

Gregory, Steven. 1998. *Black Corona: Race and the Politics of Place in an Urban Community*. Princeton: Princeton University Press.

Gusterson, Hugh. 2017. "From Brexit to Trump: Anthropology and the Rise of Nationalist Populism." *American Ethnologist* 44 (2): 209–14.

Hale, Charles R. 2006. "Activist Research v. Cultural Critique: Indigenous Land Rights and the Contradictions of Politically Engaged Anthropology." *Cultural Anthropology* 21 (1): 96–120.

Hall, Stuart. 1985. "Signification, Representation, Ideology: Althusser and the Post-Structuralist Debates." *Critical Studies in Media Communication* 2 (2): 91–114.

———. 1996. "Who Needs 'Identity?'" In *Identity: A Reader*, edited by P. Du Gay, J. Y. Evans, and P. Redman, 1–17. London: Sage.

Hall, Stuart, Chas Critcher, John Clarke, and Brian Roberts. 1978. *Policing the Crisis: Mugging, the State, and Law and Order*. London: Macmillan.

Hananoki, Eric. 2009. "'Fair and Balanced' Fox News Aggressively Promotes 'Tea Party' Protests." *Media Matters for America*, April 8, 2009. http://mediamatters.org/research/2009/04/08/report-fair-and-balanced-fox-news-aggressively/149009.

Hardisty, Jean. 1999. *Mobilizing Resentment: Conservative Resurgence from the John Birch Society to the Promise Keepers*. Boston: Beacon Press.

Hartigan, John, Jr. 1997. "Establishing the Fact of Whiteness." *American Anthropologist*, n.s., 99 (3): 495–505.

Hartmann, Douglas, Joseph Gerteis, and Paul R. Croll. 2009. "An Empirical Assessment of Whiteness Theory: Hidden from How Many?" *Social Problems* 56 (3): 403–24.

Hayek, Friedrich. 2007. *The Road to Serfdom*. Chicago: University of Chicago Press.

Hervik, Peter. 2011. "The Annoying Difference." *The Emergence of Danish Neonationalism, Neoracism, and Populism in the Post-1989 World*. New York: Berghahn Books.

Hetherington, Kevin. 1998. *Expressions of Identity: Space, Performance, Politics*. London: Sage.

Hetherington, Marc, and Jonathan Daniel Weiler. 2009. *Authoritarianism and Polarization in American Politics*. New York: Cambridge University Press.

Hinson, G. 1999. "'You've Got to Include an Invitation': Engaged Reciprocity and Negotiated Purpose in Collaborative Ethnography." Paper presented at the Ninety-Eighth Annual Meeting of the American Anthropological Association, Chicago.

Hirsch, Eric L. 1990. *Urban Revolt: Ethnic Politics in the Nineteenth-Century Chicago Labor Movement*. Berkeley: University of California Press.

Hirsh, Michael. 2010. "What Sparked the Tea Party?" *National Journal*, August 15, 2010.

Hochschild, Arlie Russell. 2016. *Strangers in Their Own Land: Anger and Mourning on the American Right*. New York: New Press.

Hofstadter, Richard. 2008. *The Paranoid Style in American Politics, and Other Essays*. New York: Vintage Books.

Holland, Dorothy, Gretchen Fox, and Vinci Daro. 2008. "Social Movements and Collective Identity: A Decentered, Dialogic View." *Anthropological Quarterly* 81 (1): 95–126.

Holland, Dorothy, William S. Lachicotte, Debra Skinner, and Carole Cain. 1998. *Identity and Agency in Cultural Worlds*. Cambridge MA: Harvard University Press.

Holland, Dorothy, and Jean Lave. 2001. *History in Person: Enduring Struggles, Contentious Practice, Intimate Identities*. Santa Fe: SAR Press.

Holland, Dorothy, Donald Macon Nonini, Catherine Lutz, Lesley Bartlett, Marla Frederick-McGlathery, Thaddeus C. Guldbrandsen, and Enrique G. Murillo. 2007. *Local Democracy under Siege: Activism, Public Interests, and Private Politics*. New York: New York University Press.

Holquist, Michael. 1990. *Dialogism: Bakhtin and His World*. London: Routledge.

Honig, Bonnie. 2001. *Democracy and the Foreigner*. Princeton: Princeton University Press.

Horwitz, Robert. 2013. *America's Right: Anti-Establishment Conservatism from Goldwater to the Tea Party*. Cambridge: Polity.

HoSang, Daniel. 2010. *Racial Propositions: Ballot Initiatives and the Making of Postwar California*. Berkeley: University of California Press.

Indivisible. N.d. "About." Accessed March 2, 2019. https://indivisible.org/about.

International Council for Local Environmental Initiatives. 2008. "FAQs about ICLEI and Its International Role." http://archive.iclei.org/index.php?id= 12366.

Isenstadt, Alex. 2009. "Town Halls Gone Wild." *Politico*, July 31, 2009. http:// www.politico.com/story/2009/07/town-halls-gone-wild-025646.

Iyengar, Shanto, and Masha Krupenkin. 2018. "The Strengthening of Partisan Affect." *Political Psychology* 39 (S1): 201–18.

Jamieson, Kathleen, and Joseph N. Cappella. 2008. *Echo Chamber: Rush Limbaugh and the Conservative Media Establishment*. Oxford: Oxford University Press.

Jasper, James. 2011. "Emotions and Social Movements: Twenty Years of Theory and Research." *Annual Review of Sociology* 37: 285–303.

Jenkins, J. Craig. 1983. "Resource Mobilization Theory and the Study of Social Movements." *Annual Review of Sociology* 9 (1): 527–53.

Jones, Robert P. 2016. *The End of White Christian America*. New York: Simon & Schuster.

Jones, Robert P., and Daniel Cox. 2010. "Religion and the Tea Party in the 2010 Elections." *PRRI* (blog), October 5, 2010. https://www.prri.org/research /religion-tea-party-2010/.

Juris, Jeffrey. 2008a. *Networking Futures: The Movements against Corporate Globalization*. Durham NC: Duke University Press.

———. 2008b. "Performing Politics: Image, Embodiment, and Affective Solidarity during Anti-Corporate Globalization Protests." *Ethnography* 9 (1): 61–97.

———. 2012. "Reflections on #Occupy Everywhere: Social Media, Public Space, and Emerging Logics of Aggregation: Reflections on #Occupy Everywhere." *American Ethnologist* 39 (2): 259–79.

Kapferer, Bruce. 1988. *Legends of People, Myths of State: Violence, Intolerance, and Political Culture in Sri Lanka and Australia*. New York: Berghahn Books.

Kazin, Michael. 1995. *The Populist Persuasion: An American History*. Ithaca NY: Cornell University Press.

Khondker, Habibul Haque. 2011. "Role of the New Media in the Arab Spring." *Globalizations* 8 (5): 675–79.

Killian, Joe. 2012. "GOP Sweep Followed Map." *Greensboro News and Record*, November 7, 2012.

Klatch, Rebecca E. 1987. *Women of the New Right*. Philadelphia: Temple University Press.

Knickerbocker, Brad. 2012. "Who Is Saul Alinsky, and Why Is Newt Gingrich So Obsessed with Him?" *Christian Science Monitor*, January 28, 2012.

Krugman, Paul. 2009. "Tea Parties Forever." *New York Times*, April 12, 2009.

Kunda, Ziva. 1990. "The Case for Motivated Reasoning." *Psychological Bulletin* 108 (3): 480.

Kurzman, C. 2008. "Introduction: Meaning-Making in Social Movements." *Anthropological Quarterly* 81 (1): 5–15.

Lachicotte, William S. 2002. "Intimate Powers, Public Selves: Bakhtin's Space of Authoring." In *Power and the Self*, edited by Jeannette Marie Mageo, 48–66. Cambridge: Cambridge University Press.

Laclau, Ernesto. 2005. *On Populist Reason*. London: Verso.

Laclau, Ernesto, and Chantal Mouffe. 1985. *Hegemony and Socialist Strategy: Towards a Radical Democratic Politics*. New York: Verso.

Lave, Jean, and Etienne Wenger. 1991. *Situated Learning: Legitimate Peripheral Participation*. Cambridge: Cambridge University Press.

Leach, Edmund. 1954. *Political Systems of Highland Burma: A Study of Kachin Social Structure*. Cambridge: Harvard University Press.

Lepore, Jill. 2010. *The Whites of Their Eyes: The Tea Party's Revolution and the Battle over American History*. Princeton: Princeton University Press.

Lewis, Charles. 1960. *Tepoztlán, Village in Mexico*. New York: Holt.

Link, William A. 2008. *Righteous Warrior: Jesse Helms and the Rise of Modern Conservatism*. New York: Macmillan.

Lipsitz, George. 1998. *The Possessive Investment in Whiteness: How White People Profit from Identity Politics*. Philadelphia: Temple University Press.

Liu, Joseph. 2011. "The Tea Party and Religion." Pew Research Center's Religion and Public Life Project, February 23, 2011. http://www.pewforum.org/2011/02/23/tea-party-and-religion/.

Lo, Clarence Y. H. 2012. "Astroturf versus Grass Roots: Scenes from Early Tea Party Mobilization." In Rosenthal and Trost 2012, 98–130.

Lowndes, Joseph. 2008. *From the New Deal to the New Right*. New Haven: Yale University Press.

———. 2012. "The Past and Future of Race in the Tea Party Movement." In Rosenthal and Trost 2012, 152–70.

Lutz, Catherine, and Lila Abu-Lughod, eds. 1990. *Language and the Politics of Emotion*. Cambridge: Cambridge University Press.

MacGillis, Alec. 2016. "Revenge of the Forgotten Class." *ProPublica*, November 10, 2016. https://www.propublica.org/article/revenge-of-the-forgotten-class.

Markman, Joe. 2009. "Crowd Estimates Vary Wildly for Capitol March." *Los Angeles Times*, September 15, 2009.

Martin, Christopher. 2013. "Tea Party's Green Faction Fights for Solar in Red States." *Bloomberg*, November 12, 2013. http://www.bloomberg.com/news/2013-11-12/tea-party-s-green-faction-fights-for-solar-in-red-states.html.

Martin, William C. 1996. *With God on Our Side: The Rise of the Religious Right in America*. Rev. ed. New York: Broadway Books.

Mayer, Jane. 2016. *Dark Money: The Hidden History of the Billionaires behind the Rise of the Radical Right*. New York: Doubleday.

McAdam, Doug. 1982. *Political Process and the Development of Black Insurgency, 1930–1970*. Chicago: University of Chicago Press.

———. 1988. *Freedom Summer*. New York: Oxford University Press.

McAdam, Doug, and Ronnelle Paulsen. 1993. "Specifying the Relationship between Social Ties and Activism." *American Journal of Sociology* 99 (3): 640–67.

McAdam, Doug, and Sidney Tarrow. 2010. "Ballots and Barricades: On the Reciprocal Relationship between Elections and Social Movements." *Perspectives on Politics* 8 (2): 529–42.

McCarthy, John D., and Mayer N. Zald. 1977. "Resource Mobilization and Social Movements: A Partial Theory." *American Journal of Sociology* 82 (6): 1212–41.

McCright, Aaron M., and Riley E. Dunlap. 2003. "Defeating Kyoto: The Conservative Movement's Impact on U.S. Climate Change Policy." *Social Problems* 50 (3): 348–73.

McDermott, R. P. 2001. "The Acquisition of a Child by a Learning Disability." In *Understanding Learning: Influences and Outcomes*, edited by Janet, Collins, and Deirdre Cook, 60–70. Thousand Oaks CA: Sage.

McGirr, Lisa. 2001. *Suburban Warriors: The Origins of the New American Right*. Princeton: Princeton University Press.

McGrath, Ben. 2010. "The Movement." *The New Yorker*, February 1, 2010.

McIntosh, Peggy. 1989. "White Privilege: Unpacking the Invisible Knapsack. *Peace and Freedom Magazine*, July/August.

McVeigh, Rory. 2004. "Structured Ignorance and Organized Racism in the United States." *Social Forces* 82 (3): 895–936.

———. 2014. "What's New about the Tea Party Movement?" In Van Dyke and Meyer 2014, 15–34.

Mead, George H. 1913. "The Social Self." *Journal of Philosophy, Psychology and Scientific Methods*, July 3.

———. 1934. *Mind, Self and Society from the Standpoint of a Social Behaviorist*. Edited by Charles W. Morris. Chicago: University of Chicago Press.

Meckler, Mark, and Jenny Beth Martin. 2012. *Tea Party Patriots: The Second American Revolution*. New York: Henry Holt.

Melucci, Alberto. 1995. "The Process of Collective Identity." In *Social Movements and Culture*, edited by Hank Johnson and Bert Klandermans, 41–63. New York: Routledge.

———. 1996. *Challenging Codes: Collective Action in the Information Age*. Cambridge: Cambridge University Press.

Melucci, Alberto, John Keane, and Paul Mier. 1989. *Nomads of the Present: Social Movements and Individual Needs in Contemporary Society*. Philadelphia: Temple University Press.

Meyer, David S., and Amanda Pullum. 2014. "The Tea Party and the Dilemmas of Conservative Populism." In Van Dyke and Meyer 2014, 73–98.

Mills, C. 2000. *The Sociological Imagination*. New York: Oxford University Press.

Montgomery, Peter. 2012. "The Tea Party and Religious Right Movements: Frenemies with Benefits." In Rosenthal and Trost 2012, 242–74.

Morgen, Sandra. 2002. *Into Our Own Hands: The Women's Health Movement in the United States, 1969–1990*. New Brunswick NJ: Rutgers University Press.

———. 2011. "Taxing Subjects: Constructing Opposition to Public Sector Workers and Services in the Era of the Tea Party in the Contemporary U.S." Paper presented at the Annual Meeting of the American Anthropological Association, Montreal, November 19, 2011.

Morris, Aldon. 1984. *The Origins of the Civil Rights Movement: Black Communities Organizing for Change*. New York: Collier Macmillan.

Murray, Charles. 1984. *Losing Ground: American Social Policy, 1950–1980*. New York: Basic Books.

Nagata, Judith. 2001. "Beyond Theology: Toward an Anthropology of 'Fundamentalism.'" *American Anthropologist* 103 (2): 481–98.

Nickerson, Michelle M. 2012. *Mothers of Conservatism: Women and the Postwar Right*. Princeton: Princeton University Press.

Niesz, Tricia, and Ramchandar Krishnamurthy. 2014. "Movement Actors in the Education Bureaucracy: The Figured World of Activity Based Learning in Tamil Nadu." *Anthropology and Education Quarterly* 45 (2): 148–66.

Omi, Michael, and Howard Winant. 2015. *Racial Formation in the United States: From the 1960s to the 1990s*. 3rd ed. New York: Routledge.

Ong, Aihwa. 1996. "Cultural Citizenship as Subject-Making: Immigrants Negotiate Racial and Cultural Boundaries in the United. *Current Anthropology* 37 (5): 737–62.

Ortner, Sherry B. 1984. "Theory in Anthropology since the Sixties." *Comparative Studies in Society and History* 26 (1): 126–66.

Parker, Christopher S. 2010. "2010 Multi-State Survey of Race and Politics." University of Washington Institute for the Study of Ethnicity, Race and Sexuality. http://depts.washington.edu/uwiser/racepolitics.html.

Parker, Christopher S., and Matt A. Barreto. 2013. *Change They Can't Believe In: The Tea Party and Reactionary Politics in America*. Princeton: Princeton University Press.

Payne, Charles M. 1995. *I've Got the Light of Freedom: The Organizing Tradition and the Mississippi Freedom Struggle*. Berkeley: University of California Press.

Pelkmans, Mathijs, and Rhys Machold. 2011. "Conspiracy Theories and Their Truth Trajectories." *Focaal* 2011 (59): 66–80. https://doi.org/10.3167/fcl.2011.590105.

Perrin, Andrew J., Steven J. Tepper, Neal Caren, and Sally Morris. 2011. "Cultures of the Tea Party." *Contexts* 10 (2): 74–75.

Phillips-Fein, Kim. 2009. *Invisible Hands: The Making of the Conservative Movement from the New Deal to Reagan.* New York: Norton.

Polletta, Francesca, and James M. Jasper. 2001. "Collective Identity and Social Movements." *Annual Review of Sociology* 27 (January): 283–305.

Portnoy, Jenna. 2014. "Cantor Faces Tea Party Fury in His Back Yard." *Washington Post,* May 10, 2014.

Pratto, Felicia, Jim Sidanius, Lisa M. Stallworth, and Bertram F. Malle. 1994. "Social Dominance Orientation: A Personality Variable Predicting Social and Political Attitudes." *Journal of Personality and Social Psychology* 67 (4): 741–63.

Preston, Julia. 2015. "Newest Immigrants Assimilating as Fast as Previous Ones, Report Says." *New York Times,* September 21, 2015.

Price, Charles. 2009. *Becoming Rasta: Origins of Rastafari Identity in Jamaica.* New York: New York University Press.

———. 2018. "An Ethnographic Life Narrative Strategy for Studying Race, Identity, and Acts of Political Significance: Black Racial Identity Theory and the Rastafari of Jamaica." In Strauss and Friedman 2018, 237–63.

Rawles, James. 2009. *Patriots: Surviving the Coming Collapse.* 4th expanded ed. Berkeley CA: Ulysses Press.

Reed, Ralph. 1993. "Casting a Wider Net: Religious Conservatives Move beyond Abortion and Homosexuality." *Policy Review,* no. 65 (June): 31.

———. 1994. *Politically Incorrect: The Emerging Faith Factor in American Politics.* Dallas: Word Pub.

Reed, T. V. 2005. *The Art of Protest: Culture and Activism from the Civil Rights Movement to the Streets of Seattle.* Minneapolis: University of Minnesota Press.

Robbins, Joel. 2013. "Beyond the Suffering Subject: Toward an Anthropology of the Good." *Journal of the Royal Anthropological Institute* 19 (3): 447–62.

Rohlinger, Deana, and Jesse Klein. 2014. "From Fervor to Fear: ICT and Emotions in the Tea Party Movement." In Van Dyke and Meyer 2014, 139–62.

Rosaldo, Renato. 1980. *Ilongot Headhunting, 1883–1974: A Study in Society and History.* Stanford CA: Stanford University Press.

Rosenthal, Lawrence, and Christine Trost, eds. 2012. *Steep: The Precipitous Rise of the Tea Party.* Berkeley: University of California Press.

Roth, Zachary. 2009. "Majority of Tea Party Group's Spending Went to GOP Firm That Created It." *Talking Points Memo,* December 28, 2009. https://

talkingpointsmemo.com/muckraker/majority-of-tea-party-group-s-spending
-went-to-gop-firm-that-created-it.

Rugh, Jacob S., and Douglas S. Massey. 2010. "Racial Segregation and the American Foreclosure Crisis." *American Sociological Review* 75 (5): 629–51.

Ryan, William. 1971. *Blaming the Victim*. New York: Pantheon Books.

Rymph, Catherine E. 2006. *Republican Women: Feminism and Conservatism from Suffrage through the Rise of the New Right*. Chapel Hill: University of North Carolina Press.

Saad, Lydia. 2015. "U.S. Liberals at Record 24%, but Still Trail Conservatives." *Gallup*, January 9, 2015. http://www.gallup.com/poll/180452/liberals-record -trail-conservatives.aspx.

Sanchez, Julian. 2010. "Epistemic Closure, Technology, and the End of Distance." *Julian Sanchez* (blog), April 7, 2010. http://www.juliansanchez.com/2010 /04/07/epistemic-closure-technology-and-the-end-of-distance/.

Sartwell, Crispin. 2010. *Political Aesthetics*. Ithaca NY: Cornell University Press.

Satterfield, Terre. 2002. *Anatomy of a Conflict: Identity, Knowledge, and Emotion in Old-Growth Forests*. Vancouver: UBC Press.

Schatz, Edward. 2009. *Political Ethnography: What Immersion Contributes to the Study of Power*. Chicago: University of Chicago Press.

Schlozman, Daniel. 2015. *When Movements Anchor Parties: Electoral Alignments in American History*. Princeton: Princeton University Press.

Schuessler, Jennifer. 2012. "Giving Incredibility Its Due, Historically Speaking." *New York Times*, July 19, 2012.

Scott, James. 1985. *Weapons of the Weak: Everyday Forms of Peasant Resistance*. New Haven: Yale University Press.

———. 1990. *Domination and the Arts of Resistance: Hidden Transcripts*. New Haven: Yale University Press.

Shapira, Harel. 2013. *Waiting for José: The Minutemen's Pursuit of America*. Princeton: Princeton University Press.

———. 2017. "Who Cares What They Think? Going about the Right the Wrong Way." *Contemporary Sociology* 46 (5): 512–17.

Sharlet, Jeff. 2010. "Is the Tea Party Becoming a Religious Movement?" CNN Opinion, October 27, 2010. http://www.cnn.com/2010/OPINION/10/27 /sharlet.tea.party.evangelical/index.html.

Silver, Nate, and Allison McCann. 2014. "Are White Republicans More Racist Than White Democrats?" *FiveThirtyEight*, April 30, 2014. http://fivethirtyeight .com/features/are-white-republicans-more-racist-than-white-democrats/.

Skocpol, Theda, and Vanessa Williamson. 2012. *The Tea Party and the Remaking of Republican Conservatism*. New York: Oxford University Press.

Skousen, W. Cleon. 1981. *The Five Thousand Year Leap: Twenty-Eight Ideas That Changed the World*. Salt Lake City: Freemen Institute.

Snow, David A., and Robert D. Benford. 1988. "Ideology, Frame Resonance, and Participant Mobilization." *International Social Movement Research* 1 (1): 197–217.

Spitulnik, Debra. 2002. *Mobile Machines and Fluid Audiences: Rethinking Reception through Zambian Radio Culture*. Berkeley: University of California Press.

Steele, Shelby. 2011. "Obama and the Burden of Exceptionalism." *Wall Street Journal*, September 1, 2011.

Stein, Arlene. 2001. *The Stranger Next Door: The Story of a Small Community's Battle over Sex, Faith, and Civil Rights*. Boston: Beacon Press.

Stenner, Karen. 2005. *The Authoritarian Dynamic*. New York: Cambridge University Press.

Stock, Catherine. 1996. *Rural Radicals: Righteous Rage in the American Grain*. Ithaca NY: Cornell University Press.

Stolcke, Verena. 1995. "Cultural Fundamentalism." *Current Anthropology* 36: 1–24.

Strauss, Claudia. 1990. "Who Gets Ahead? Cognitive Responses to Heteroglossia in American Political Culture." *American Ethnologist* 17 (2): 312–28.

———. 1997. "Partly Fragmented, Partly Integrated: An Anthropological Examination of 'Postmodern Fragmented Subjects.'" *Cultural Anthropology* 12 (3): 362–404.

Strauss, Claudia, and Jack R. Friedman, eds. 2018. *Political Sentiments and Social Movements: The Person in Politics and Culture*. New York: Palgrave Macmillan.

Street, Paul. 2001. "The White Fairness Understanding Gap." *Z Magazine*, October 1, 2001. https://zcomm.org/zmagazine/the-white-fairness-understanding-gap-by-paul-street/9-11.

Street, Paul, and Anthony R. DiMaggio. 2011. *Crashing the Tea Party: Mass Media and the Campaign to Remake American Politics*. Boulder CO: Paradigm Publishers.

Strzelczyk, Scott, and Richard Rothschild. 2009. "Articles: UN Agenda 21—Coming to a Neighborhood near You." *American Thinker*, October 28, 2009. http://www.americanthinker.com/2009/10/un_agenda_21_coming_to_a_neigh.html.

Stutz, Terrence. 2010. "Fox News Tries to Clarify Erroneous Reports about Texas Social Studies Curriculum Debate." *Dallas Morning News*, March 12, 2010.

Taber, Charles S., and Milton Lodge. 2006. "Motivated Skepticism in Political Information Processing." *American Journal of Political Science* 50 (3): 755–69.

Taylor, Verta. 1989. "Social Movement Continuity: The Women's Movement in Abeyance." *American Sociological Review* 54 (5): 761–75.

Taylor, Verta, and Nancy E. Whittier. 1999. "Collective Identity in Social Movement Communities: Lesbian Feminist." In *Waves of Protest: Social Movements since the Sixties*, edited by Jo Freeman, 163–87. Lanham MD: Rowman & Littlefield.

Tea Party Patriots. 2014a. "Dave Brat Powered to Victory over Eric Cantor by Grassroots." June 11, 2014. https://www.teapartypatriots.org/news/dave -brat-power-to-victory-over-eric-cantor-by-grassroots/.

———. 2014b. "We Stand with Hobby Lobby and Conestoga Woods." March 24, 2014. https://www.teapartypatriots.org/news/we-stand-with-hobby-lobby -and-conestoga-woods/.

Terbush, Jon. 2013. "The Green Tea Coalition: Why the Sierra Club and the Georgia Tea Party Keep Teaming Up." *The Week*, November 20, 2013. http:// theweek.com/article/index/253115/the-green-tea-coalition-why-the-sierra -club-and-the-georgia-tea-party-keep-teaming-up.

Teske, Nathan. 1997. *Political Activists in America: The Identity Construction Model of Political Participation*. Cambridge: Cambridge University Press.

Thelen, David. 1990. *Memory and American History*. Bloomington: Indiana University Press.

Trapenberg-Frick, Karen. 2013. "The Actions of Discontent: Tea Party and Property Rights Activists Pushing Back against Regional Planning." *Journal of the American Planning Association* 79 (3): 190–200.

———. 2018. "No Left or Right, Only Right or Wrong." *Planning Theory and Practice* 19 (3): 454–57.

Trapenberg-Frick, Karen, David Weinzimmer, and Paul Waddell. 2015. "The Politics of Sustainable Development Opposition: State Legislative Efforts to Stop the United Nation's Agenda 21 in the United States." *Urban Studies* 52 (2): 209–32.

Tretjak, Kaja. 2013. "Opportunity and Danger: Why Studies of the Right Are Crucial for US Anthropology and Beyond." *North American Dialogue* 16 (2): 60–68.

Urrieta, Luis. 2007. "Figured Worlds and Education: An Introduction to the Special Issue." *Urban Review* 39 (2): 107–16.

Van Dyke, Nella, and David S Meyer. 2014. *Understanding the Tea Party Movement*. New York: Ashgate.

Virchow, F. 2007. "Performance, Emotion, and Ideology: On the Creation of 'Collectives of Emotion' and Worldview in the Contemporary German Far Right." *Journal of Contemporary Ethnography* 36 (2): 147–64.

Vogel, Kenneth P. 2010. "Tea Party vs. Tea Party Caucus." *Politico*, August 2, 2010. http://www.politico.com/news/stories/0810/40528.html.

Voloshinov, V. 1986. *Marxism and the Philosophy of Language.* Cambridge MA: Harvard University Press.

Vygotsky, Lev. 1978. *Mind in Society.* Translated by M. Cole. Cambridge MA: Harvard University Press.

Walgrave, Stefaan, and Jan Manssens. 2000. "The Making of the White March: The Mass Media as a Mobilizing Alternative to Movement Organizations." *Mobilization: An International Quarterly* 5 (2): 217–39.

Wallsten, Peter, and Lyndsey Layton. 2013. "Tea Party Groups Rallying against Common Core Education Overhaul." *Washington Post*, May 30, 2013.

Walsh, Katherine Cramer. 2004. *Talking about Politics: Informal Groups and Social Identity in American Life.* Chicago: University of Chicago Press.

———. 2009. "Scholars as Citizens: Studying Public Opinion through Ethnography." In *Political Ethnography: What Immersion Contributes to the Study of Power*, edited by Edward Schatz, 165–82. Chicago: University of Chicago Press.

Warner, Michael. 2005. *Publics and Counterpublics.* New York: Zone Books.

Westermeyer, William H. 2009. "Toward an Anthropological Understanding of Citizen Political Participation." Unpublished manuscript, Department of Anthropology, University of North Carolina–Chapel Hill.

———. 2016. "Local Tea Party Groups: The Vibrancy of the Movement." *Political and Legal Anthropology Review* 39 (S1): 121–38.

Whittemore, Andrew. 2012. "Why Planners Need to Take Agenda 21 Criticism More Seriously." *CityLab*, February 7, 2012. http://www.theatlanticcities.com/neighborhoods/2012/02/why-planners-need-take-agenda-21-criticism-more-seriously/1159/.

———. 2013. "Finding Sustainability in Conservative Contexts: Topics for Conversation between American Conservative Élites, Planners and the Conservative Base." *Urban Studies* 50 (12): 2460–77.

Whittenburg, James P. 1977. "Planters, Merchants, and Lawyers: Social Change and the Origins of the North Carolina Regulation." *William and Mary Quarterly* 34 (2): 215–38.

Wilcox, Clyde. 1992. *God's Warriors: The Christian Right in Twentieth-Century America.* Baltimore: Johns Hopkins University Press.

Wilcox, Clyde, and Carin Robinson. 2011. *Onward Christian Soldiers?: The Religious Right in American Politics (Dilemmas in American Politics).* Boulder CO: Westview Press.

Wilentz, Sean. 2010. "Confounding Fathers." *The New Yorker*, October 18, 2010.

Williams, Daniel K. 2012. *God's Own Party: The Making of the Christian Right.* Oxford: Oxford University Press.

Williams, Joan C. 2016. "What So Many People Don't Get about the U.S. Working Class." *Harvard Business Review*, November 10, 2016. https://hbr.org/2016/11/what-so-many-people-dont-get-about-the-u-s-working-class.

Williamson, V., T. Skocpol, and J. Coggin. 2011. "The Tea Party and the Remaking of Republican Conservatism." *Perspectives on Politics* 9 (1): 25–43.

Wilson, Angelia R., and Cynthia Burack. 2012. "'Where Liberty Reigns and God Is Supreme': The Christian Right and the Tea Party Movement." *New Political Science* 34 (2):172–90.

Wolford, Wendy. 2010. *This Land Is Our Land Now: Spatial Imaginaries and the Struggle for Land in Brazil.* Durham NC: Duke University Press.

Wortham, Stanton. 2006. *Learning Identity: The Joint Emergence of Social Identification and Academic Learning.* Cambridge: Cambridge University Press.

Yang, Guobin. 2000. "Achieving Emotions in Collective Action: Emotional Processes and Movement Mobilization in the 1989 Chinese Student Movement." *Sociological Quarterly* 41 (4): 593–614.

Zernike, Kate. 2010. *Boiling Mad: Inside Tea Party America.* New York: Times Books.

Zernike, Kate, and Megan Thee-Brenan. 2010. "Poll Finds Tea Party Backers Wealthier and More Educated." *New York Times*, April 14, 2010.

Index

Atlanta Braves, 162
Atlanta Green Tea Coalition, 161–62
Atlanta Tea Party Patriots, 161
Ayers, William, 20

Bachmann, Michele, 36–37, 49, 183n1
Bakhtin, Mikhail, 31
Balboa High School, 72–73
Balibar, Etienne, 96, 99
Bannon, Steve, 179
Barker, David C., 54
Barreto, Matt A., 94, 95, 96, 188n13
Barton, David, 43, 51, 56, 91
Beck, Glenn: on Agenda 21, 163–66; "disaster" predicted by, 4; emotional displays of, 59; guests of, 129; Hamilton County Tea Party's link to, 5; historical references by, 40, 42, 188n2; influence of, 16, 117, 162; politico-religious views of, 51–52, 56; rallies organized by, 116; recognition of blacks, 91. See also *The Glenn Beck Program*
Bellah, Robert, 122
Bellott, Bruce, 127
Berry, Jeffrey, 178
Bible: American end times in, 54, 85, 136; founding documents compared to, 43, 48, 50–52, 188n3; on greed, 86; quoting of, 137; reading in schools, 84
Bilderberg group, 136
Bill of Rights, 50
Black Lives Matter, 187n1
Black Power movement, 188n11
blacks: attitudes toward Tea Party, 90, 91, 94, 107–8, 111–12; collective identity of, 109, 114; dependence on government, 93–94, 105, 106, 107; enslavement and oppression

of, 91–92, 186nn5–6; in Hamilton County, 149, 150; perceived culture of, 105–6, 108, 110, 111, 112; self-segregation of, 108–9; in Tea Party movement, 82, 108, 112, 187n2; whites' attitudes toward, 95–97, 99, 101, 113, 187n4, 187n7, 188n12
The Blaze, 129
Bobo, Lawrence D., 187n7
Boehner, John, 175
Bonilla-Silva, Eduardo, 97, 101, 102, 105, 108, 113
Boston Tea Party, 23, 29
Bourdieu, Pierre, 31, 152, 180
Braunstein, Ruth, 12, 134, 185n8
Breitbart News, 179
Brody, David, 53
Brooklyn Heights, 141
Buckley, William F., 186n3
The Bullet Proof George Washington (Barton), 51
Burghart, Devin, 94, 95
Burgoyne County NC, 13
Burgoyne County Tea Party: Constitution revered by, 125, 126, 155, 188n3; leadership of, 153–54, 156–57; members and activities of, 28, 121–22, 124–27, 133–34, 145, 153, 155–57, 160, 189(ch5)n5; opposition to Agenda 21, 165; at rallies, 35–37, 39; and Republican Party, 155–56, 169; Timothy Johnson's speech to, 112
Burke, Meghan, 97, 98
Bush, George W., 21, 75–76, 91, 93, 161
Bush, Jeb, 181
Bush, Melanie, 99, 100–101
Butterfield, C. K., 1–2

Cain, Carol, 33, 58

Cain, Herman, 107–8, 113
California, 69, 94, 190(ch5)n6
Cantor, Eric, 169
capitalism, 85–86, 138. *See also* economy
capital punishment, 102
Carlson, Gretchen, 141–42
Carman, Christopher Jan, 54
Carroll County MD, 163
Carson, Ben, 113, 179
Carter, Jimmy, 72
Chaney, James, 187n6
Charlotte NC, 13, 28
Chicago, 20, 23
Chicago Mercantile Exchange, 22
Children's Miracle Network, 158
China, 186n1
Christian Coalition, 8, 144–45, 189n2
Christianity: in American history, 42, 51, 52; of black conservatives, 112; consequences of rejection of, 138, 140; and constitutional education, 49–51; fundamentalism of, 44, 48, 83; and race, 103; relationalism in, 106; role in Tea Party formation and success, 24; of Tea Partyists, 12, 33, 54–55, 80–87, 147, 154, 157–59, 178, 185n9, 185n10; at Tea Party meetings, 122, 140–41; worldview of, 32. *See also* morality; prayers
Christian Right, 53–56, 159, 173, 185n9. *See also* conservatives
Citizens for Sound Economy, 26
citizenship, 46–48, 70, 78–79, 120, 126, 154, 167, 168. *See also* community; patriotism
civil rights movement, 97, 106, 110, 144, 173, 187n6
Civil War, 74, 82, 186nn5–6

climate change, 166
Clinton, Bill, 2, 85
Clinton, Hillary, 179, 181
CNBC, 22–23
Cohen, Abner, 174
Cohen, Jean, 24
collectivism. *See* community
College of William and Mary, 43
Common Core standards, 161
communism, 5, 49, 131, 144, 166, 186n7
communities of practice, 118, 123–24, 146. *See also* figured worlds
community, 68, 70, 109, 110, 114–18. *See also* citizenship; grassroots networks; local Tea Party Groups (LTPGS)
computer and information technology (CIT), 26, 124, 127, 136–39, 141, 163, 170–73. *See also* Facebook; media; social media; Vimeo; YouTube
conceal and carry, 133. *See also* Second Amendment
Concord Bridge, 129, 189(ch4)n4
Confederacy, 74. *See also* Civil War
Confederate flag, 30
conservatives: blacks as, 94, 107–8, 110; books favored by, 109; Christianity of, 81–86, 154; concerns of, 19–25, 28, 29, 161; conspiracy theories of, 166; Constitution revered by, 49; defense against liberals, 130, 131, 133; differences among, 69, 135, 137–38, 142, 159, 186n3, 186n4; for Donald Trump, 179, 181; fiscal vs. social, 13, 178; identities of, 62, 74; liberalism of, 81, 154; opposition to Barack Obama, 26, 100; political activism of, 144–45, 168; and race,

conservatives (*cont.*)
80, 92, 97, 98, 100, 103, 187n4;
symbolic forms of, 174–75; women
as, 62, 154–55. *See also* Christian
Right; neoconservatives; political
identity; Republican Party
conspiracy theories, 136–38, 163–66
Constitution League, 49
Coulter, Ann, 107
county boards of commissioners, 39,
135, 150–52
courts, 179
Cowan, Bill, 129
Crapanzano, Vincent, 48–49
Cruz, Ted, 179
culture. *See* American culture; figured
worlds; political culture; political
identity; poverty, culture of; social
identity

Dagnino, Evelina, 184n1
Daro, Vinci, 135
Daughtry, Tim, 129–33, 142, 180, 189n3
Dean, Howard, 172, 173
Declaration of Independence, 40, 42,
43, 50
De Mint, Jim, 183n1
Democracy for America (DFA), 172
Democratic Party: blacks' loyalty to,
94, 106–8, 110; in Hamilton County,
149, 150, 151; and Indivisible
movement, 190n4; Obama-era
policy of, 1; racial views of, 187n4,
188n9; and social movements, 173;
Tea Partyists' attitudes toward,
73–74, 76, 135, 150. *See also*
politicians
Department of Education, 179
Department of Housing and Urban
Development, 179

Deplorables United for Trump, 180
DeVos, Betsy, 179
Diani, Mario, 7
Disch, Lisa, 188n12
Dixon NC, 163, 164, 169
Douglass, Frederick, 114
Durkheim, Émile, 118

East River, 141
economy: Christian views of, 24, 52,
54, 56, 82–83; concerns about, 1,
20, 21, 23; control of, 136, 137;
decline in North Carolina, 186n1;
fundamentalist views of, 34, 35, 37,
48; Hawthorne Tea Party's focus
on, 140; state government
intervention in, 69; Tea Party's
stance on, 113–14, 134, 137–38;
women's views of, 55, 154–55. *See
also* capitalism; taxes
Edelman, Marc, 176
Edsall, Thomas, 180
electoral politics: local activism in,
143–47, 152, 155–56, 159, 163, 167,
189(ch5)n5; media effect on, 52–53,
173–74; race in, 106–7; and social
movements, 172–73; Tea Party
candidates in, 96, 139, 152–53, 168;
Tea Partyists' attitudes toward, 70,
75, 136, 138. *See also* politicians
Emerson, Michael O., 24, 54, 106
emotion: as component of identity, 30,
31, 33, 34, 37, 62; of male Tea Party
consultants, 59, 185n11; of Pierce
County Tea Party, 157; in social
movement theory, 56–58; at Tea
Party events, 116–17, 124, 127–29
environmental problems, 166
Environmental Protection Agency, 66
epistemic closure, 141

Escobar, Arturo, 184n1
euthanasia, 81
evolution education, 55, 140. *See also* schools

Facebook, 5, 8, 15, 137, 150, 171, 180. *See also* computer and information technology (CIT); social media
Faith and Freedom Coalition, 56
Falwell, Jerry, 50, 81
Far Right nationalism, 184n5
Fayetteville NC, 28
Federal Communications Commission, 183n3
Federalist papers, 50
feminism, 57. *See also* women
figured worlds: of Burgoyne County Tea Party, 124, 125, 153; cultural citizenship in, 46–47; cultural resources of, 30–33, 62–63, 100, 146; emotion in, 56, 58–60; interaction within, 117–19, 128, 134, 160; occupation of multiple, 54, 55; religion in, 51, 52, 53, 122, 140, 185n9; of Tea Partyists, 34–35, 37, 38, 40, 41, 60, 70–71, 87, 89, 93, 99, 103, 104, 107, 108, 113–15, 133, 142, 155, 161, 162, 167; Tea Party guest speakers in, 129. *See also* communities of practice; symbolism
First Amendment, 185n10. *See also* U.S. Constitution
Fisher, Ada, 111
The Five Thousand Year Leap (Skousen), 51–53, 188n3
Fort Dix, 105
foundational stories, 66
Fox, Gretchen, 135
Fox News: "disaster" predicted by, 4; and electoral politics, 173;

influence of, 117, 141, 162, 167; personalities from, 129; role in Tea Party formation and success, 3, 4, 8, 25, 26, 60, 124, 170
framing, 29–30, 56, 117
Frank, Thomas, 87
Frankenberg, Ruth, 98, 99
Frankfurt School, 132
Franklin, Benjamin, 23, 25, 42–43, 51, 120, 121, 188n2
Franklin County NC, 13, 28
Franklin County Tea Party, 111, 139–42
Frederick Douglass Foundation, 112
"Freedom Summer," 117
FreedomWorks: avoidance of social issues, 55; distribution of information, 15, 167; organizational efforts of, 66, 116, 144; and race, 94; and religion, 86; role in Tea Party formation and success, 26, 29, 60, 95, 124
fundamentalism: collective identity through, 67; as cultural practice, 34, 37, 44, 45, 48; definition of, 44; faith-based, 81, 83, 159; figured worlds of, 54, 62, 108; of historical views, 43, 50, 78; at Tea Party meetings, 125
The Fundamentals, 44
furniture industry, 83, 85, 86, 157, 186n1

Gadsden's flag, 30, 37
General Social Survey, 187n4
Georgia, 161
Georgia Power, 161
Gerlach, Luther, 7
Giddens, Anthony, 21
Gingrich, Newt, 168
Ginsburg, Faye, 62
The Glenn Beck Program, 51, 163–64, 188n2. *See also* Beck, Glenn

local Tea Party Groups (LTPGS) (*cont.*)
123, 124, 126, 128–29, 137, 139,
143–46, 153, 178; and national
groups, 95; national influence of,
165, 166, 168; new grievances of,
160–63, 165; racial views of, 90, 96;
religion in, 51, 55, 185n9; as research
subjects, 13, 14, 16–17, 183n2; role in
Tea Party formation and success, 3,
6, 11, 16–17, 29, 118–19, 133, 142, 143,
162, 169–71; social media use by, 8;
women's roles in, 155. *See also*
community; grassroots networks;
Tea Party movement (TPM)
Losing Ground (Murray), 106
Lowndes, Joseph, 97, 113, 187n5
Lutz, Catherine, 56

Malaysia, 73
Martin, Jenny Beth, 26, 76
Martyrs' Day, 72–73
Marxism, 20, 77, 130–32, 180, 181
McAdam, Doug, 7, 117–18, 172, 173,
190n5
McCain, John, 81
McConnell, Mitch, 175
McCrory, Pat, 188n8
McGirr, Lisa, 69
McVeigh, Rory, 57
Mead, G. H., 31
Meckler, Mark, 76
media: constitutional education
advertised through, 50; control of,
136; and electoral politics, 20–21,
173–74, 180; figured worlds of, 32, 59,
60; influence on Tea Partyists, 5–6,
124, 128, 141, 161, 166; local Tea Party
groups' use of, 156, 162; politico-
religious references in, 51; racial
discourse in, 94, 100; regulation of,

183n3; research on role in social
movement, 190n2; role in Tea Party
formation and success, 2–8, 19, 22,
25–30, 117, 120, 121, 124, 127, 162, 171;
Tea Party movement portrayed in,
169; Trump support through, 182.
See also computer and information
technology (CIT); social media
Medicare, 21, 188n12
Melucci, Alberto, 134, 184n5
Merrell, Benjamin, 74
Mexicans, 47, 125. *See also* immigration; Latinos
millennial dispensationalism, 54
Mills, C. Wright, 63
Minnesota, 36, 183n1
morality: blamed for financial
problems, 23–25, 82–83; of
populists, 77; and race, 95–96, 100,
101, 187n4; role in Tea Party
formation and success, 29; of Tea
Partyists, 24, 25, 30, 33, 34, 52, 53,
81–82, 114, 154–55; threats to
traditional American, 54–55, 69,
94–96, 98, 108, 113, 129, 158. *See
also* Christianity; social issues; Tea
Party movement (TPM): values of
Moral Majority, 81, 103
Morgen, Sandra, 24, 66
Morris, Aldon, 7
mortgage crisis, 22–23, 99
MoveOn.org, 171
multiculturalism, 71–72, 90, 158
Mulvaney, Mick, 179
Murray, Charles, 106
Muslims, 92, 141

Nagata, Judith, 44
National Association for Constitutional Government, 49

National Center for Constitutional Studies, 53, 188n3

nationalism, 38, 99, 182, 184n5. *See also* American culture

National Review, 186n3

National Rifle Association, 8

National Security Agency, 15

national Tea Party organizations (NTPOs): avoidance of social issues, 55; characteristics of, 12; decline of, 178; and local Tea Party groups, 29, 95, 124, 128, 170; origins of, 26; racist views in, 94; at rallies, 35, 37, 116, 188n1; as research subjects, 15; role in Tea Party formation and success, 3, 162; social media use by, 8. *See also* Tea Party movement (TPM)

neoconservatives, 110, 188n11. *See also* conservatives

neoliberalism, 93, 101–2

Newby, Paul, 102–3

New Deal, 24, 62, 69, 101, 173

New Jersey, 139

New Left, 188n11

New Right, 69, 144, 166, 186n3, 190n5

the New School, 132

New Social Movements, 7

Nixon, Richard, 93, 97

Normandy invasion, 122

North American Free Trade Agreement (NAFTA), 85, 186n1

North Carolina: Civil War politics in, 74, 186nn5–6; complaints about government in, 68–69; Constitution education in, 4; counties in, 167, 183n2, 190(ch5)n6; economic decline in, 186n1; political activism in, 63; political representation in, 1, 79, 139, 153, 178, 186n7; repeal of Racial Justice Act in, 188n8; Tea Party meeting places in, 121; union rally in, 184n2

North Carolina Supreme Court, 102

Obama, Barack: administration of, 120, 161; Ben Carson's rebuke of, 113; blacks' support for, 108; characterization of, 36, 37, 129; Glenn Beck's criticism of, 51; "green jobs czar" under, 5; health care plan of, 1, 148; in prayer, 122; presidential campaign of, 173; racism toward, 30, 90, 95; Tea Party's opinion of, 11, 20–22, 26, 28, 64, 75, 157, 166, 175, 180, 188n13

Occupy movement, 8, 170–71, 173, 190n3

Office of Management and Budget, 179

O'Hair, Madalyn Murray, 84

Ohio, 36

Omi, Michael, 101

O'Reilly, Bill, 5, 162

Palin, Sarah, 79, 148, 168

Panama Canal Zone, 70–73

Parker, Christopher S., 94, 95, 96, 188n13

Patient Protection and Affordable Care Act, 2, 113. *See also* health care reform

patriotism: collective identity through, 62, 67, 98, 128; as cultural practice, 33, 34, 37, 184n2; and emotion, 56, 59, 128; historical connotations of, 37–44; meaning to Tea Partyists, 104, 154, 184n5; and race, 93, 99; and religious identity, 185n9; role in Tea Party formation and success, 23–25, 29, 70, 71, 75; at Tea Party meetings, 125. *See also* American culture; American history; citizenship

vs. cultural, 105, 108, 110–11, 113–14;
in Tea Party movement, 12, 17, 21,
30, 38, 57, 80, 89, 94–97, 113,
186n6, 187n1, 187n5
Racism without Racists (Bonilla-Silva),
113
Raleigh NC, 66, 125, 184n2
Rastafarian movement, 61
Rawles, James, 4
Reagan, Ronald, 81, 97, 103, 183n3,
187n6. *See also* Lincoln-Reagan
fund-raising dinners
Reed, Ralph, 56, 144–45
Reed, T. V., 128
Regulators, 74, 75
religion. *See* Christianity; prayers
Republican National Committee, 111,
165
Republican Party: on abortion, 83;
and Agenda 21, 165, 166, 173;
attitude toward Donald Trump, 181;
blacks in, 110, 111, 112; Christian
Coalition in, 144; in Civil War North
Carolina, 186n6; convention
speakers in North Carolina, 129;
Donald Trump's appeal to, 168, 174;
history of, 74; media influence on,
190(conclusion)n6; PAC created
by, 94; on public assistance, 107;
racial views of, 95, 106, 188n9; role
in Tea Party formation, 2, 3, 78,
174–75; Tea Partyists' participation
in, 27, 136, 144, 148, 155, 160, 163,
178, 189(ch5)n5; Tea Party's
criticism of, 34, 49, 55, 75–76, 78,
86, 119, 121, 124, 135, 152, 183n1; Tea
Party's support of, 35, 139, 152–53;
use of Tea Party culture, 168;
women in, 148, 149, 154, 155. *See
also* conservatives; politicians

ResistNet, 116
Reston NC, 89–90
Restoring Honor rally, 91, 187n3
Revere County NC, 13
Revere County Tea Party, 45, 49, 122,
129, 189n3
Revolutionary Anarchist Clown Army,
58
Revolutionary War, 74
Reynolds Tobacco, 68
the Right. *See* conservatives; Republi-
can Party
RINOs. *See* Republican Party: Tea
Party's criticism of
Rio Earth Summit, 162
R.J. Reynolds, 68
Road to Serfdom (Hayek), 109, 110
Roe v. Wade, 83. *See also* abortion
Romney, Mitt, 107
Roosevelt, Franklin Delano, 20, 122, 130
Rosaldo, Renato, 41
Rules for Radicals (Alinsky), 16
The Rush Limbaugh Show, 50. *See also*
Limbaugh, Rush
Ryan, Paul, 175

Sanchez, Julian, 141
Sanders, Bernie, 173
Santelli, Rick, 22–29, 55, 60, 89, 99
Satterfield, Terre, 31–32, 56
Schatz, Edward, 62
schools: curriculum in, 141–42, 161,
166; Hamilton County budget for,
151; liberals' control of, 43, 132, 137;
as local concern, 143, 144, 147;
prayer in, 56, 84. *See also* evolution
education; U.S. Constitution:
education about
Schwerner, Michael, 187n6
Scott, James, 73

grievances of, 161; personal experiences of, 63–65, 74, 87, 88, 89, 134, 153; as political activists, 145, 147, 162, 189n2; racial views of, 91–93, 111, 113, 188n13; religious identity of, 53, 54, 80–81, 185n7; as research subjects, 12–16, 96, 184n8; role in Tea Party formation and success, 29–30, 87; self-image of, 5, 10–11, 19–20, 27, 36, 57, 104, 120–21, 182, 184n2, 189(ch5)n4

Tea Party movement (TPM): appeal to blacks, 111–13; appeal to Christians, 86; components of, 3, 30, 166–67, 183n1; culture of, 5–6, 9–11, 30, 32, 33, 38, 44, 100–101, 115, 168; influence on other movements, 190n4; influence on party politics, 173; in media, 2–3, 22, 27–28, 171, 182; origins of, 2–3, 19, 22, 29; political identities built through, 117; as "political" organization, 186n2; regaining country through, 84–85, 138; as social movement network, 7–8, 28–30, 88, 162, 169–70; study of, 174–76, 184n5, 185n7; symbols of, 6, 22, 25, 28, 30, 33, 34, 37, 51, 60, 69–70, 73, 120, 123, 174–75, 182; and Trumpism, 18, 172, 177–81; values of, 5, 23, 24, 27, 28, 34, 40–42, 48, 52–56, 63–65, 69, 106, 111, 114, 120, 154, 158, 179–80; women in, 155. See also local Tea Party Groups (LTPGs); national Tea Party organizations (NTPOs)

Tea Party Patriots: anger of, 57; avoidance of social issues, 55, 185n10; and local Tea Party groups, 170; origins of, 26; and race, 94; rallies organized by, 116; role in Tea

Party formation and success, 3, 4, 95; supporters of, 26, 28

Temporary Assistance for Needy Families (TANF), 188n12

Texas, 141–42

Thurmond, Strom, 188n9

Tillis, Thom, 178

Time magazine, 20

tobacco industry, 66–68

troubles, definition of, 63

Trump, Donald: economic policy of, 138; and party politics, 168, 174; reactions to election of, 176, 187n11; social movement associated with, 172; supporters of, 79, 87, 177–82; Tea Party movement's effect on, 18, 175

Twitter, 8, 26, 171, 182. See also social media

United Nations, 85, 162, 166

University of Chicago, 20

U.S. Army, 72, 103–5, 116

U.S. Chamber of Commerce, 2

U.S. Congress: constituent services of, 186n8; debt ceiling debate in, 35; North Carolina representation in, 79; Republican Party sweep of, 190(conclusion)n6; Tea Party candidates in, 96, 153; Tea Party Caucus in, 49, 183n1; Tea Party criticism of, 2, 175

U.S. Constitution: education about, 4, 10, 48–50, 53, 140, 142, 189n3; Judeo-Christian principles of, 50–52, 82, 84–86; republic provided by, 120; on states' rights, 187n6; Tea Party adherence to, 1, 5, 25, 37, 41, 46, 48–49, 104, 125, 154, 161, 179; as Tea Party symbol, 33, 34, 37, 39, 125, 126, 155–58, 161, 175, 188n3. See also First Amendment

U.S. government: and American cultural loss, 25–26, 34, 44, 54, 55, 65, 71–73; dependencc on, 93–94, 104–8, 113; and economic problems, 22–25, 66–67, 86, 136–38; and immorality, 83–84, 158; shutdowns of, 96, 134, 175; Tea Partyists' distrust of, 70, 76–77, 120, 135–36, 154, 161, 166. *See also* politicians

U.S. House of Representatives, 169, 183n1

U.S. Navy, 41

U.S. Senate, 178

U.S. Supreme Court, 179

Value Voters Summit, 53

videos, 5, 6, 20, 51, 127, 128, 150, 157, 162, 169. *See also* media; Vimeo; YouTube

Viguerie, Richard, 190(conclusion)n6

Vimeo, 157. *See also* computer and information technology (CIT); videos

Virchow, F., 127

Virginia, 169, 190n1

Vygotsky, Lev, 31

WallBuilders, 51

Walsh, Katherine Cramer, 87

Washington, George, 25, 51, 114, 141

Washington DC, 35–37, 116–17, 188n1

"We Ain't Going Away" (Bellott), 127

Weather Underground, 20

Wenger, Etienne, 146

West, Alan, 108, 113, 188n10

What's the Matter with Kansas? (Frank), 87

whites: on black rights, 97, 103; characteristics of, 98–99; in Civil War North Carolina, 186nn5–6; "color blindness" of, 93, 99, 101–2, 113; on discrimination, 110; moral values of, 96, 100; nationalism of, 184n5; in Tea Party movement, 29, 90, 94, 98, 99, 101, 111–12, 182, 185n9

Whittier, Nancy E., 134

Williams, Mark, 95

Williamson, V., 12, 95–97, 156

Wilson, Rev., 50–51, 54, 82

Winant, Howard, 101

Winston-Salem NC, 66, 68

women, 55, 62, 139, 154–55, 189(ch5) n4. *See also* feminism

World Trade Association, 186n1

worldviews, 32, 33

World War I, 62

Wright, Jeremiah, 20, 21

Yang, Guobin, 58

YouTube, 5, 6, 127, 150. *See also* computer and information technology (CIT); videos

Zeskind, Leonard, 94, 95

In the Anthropology of Contemporary North America series:

To order or obtain more information on these or other University of Nebraska Press titles, visit nebraskapress.unl.edu.

Printed in the USA
CPSIA information can be obtained
at www.ICGtesting.com
LVHW042328180823
755636LV00005B/464